Teaching English, Language and Literacy

English is one of the most fascinating, controversial and challenging subjects of the school curriculum. There has been a wide range of literature published in the field of primary English teaching, but no book has attempted a comprehensive overview of the subject. For anyone interested in the teaching of English this book is an essential introduction to the issues, ideas, theory and practice.

The new curriculum for people involved in the training of teachers has resulted in the expectation that all primary teachers acquire a challenging level of English subject knowledge; both teaching methods and content. The National Literacy Strategy also requires new levels of knowledge. This book consists mainly of short chapters that cover the variety of aspects that make up the English curriculum. All these chapters include clear examples of practice, coverage of key issues, analysis of research, and reflections on national policy. The short chapters are complemented by four longer ones: the first of these addresses the important subject of the history of English and English teaching. The other three look at children's development in reading, writing and talking and relate this development to teaching approaches.

This is a comprehensive account of the Teaching of English and includes a critical evaluation of the impact of the National Literacy Strategy and the National Curriculum 2000. It is an essential introduction to the Teaching of English for all primary students.

Dominic Wyse is Principal Lecturer in Primary English and School-Based Research at Liverpool John Moores University. **Russell Jones** is Senior Lecturer in Primary Education at Manchester Metropolitan University, specialising in English. They have worked as primary teachers and subject leaders and have substantial experience of working with students and teachers.

Teaching English, Language and Literacy

Dominic Wyse and Russell Jones
With contributions from Roger Bainbridge
and Charles Sarland

London and New York

First published 2001
by RoutledgeFalmer
11 New Fetter Lane, London EC4P 4EE

Simultaneously published in the USA and Canada
by RoutledgeFalmer
29 West 35th Street, New York, NY 10001

Reprinted 2002 (twice), 2003

RoutledgeFalmer is an imprint of the Taylor & Francis Group

© 2001 Dominic Wyse and Russell Jones

Typeset in 10/12 Sabon by
Macreth Media Services, Hemel Hempstead, Herts
Printed and bound in Great Britain by
St Edmundsbury Press Ltd, Bury St Edmunds, Suffolk

British Library Cataloguing in Publication Data
A catalogue record for this book is available from the British Library

Library of Congress Cataloging in Publication Data
A catalog record for this book has been requested

ISBN 0-415-20091-1 (hbk)
ISBN 0-415-20092-X (pbk)

To Jackie, Esther and Oliver

Alan, Steve, Nigel, John and Adrian

Contents

Figures

Tables

Foreword

Books about literacy and language teaching serve many different purposes. Some present original research into an aspect of teaching and learning; some focus on a particular issue; others attempt to summarise what is currently known in this field, drawing out the major implications for teachers and teachers in training.

Books of the last type are difficult to write well, demanding as they do an almost encyclopaedic knowledge of this vast area and it is perhaps not surprising that a few such books come to dominate reading lists for long periods. During the 1980s the key book of this type was Diana Hutchcroft's *Making Language Work*, but in the 1990s this was largely replaced as the standard text by our own *Literacy and Language in the Primary Years*.

With the publication of *Teaching English, Language and Literacy*, Dominic Wyse and Russell Jones could well have produced the standard text for the 2000s. The book is comprehensive, up-to-date, critical and authoritative. It is also, above all, well written. It will undoubtedly become standard reading for the next generation of teachers in training and practising teachers will also learn a great deal from dipping into its contents. As the co-author of the book it will replace, I was less than ecstatic at the arrival of this volume: as a student, researcher and teacher of literacy and language education, I am delighted to have this book on my shelf.

Professor David Wray
Institute of Education, University of Warwick

Preface

English is one of the most fascinating, controversial and challenging subjects of the school curriculum. The fact that English is the language that we speak also makes it a subject that is closely linked with our identities and this is one of the reasons that it often engenders passionate views. Another reason that it is important is that all teachers have to be teachers of English because we communicate our knowledge in all subjects by talking, reading and writing about them. In the primary education curriculum great stress is put on the learning of English because it is a bridge to all other learning.

Since the Education Reform Act 1988 the primary curriculum has been the subject of intense focus. In 1998 two initiatives dramatically changed the face of primary education. The most significant was the National Literacy Strategy, but for students and their teachers the government Circular 4/98 established a radical new curriculum for initial teacher education. For the first time a circular explicitly detailed the kind of subject knowledge about English that *all* students had to acquire in order to qualify as teachers. This book is a comprehensive introduction to the ideas, concepts and knowledge that are part of the study of English teaching. As you will see from the Appendix the book addresses all aspects of Annex C (the English requirements) from 4/98, but it also tackles a wide range of other aspects of the teaching of English.

Teaching English, Language and Literacy has been written for all primary education students and their teachers. It is designed as a reader that will enhance and consolidate the learning in core-curriculum English programmes and as an essential guide to the teaching of English. The moves towards greater partnership between university education departments and schools mean that there is a pressing need for a book that offers a comprehensive overview of the subject to enable teacher mentors to up-date their professional knowledge in specific areas when appropriate. The structure of this book is designed to support that very process.

The book is divided into five parts: Introduction; Reading; Writing; Speaking and Listening, and General Issues. The bulk of the book consists of short chapters that cover the variety of aspects that make up the English curriculum. All these chapters include clear examples of practice, coverage of key issues, analysis of research, and reflections on national policy. The short chapters are complimented by four longer ones that begin parts I to IV. The first of these addresses the important subject of the history of English and English teaching. The other three look at children's development in reading, writing and talking and relate this development to teaching approaches. The structure of the longer chapters allowed us to tackle some of the most important aspects of the English curriculum in depth and at a higher level. Part V is made up of issues that tend to be applicable to all three modes of reading, writing and speaking and listening. The exception to this structure is 'Theories of Learning' which is located in the introduction because of our view that learning theories should underpin your understanding of the curriculum as a whole.

One of the innovative features of the book is its comprehensive nature. The subject of English is an area that boasts an impressive array of scholarship and practice. While there are many books that have addressed the modes of reading, writing and speaking and listening separately, there are very few which address the complete subject area. By doing this we have accepted that inevitably some parts of the subject are only touched on briefly. In recognition of this you will find more than ninety descriptions of recommended books and papers for further reading which appear in the 'annotated bibliographies' for every chapter. A novel feature of these bibliographies is a system of coding which allows you to judge the reading level and the balance between theory and practice:

*   Mainly focused on classroom practice
**   Close balance between theory and practice
*** Research and theory based

L1 Introductory reading.
L2 Intermediate reading
L3 Advanced reading

The dramatic and swift changes to the English curriculum caused by the National Literacy Strategy (NLS) have required much rethinking from educators. This book is the first to include analysis of the implementation of the NLS and its relationship to previous practice and research. Recent years have seen many significant documents and materials being produced by government agencies such as the Qualifications and Curriculum Authority (QCA), The Office for Standards in Education (OFSTED) and the National Literacy Centre. In the best of these documents rigorous academic arguments are being put forward to defend particular approaches to the curriculum. In other documents, such as the National Curriculum 2000, major policy changes have been signalled, of which books like this must take account. So you will see reflections on both national documentation and on a range of high quality, classroom-focused research. We cannot conceive of effective teaching which does not take into account research findings, but if further justification were required the following standard statement taken from Circular 4/98 provides an official rationale:

> **For all courses, those to be awarded Qualified Teacher Status must, when assessed, demonstrate that they:**
> d. v. are aware of, and know how to access, recent inspection evidence and classroom relevant research evidence on teaching primary pupils in the subject, and know how to use this to inform and improve their teaching;

We are fully in support of the idea that teaching should be an evidence-based activity. Each chapter in the book is underpinned by our reading of research. Most chapters include references to 'peer-reviewed' journals (a process which contributes to a higher quality of research) not just books. The academic standard of some books needs to be questioned particularly those that are not subject to a rigorous review process. However, the fact that books and their ideas often communicate to a wider audience is important, and for that reason we have carefully selected references to both books and papers. So in addition to the annotated bibliographies each chapter contains its own reference list which includes a range of texts that we think are worthy of further study.

In addition to our inclusion of papers, books and official publications we also make reference to a range of websites. This is always a tricky business. This book took one and a half years to complete and in that time information and communications technology (ICT) has continued to develop at an extreme pace. In the light of this we have chosen sites that we think will stand the test of time.

The most important part of reading a book like this is that it will enable you to become a better teacher. No book can offer a magic solution to becoming an effective teacher. Teaching skills and knowledge – like most learning – requires practical engagement with the subject in partnership with experienced professionals. However, in order to establish direct and explicit links with practice we use case-studies, analysis of resources, reflections on children's work, teacher's thoughts, examples of teaching, and each chapter concludes with 'practice points' which have been written to focus attention on some of the most important practical ideas of which you should be aware.

The issue of subject knowledge continues to be debated. 'Effective teachers...' funded by the TTA illustrated the important idea that particular kinds of subject knowledge were associated with effective teachers.

> Despite this apparent lack of explicit, abstract knowledge of linguistic concepts, these teachers were observed to use such knowledge implicitly in their teaching, particularly that connected with phonics. Our interpretation of this contradiction is that effective teachers knew the material that they were teaching in a particular way . . . they appeared to know and understand the material in the form in which they taught it to the children, which was usually as material which helped these

children read and write. The effective teachers' knowledge about content and their knowledge about teaching and learning strategies were integrated. The knowledge base of these teachers thus was their pedagogical content knowledge.

(Medwell et al, 1998: 76)

This book covers a wide range of essential knowledge. If we consider technical vocabulary alone, there are hundreds of definitions supplied in the 'glossaries' that are a feature of every chapter. So if you are unsure about the meaning of a particular word as you are reading you do not need to reach for a dictionary because most of the key words are defined for you at the end of the chapter. Another aspect of knowledge that has been played down in recent years is the knowledge of *issues*. It is the knowledge of these key issues that are vital to both effective teaching and success in the education profession. In order to maintain the tradition of English as a vibrant subject it is necessary for all teachers to continue to fully engage with the issues and ideas that are explored in this book.

Note
Throughout this book the following icons are used to assist the reader:
➡   Recommends the reader looks at another chapter in the book.
☞   These words are included in the glossary.

Part I

Introduction

Chapter 1

The history of English, language and literacy

One of the important aspects of historical knowledge is that it enables us to better understand the present. This chapter briefly examines three important historical angles: the history of English as a language; the history of the teaching of English; and the history of recent national initiatives to improve the teaching of English. We conclude in the present by looking at the creation of the National Literacy Strategy (☞).

The three words 'English', 'Language' and 'Literacy' in the title of this book are significant because they are central to many of the recent debates that have raged about the teaching of English in primary schools. During the 1970s and 1980s the teaching of 'language' was the focus. The job of primary schools was to foster the development of children's language through reading, writing and, to a lesser extent, talking. This focus included the need to support multilingual children's development in English and other languages. The teachers who coordinated the subject were known as 'language coordinators'. The teaching of language in primary schools was seen as different in many respects from the teaching of English that secondary schools carried out.

With the coming of the Education Reform Act 1988 'English' was re-established as the main focus for primary education, however, this was still to be concerned with the teaching of the three language modes of reading, writing and talking. 'Speaking and Listening' became of equal importance to reading and writing for the first time, and this was prescribed by the National Curriculum. Coordinators were now to be called 'English' coordinators. Since then the advent of the National Literacy Strategy in 1997 has resulted in a heavy focus on 'Literacy'. You will probably have guessed that subject leaders were renamed 'literacy coordinators'.

The first part of this chapter looks at some of the historical aspects of the subject that have shaped its development. It is vital that all teachers have a historical perspective on their work, at the very least this can give you a means to critically examine modern initiatives and to check how 'new' they really are. We start with a brief look at some of the significant moments in the development of the English language and reflect on their continuing relevance to classroom teaching. This is followed by reflections on the history of the *teaching* of English. We conclude with an outline of some of the recent major national projects that have been undertaken and finish right up-to-date with a look at the National Literacy Strategy.

THE ENGLISH LANGUAGE

English, like all languages, is constantly changing. When the editor of the Oxford English dictionary was interviewed in 1998 he commented on the fact that 'phwoarr' had recently been included in the dictionary, defined as an exclamation of sexual attraction. Each time publishers produce new editions of dictionaries, new words – and new meanings for old words – are added in recognition that language is always changing. For teachers, the idea that language is always changing is an important one. If we place too heavy an emphasis on absolute and fixed 'rules', we may be teaching in a linguistically inaccurate or inappropriate way. Modern teaching needs to recognise those features of the language that are stable and those that are subject to constant change. Two more examples illustrate the kinds of change that continue to happen. You may have been taught to start a formal letter like this: 'Dear Mrs Jones,' including the comma and the idea that the first line of a paragraph should be indented. Yet modern business conventions have resulted in the use of the comma in this context becoming redundant and the indent being omitted, in order to save time. On the other hand most books still do indent the first line of a paragraph, but often they only use *one* inverted comma for indicating direct speech – you may have been taught to use two speech marks. Frank McCourt does not use any speech marks at all for the dialogue in his novel *'Angela's Ashes'*.

The increasing standardisation of the language has resulted in changes to the pace and nature of change. Dictionaries themselves have a major role in the standardisation of the language, and it is interesting to note that standard American English is represented by *Webster's Dictionary* but Standard (English) English is represented by the *Oxford English Dictionary* or *Chambers Dictionary* for many things. The significant influence of publishing has also resulted in standard reference works that lay down particular conventions. So if you have ever wondered how to reference properly using the 'Harvard' method (☞) try *The Chicago Manual of Style*, but if you want to know about the referencing of electronic sources try the international standard held by the National Library of Canada.

If we look back in time we can see that this process of change is by no means a recent phenomenon. It was during the fifth century that the Anglo-Saxons settled in England, and as always happens when people settle they brought changes to the language, which was at that time 'old English'. The texts that have survived from the period are in four main dialects (☞): West Saxon, Kentish, Mercian, and Northumbrian. West Saxon became the standard dialect at the time, but is not the direct ancestor of modern standard

English (☞) which is mainly derived from an Anglian dialect (Barber, 1993). If we take the modern word 'cold' as an example, the West Saxon version was 'ceald' but the Anglian was 'cald', which is the stronger influence.

In the ninth century the Vikings bought further changes to the language. Placenames were affected: 'Grimsby' meant Grim's village and 'Micklethwaite' meant large clearing. The pronunciation of English speech was also affected, and it is possible to recognise some Scandinavian influenced words because of their phonological form (☞). It is suggested that 'awe' is a Scandinavian word and that this came from changes of pronunciation to the Old English word 'ege'. One of the most interesting things about Scandinavian loanwords (☞) is that they are so commonly used: sister, leg, neck, bag, cake, dirt, fellow, fog, knife, skill, skin, sky, window, flat, loose, call, drag and even 'they' and 'them' (Barber, 1993).

In more recent times words from a range of countries have been borrowed. Here are a small selection of examples: French – elite, liaison, menu, plateau; Spanish and Portuguese – alligator, chocolate, cannibal, embargo, potato; Italian – concerto, balcony, casino, cartoon; Indian – bangle, cot, juggernaut, loot, pyjamas, shampoo; African languages – banjo, zombie, rumba, tote. However, for many of these words it is difficult to attribute them to one original country. To illustrate the complexities consider the word 'chess':

> 'Chess' was borrowed from Middle French in the fourteenth century. The French word was, in turn, borrowed from Arabic, which had earlier borrowed it from Persian 'shah' 'king'. Thus the etymology (☞) of the word reaches from Persian, through Arabic and Middle French, but its ultimate source (as far back as we can trace its history) is Persian. Similarly, the etymon of 'chess', that is, the word from which it has been derived, is immediately 'esches' and ultimately 'shah'. Loanwords have, as it were, a life of their own that cuts across the boundaries between languages.
>
> (Pyles and Algeo, 1993: 286)

The influence of loanwords is one of the factors that has resulted in some of the irregularities of English spelling. David Crystal (1997) lists some of the other major factors. Above we referred to the Anglo-Saxon period; at that time there were only 24 graphemes (letter symbols) to represent 40 phonemes (sounds). Later 'i' and 'j', 'u' and 'v' were changed from being interchangeable to having distinct functions and 'w' was added but many sounds still had to be signalled by combinations of letters.

After the Norman conquest French scribes – who had responsibility for publishing texts – respelled a great deal of the language. They introduced new conventions such as 'qu' for 'cw' (queen), 'gh' for 'h' (night) and 'c' before 'e' or 'i' in words such as 'circle' and 'cell'. Once printing became better established in the West this added further complications. William Caxton (1422–91) is often credited with the 'invention' of the printing press but that is not accurate. During the seventh century the Chinese printed the earliest known book *The Diamond Sutra*, using inked wooden relief blocks. By the beginning of the fifteenth century the process had developed in Korea to the extent that printers were manufacturing bronze type sets of 100,000 pieces. In the West, Johannes Gutenberg (1390s–1468) is credited with the development of moveable metal type in association with a hand-operated printing press.

Many of the early printers working in England were foreign (especially from Holland) and they used their own spelling conventions. Also, until the sixteenth century, line justification (☞) was achieved by changing words rather than by adding spaces. Once printing became established, the written language did not keep pace with the considerable changes in the way words were spoken, resulting in weaker links between sound and symbol.

Samuel Johnson's dictionary published in 1755 was another important factor in relation to English spelling. His work resulted in dictionaries becoming more authoritarian and used as the basis for 'correct' usage. Noah Webster the first person to write a major account of American English compared Johnson's contribution to Isaac Newton's in mathematics. Johnson's dictionary was significant for a number of reasons. Unlike dictionaries of the past that tended to concentrate on 'hard words', Johnson wanted a scholarly record of the whole language. It was based on words in use and introduced a literary dimension drawing heavily on writers such as Dryden, Milton, Addison, Bacon, Pope and Shakespeare (Crystal, 1997: 109).

Shakespeare's remarkable influence on the English language is not confined to the artistic significance of his work, many of the words and phrases of his plays are still commonly used today:

> He coined some 2,000 words – an astonishing number – and gave us countless phrases. As a phrasemaker there has never been anyone to match him. Among his inventions: one fell swoop, in my mind's eye, more in sorrow than in anger, to be in a pickle, bag and baggage, vanish into thin air, budge an inch, play fast and loose, go down the primrose path, the milk of human kindness, remembrance of things past, the sound and fury, to thine own self be true, to be or not to be, cold comfort, to beggar all description, salad days, flesh and blood, foul play, tower of strength, to be cruel to be kind, and on and on and on and on. And on. He was so wildly prolific that he could put two in one sentence, as in Hamlet's observation: 'Though I am native here and to the manner born, it is custom more honoured in the breach than the observance.' He could even mix metaphors and get away with it, as when he wrote: 'Or to take arms against a sea of troubles.'
>
> (Bryson, 1990: 57)

THE TEACHING OF ENGLISH

The establishment of state education as we know it can be conveniently traced back to the 1870 Elementary Education Act. Before that, the education of working class children in this country was largely in the hands of the voluntary sector: church schools, factory schools, and, in the earlier part of the nineteenth century, schools run by the oppositional Chartist and Owenite

Co-operative movements. The 1870 Act led to the establishment of free educational provision in elementary schools for all children from the age of 5 up to the age of 12. Education up to the age of 10 was compulsory, but if children had met the standards required they could be exempted from schooling for the final years. State schools and voluntary sector schools existed side by side from that date, a distinction that is still found today. Class differences were firmly established: the elementary and voluntary schools were schools for the labouring classes and the poor. The middle and upper classes expected to pay for the education of their children; secondary education in the form of the grammar and public schools was not available to the bulk of the population.

The curriculum in the voluntary schools and later in the elementary schools was extremely limited. Writing meant copying or dictation (DES, 1967: S601). Oral work involved such things as the children learning by heart from the Book of Common Prayer, which included: 'To order myself lowly and reverently to all my betters' and 'to do my duty in that state of life, unto which it shall please God to call me' (Williamson, 1981: 79).

The elementary schools emerged at a time when the government exerted considerable control over the curriculum through the 'Revised Code' established in 1862, better known as 'payment by results'. This was administered through frequent tests in reading, writing, and arithmetic – the three Rs. If the children failed to meet the required standards, the grant was withdrawn and the teachers did not get paid. Under such conditions curriculum development was impossible because schools had to focus so much on the tests in order to get paid (Lawson and Silver, 1973).

Though the code was abolished in 1895, and the statutory control of the curriculum relinquished in 1902, the effects lasted well into the twentieth century, leading one inspector to comment that 30 years of 'code despotism' meant that 'teaching remained as mechanical and routine ridden as ever'. (Holmes, 1922). Despite these criticisms, however, the introduction of universal compulsory education meant that literacy rates climbed steadily until, by the end of the nineteenth century, some 97% of the population were literate. However, it should be remembered that definitions of what constitutes 'literate' continue to change.

'English' as a subject 1900–39

At the start of the twentieth century the term 'English' referred to grammar. Reading and writing were not even seen as part of 'English'. The emergence of English as a school subject in its own right occurred in the first years of the twentieth century. A major landmark in the development of the subject was the Newbolt Report on 'The Teaching of English in England' (Board of Education, 1921). Sampson, a member of the Newbolt committee, writing in the same year (1921) had identified the following 'subjects' still being taught in elementary schools across the land:

> . . . oral composition, written composition, dictation, grammar, repro-

duction, reading, recitation, literature, spelling, and handwriting.
(Shayer 1972: 67)

The Newbolt report sought to change that and to bring together:

> ... under the title of English, 'taught as a fine art', four separate con-
> cepts: the universal need for literacy as the core of the curriculum, the
> developmental importance of children's self expression, a belief in the
> power of English literature for moral and social improvement, and a con-
> cern for 'the full development of mind and character'.
> (Protherough and Atkinson, 1994: 7)

This was how English became established as a subject in the secondary curriculum, and placed at the centre of the curriculum for all ages. Famously the
Newbolt report suggested, of elementary teachers, that 'every teacher is a
teacher *of* English because every teacher is a teacher *in* English' (Shayer,
1972: 70). The committee recommended that children's creative language
skills should be developed. They recommended the study of literature in the
elementary schools. In addition they recommended the development of children's oral work, albeit in the form of 'speech training', which they saw as
the basis for written work. Finally they challenged the nineteenth century
legacy of educational class division, placing English at the centre of an educational aim to develop the 'mind and character' of *all* children.

Change on the ground was slow to occur but it was happening. The old
practice of reading aloud in chorus was disappearing, silent reading was
being encouraged and, in the 1920s, textbooks were published that encouraged children's free expression and that questioned the necessity for formal
grammar teaching. However, although within the pages of the Newbolt
report there was evidence of the uselessness of grammar teaching, the committee had the strong feeling that self-expression could go too far, and that
the best way for children to learn to write was to study grammar and to copy
good models.

The Hadow reports

The years 1926, 1931, and 1933 saw the publication of the three Hadow
reports on secondary, primary and infant education respectively, the second
(Board of Education, 1931) focused on the 7–11 age range. It had a number
of specific recommendations about the curriculum in general and English in
particular. Famously, it stated:

> We are of the opinion that the curriculum of the primary school is to be
> thought of in terms of activity and experience rather than of knowledge
> to be acquired and facts to be stored.
> (Board of Education, 1931: 139)

In English oral work was seen as important, with an emphasis on speaking
'correctly', and including 'oral composition', getting the child to talk on a
topic of their choice or one of the teacher's. 'Reproduction' involved getting

the child to recount the subject matter of the lesson they had just been taught.

Class libraries were encouraged, and silent reading was recommended, though not in school time except in the most deprived areas. And the aim?

> In the upper stage of primary education the child should gain a sense of the printed page and begin to read for pleasure and information.
> (Board of Education, 1931: 158).

As for writing, children's written composition should build on oral composition and children should be given topics that interested them. Spelling should be related to the children's writing and reading:

> Any attempt to teach spelling otherwise than in connection with the actual practice of writing or reading is beset with obvious dangers.
> (ibid: 160)

The abstract study of formal grammar was rejected, though some grammar was to be taught. Bilingualism was addressed in the Welsh context, and teaching in the mother tongue was recommended. Welsh-speaking children were expected to learn English and, strikingly, English-speaking children were expected to learn Welsh.

The third Hadow report (Board of Education, 1933) drew on ideas current at the time to suggest that formal instruction of the three Rs traditionally started too early in British schools, and recommended that for infant and nursery children:

> The child should begin to learn the 3 Rs when he (sic) wants to do so, whether he be three or six years old.
> (Board of Education, 1933: 133)

The report noted three methods of teaching reading that were used at the time: 'look and say', 'phonics' and more contextualised meaning-centred 'sentence' methods. It recommended that teachers should use a mix of the three as appropriate to the child's needs. Writing should start at the same time as reading, and children's natural desire to write in imitation of the adult writing they saw around them at home or at school should be encouraged. The child should have control over the subject matter and his or her efforts should be valued by the teacher as real attempts to communicate meaning.

The report emphasised the importance of imaginative play, and noted, 'Words mean nothing to the young child unless they are definitively associated with active experience' (Board of Education, 1933: 181) and, 'Oral lessons should be short and closely related to the child's practical interests' (1933: 182). While 'speech training' was important, drama work was recommended for the development of children's language, and nursery rhymes and game songs were encouraged alongside traditional hymns. Stories should be told and read to the children.

The Hadow reports read as remarkably progressive documents for their time, and the principles of child-centred education that are explicit in many of their recommendations continued to inform thinking in primary language teaching for the next 50 years.

Progressive education (☞) 1931–75

The central years of the twentieth century can perhaps be characterised as the years of progressive aspiration so far as primary language was concerned. The progressive views of the Hadow reports began to be reflected in the Board of Education's regular guidelines, and teachers were on the whole free to follow them as they pleased. The 1944 Education Act itself offered no curriculum advice, except with regard to religious education, and central guidance on the curriculum ended in 1945. The primary curriculum in particular came to be regarded as something of a 'secret garden' to quote a Tory minister of education from the 1960s (Gordon et al, 1991: 287)

The 1944 Education Act finally established primary schools in place of elementary schools, though it would be another 20 years before the last school that included all ages of children closed. At secondary level a three-layered system of grammar, technical, and secondary modern schools was established, and a new exam, the 11+, was devised to decide which children should go where. Like the scholarship exam before it, the 11+ continued to restrain the primary language curriculum, particularly with the older children, in spite of the fact that more progressive child-centred measures were gaining ground with younger children. With the reorganisation of secondary schools along comprehensive lines in the 1960s (encapsulated in circular 10/65) the 11+ was abolished and the primary curriculum was technically freed from all constraint.

In retrospect the Plowden Report on primary education (DES, 1967) can be seen as centrally representative of the progressive aspiration of 'child-centred education'. Its purpose was to report on effective primary education of the time, and it was concerned to see to what extent the Hadow recommendations had been put into effect. It functioned as much to disseminate effective practice as it did to recommend future change. The child was central: 'At the heart of the educational process lies the child' (1967: S9); and language was crucial: 'Spoken language plays a central role in learning' (1967: S54) and 'The development of language is, therefore, central to the educational process' (1967: S55).

Like its predecessors, the report emphasised the importance of talk; like its predecessors, it emphasised the fact that effective teachers of reading used a mix of approaches. Drama work and story telling were to be encouraged, the increased importance of fiction and poetry written for children and the development of school libraries were all emphasised. The report applauded wholeheartedly the development of personal 'creative' writing (➡ Chapter 12, The Development of Writing) from the children, characterising it as a dramatic revolution (1967: S601). About spelling and punctuation the committee was more reticent, noting only that when inaccuracy impeded communication then steps should be taken to remedy the deficiencies (1967: S602). Knowledge about language was seen as an interesting new area but 'Formal study of grammar will have little place in the primary school' (1967: S612).

The Plowden Report was followed by the Bullock Report on English (DES, 1975). So far as primary age children were concerned this spelt out in more detail much of what was already implicit in Plowden. Central to both the reports was an emphasis on the 'process' of language learning. From such a perspective children's oral and written language would best develop in meaningful language use. A couple of quotes from the Bullock report will illustrate the point. Of the development of oral language it suggested:

> Language should be learned in the course of using it in, and about, the daily experiences of the classroom and the home.
>
> (DES, 1975: 520)

Where writing was concerned:

> Competence in language comes above all through its purposeful use, not through working of exercises divorced from context.
>
> (DES, 1975: 528

So far as bilingual children and children from the ethnic minorities were concerned the Plowden Report had already recognised the contribution that such children could make to the classroom, and the Bullock committee was concerned that such children should not find school an alien place:

> No child should be expected to cast off the language and culture of the home as he [sic] crosses the school threshold, nor to live and act as though home and school represent two totally separate and different cultures which have to be kept firmly apart. The curriculum should reflect many elements of that part of his life which a child lives outside school.
>
> (DES, 1975: S20.5)

Back to basics: 1976 onwards

The ideas of progressive education remained important – despite increasingly frequent attacks – until the 1970s when things started to change. Britain was declining in world economic importance and the oil crisis of the early 1970s was followed by an International Monetary Fund (IMF) loan which saw the Labour government of the time having to cut back on public spending. Effective child-centred education is teacher intensive and requires small classes, and the previous decades had seen reductions in class size. That was no longer compatible with the financial constraints of the time and class sizes began to increase again. A more regulated curriculum is easier to cope with in such circumstances.

The national curriculum itself was established by the 1988 Education Reform Act, which in the process gave the secretary of state considerable powers of direct intervention in curriculum matters. Following the act, curriculum documents were drawn up for all the major subject areas. In line with the recommendations of the TGAT report (DES, 1987: S227), attainment in each subject was to be measured against a ten-level scale and tested at ages 7, 11, 14 and 16. As the curriculum was introduced into schools it became clear that each subject group had produced documents of considerable complexity. Discontent in the profession grew and a slimmed down version was introduced in 1995.

The original English document was prepared by a committee under the chairmanship of Brian Cox (DES, 1989,1990; Cox, 1991) English was to be divided up into five 'attainment targets': Speaking and Listening, Reading, Writing, Spelling, and Handwriting. These were reorganised to three in Sir Ron Dearing's 1995 rewrite, as Spelling and Handwriting were incorporated into Writing (DFE, 1995). In 1998 the Framework for Teaching (DfEE, 1998) was introduced and primary teachers found themselves confronted with their third major change in eight years.

Since 1988 the subject of English has suffered more than most from direct political intervention (Cox, 1995). This is illustrated by increasing demands for a return to traditional grammar teaching, in an increasing emphasis on Standard English, in views about which texts were to be studied in school, and latterly in intervention in the methods of teaching children to read and write.

RECENT NATIONAL PROJECTS

During the mid to late 1980s a number of large-scale projects were undertaken which aimed to improve the teaching and learning of English. The Schools Council, a body responsible for national curriculum development, had been replaced by the School Curriculum Development Committee (SCDC); the SCDC initiated the National Writing Project. This was in two phases: the development phase took place from 1985–88 and the implementation phase from 1988–89, although the Education Reform Act 1988 and the resulting National Curriculum and testing arrangements changed the focus of implementation.

One of the key problems was that many children were being turned off by writing, and this was supported by some evidence from the Assessment of Performance Unit (APU). The APU found that as many as four in ten children did not find writing an enjoyable experience and 'not less than one in ten pupils [had] an active dislike of writing and endeavour[ed] to write as little as possible' (APU, 1988: 170). Somewhat later the National Writing Project gathered evidence that many children, particularly young children, tended to equate writing with transcription skills rather than composition.

The National Writing Project involved thousands of educators across the country. One of the main messages from the project was that writers needed to become involved in writing for a defined and recognisable audience not just because the teacher said so. Connected to these ideas was the notion that writing should have a meaningful purpose. With these key concepts in place teachers began to realise that writing tasks which were sequentially organised in school exercise books and consisting of one draft – or at best 'rough copy/neat copy' drafts – were not helping to address the audiences and purposes that needed to be generated.

The National Oracy Project was also initiated by SCDC and partly overlapped with the National Writing Project. During the period from 1987–91, 35 local education authorities were involved in the oracy project. The recognition that oracy, or speaking and listening as it came to be called, needed a national initiative was in itself significant. Since the late 1960s a number of enlightened educators had realised that talking and learning were very closely linked and that the curriculum should reflect that reality. But these people were in a minority and most educators continued to emphasise reading and, to a lesser extent, writing. The major achievement of the oracy project was to secure recognition that talk was important and that children could learn more if teachers understood the issues, and planned activities to support the development of oracy. As Wells pointed out:

> The centrality of talk in education is finally being recognised. Not simply in theory – in the exhortations of progressive-minded academics – but mandated at all levels and across all subjects in a national curriculum.
>
> (Wells, 1992: 283)

The other large national project that we will touch on is the Language in the National Curriculum (LINC) project. In 1987 a committee of inquiry was commissioned to make recommendations about the sort of knowledge about language that it would be appropriate to teach in school. The Kingman Report, as it was known (DES, 1988), disappointed the right-wing politicians and sections of the press when it failed to advocate a return to traditional grammar teaching. The Cox Report (DES, 1989) ran into similar problems for the same reason, but both the 1990 and the 1995 orders for English in the National Curriculum (DES, 1990; DFE, 1995) contented themselves with general recommendations to use grammatical terms where and as the need arose. Between 1989 and 1992 most schools in England were involved with the LINC project. Its main aim was to acquaint teachers with the model of language presented in the Kingman Report. Kingman's work reaffirmed the idea that children and teachers should have sufficient 'knowledge about language' or 'KAL' if they were to become successful language users.

One of the strong features of the materials that were produced by the LINC project was that they were built on an explicit set of principles and theories:

Principles
1   Teaching children should start positively from what they can already do.
2   The experience of using language should precede analysis.
3   Language should be explored in real purposeful situations not analysed out of context.
4   An understanding of people's attitudes to language can help you understand more about values and beliefs.

Theories:
1   Humans use language for social reasons.
2   Language is constantly changing.
3   Language is a cultural phenomenon.
4   There are important connections between language and power.
5   Language is systematically organised.
6   The meanings of language depend on negotiation.

It may have been that some of these philosophies resulted in the politicians of the time refusing to publish the materials. In spite of this the materials were photocopied and distributed widely and various publications independent of government were produced which continue to be influential e.g. Carter, 1990.

The National Literacy Strategy

Most political education initiatives are introduced following claims that standards are falling, and the National Literacy Strategy was no exception. However, in spite of regular claims by the media, teachers, business people, politicians, etc., there is no evidence that standards of literacy have declined in England as Beard (1999) pointed out; something that Campbell (1997) also commented upon.

> On the current moral panic over the impact of the reforms on standards of attainment in literacy and numeracy, there are two things to say. First, no-one can be sure about standards in literacy and numeracy because of the failure – unquestioned failure – of the national agencies (NCC, SEAC and now SCAA) to establish an effective, credible and reliable mechanism for the national monitoring of standards over time since 1989.
> (Campbell, 1997: 22)

Although what evidence there is indicates that standards have not fallen, the evidence from comparisons of reading in different countries places England and Wales in a middle group of countries and out-performed by countries like Finland, France and New Zealand, and politically this is offered as one of the reasons for the need for higher standards. Related to this, perhaps the real political rationale for the literacy strategy, is Britain's declining international economic success. Politicians have made clear connections between standards in education and future economic prosperity. Of course, it does not necessarily follow that an education system that primarily serves economic competitiveness is the right one for the majority of its learners.

In addition to the links with economic prosperity the other major strand to the rationale for the National Literacy Strategy is the research evidence from the school effectiveness (☞) and school improvement (☞) literature. There is a significant body of research that has suggested a wide range of features that are part of 'good' schools. In the UK David Reynolds has been an influential figure in relation to this research. In his paper that looks at literacy and effectiveness a number of significant points are made. Information from research and practice strongly supports the idea that for curriculum change to be effective there must be high levels of ownership by the 'end users'. Reynolds (1998) suggests that in relation to the National Literacy Strategy there has been a lack of teacher input related to decisions on: choice of appropriate knowledge, consultation, and school level organisation of the strategies. It is important that all teachers continue to ask questions about the levels of genuine consultation that are being offered. Reynolds also adds that 'Reading recovery' (➡ Chapter 10, 'Reading recovery') and 'Success for all' are two programmes that are unique in that they have resulted in the highest gains in reading ever seen in educational research and unusually they have affected the low-scoring children in particular. In spite of this fact, reading recovery is no longer being used as a national strategy.

The idea that standards can be improved is, of course, always true. The performance of children in England and Wales as assessed by international comparisons of reading attainment has resulted in the recognition of what has been called a 'long tail of underachievement'. These findings have in part been seen as a rationale for the National Literacy Strategy.

> The Literacy Task Force was established on 31 May 1996 by David Blunkett, then Shadow Secretary of State for Education and Employment. It was charged with developing, in time for an incoming Labour government, a strategy for substantially raising standards of literacy in primary schools over a five to ten year period.
>
> (Literacy Task Force, 1997: 4)

The members of the Literacy Task Force were as follows: Professor Michael Barber (Chair) – Head of the Standards and Effectiveness Unit, Department for Education and Employment; John Botham – Headteacher, Greenwood Junior School, Nottingham; Ken Follett – Novelist; Simon Goodenough – Chair of governors, Queen Elizabeth Community College, Devon; Mary Gray – Retired Headteacher, Fair Furlong School, Bristol; David Pitt-Watson – Deloitte Et Touche; David Reynolds – Professor of Education, University of Newcastle; Anne Waterhouse – Headteacher, Asmall County Primary School, Lancashire; Diane Wright – Parent. It is interesting to note that none of the task force members had a national reputation for their academic expertise in the teaching of English.

The literary task force produced a final report that suggested how a National Literacy Strategy could be implemented. The recommendations heralded some of the most profound changes to English teaching. The single most important driving force behind the strategy is the setting of targets: specifically that by 2002, 80% of 11-year-olds should reach the standard expected for their age in English (i.e. Level 4) in the Key Stage 2 National Standard Assessment Tasks (SATs). This target-setting has resulted in local education authorities negotiating targets with central government, and schools negotiating with their authorities. While such targets may enforce a common sense of direction there are problems that have long been recognised, such as the narrowing of the curriculum as teachers prepare students for the tests. Searching questions have also been asked about the implications for areas where there are high levels of deprivation and whether it is possible to evaluate not just crude test scores but whether schools are 'adding value'. This is particularly pertinent for schools who achieve high *gains* in achievement but whose children start from low levels. In order to achieve the targets schools were guaranteed professional development opportunities if they fulfilled certain demands: set literacy targets and agree them with the LEA; devote a structured hour each day to literacy for all pupils; produce a school literacy action plan for the next two years; produce detailed and practical schemes of work for literacy in line with the National Curriculum requirements, and comparable to that used in the National Literacy Project (☞).

Overall the National Literacy Strategy is an ambitious and wide-ranging vision. Part of the philosophy includes the importance of appealing to the community as a whole not just making changes to schools; so business and the wider community were included as partners in the process. Initiatives to help this included a National Year of Reading, summer literacy schools, special soap-opera scripts focusing on literacy, extra money for books and so on.

The National Literacy Project

Another of the key features of the strategy is the 'Framework for Teaching' which was developed through the introduction of the National Literacy Project between 1996 and 1998. The project's main aim was to raise the standards of literacy in the participating schools so that they raised their achievements in line with national expectations. The project established for the first time a detailed scheme of work with term by term objectives that were organised into text level, sentence level and word level. These were to be delivered through the use of a daily literacy hour. The timings for the hour were slightly more flexible than those in the current literacy hour. The project was supported by a national network of centres where literacy consultants were available to support project schools.

The National Literacy Project was important because it has been claimed that its success was the reason that the National Literacy Strategy adopted the ideas of a Framework for Teaching and a prescribed literacy hour. However, it should be remembered that the schools who were involved in the project were schools who had identified weaknesses in their literacy teaching and this has to be taken into account when any kind of evaluation is made about the success of the project. The other important point to bear in mind is that it was originally conceived as a five-year project; after that time, evaluations were to be carried out. One of the features of these evaluations was that they were supposed to measure the success of the three years of the programme when schools were no longer *directly* involved in the project. In the event, the approaches of the National Literacy Project were adopted as part of the National Literacy Strategy in 1998. This occurred *before* any independent evaluation had been carried out and long before the planned five-year extent of the National Literacy Project.

The only *independent* evaluation of the project carried out by the National Foundation for Educational Research (NFER) found that:

> The analyses of the test outcomes have indicated that, in terms of the standardised scores on reading tests, the pupils involved in Cohort 1 of the National Literacy Project have made substantial gains. All three year groups showed significant and substantial increases in scores from the beginning to end of the project.
>
> (Sainsbury et al, 1998: 21)

This outcome illustrates definite progress in the fairly restricted parameters of standardised reading tests. It is not possible to conclude that the specific approach of the National Literacy Project was more beneficial than other approaches as this variable was not controlled. It is possible that the financial investment, extra support and a new initiative were the dominant factors in improved test scores rather than the particular characteristics of the recommended teaching methods. One area of concern about the findings from the evaluation was that pupils eligible for free school meals, pupils with special educational needs, pupils with English as an additional language (EAL) at the 'becoming familiar with English stage', and boys, made less progress than other groups. This is a concern that is mirrored by worries that the Framework for Teaching does not cater for individual needs well enough. It distorts the long-held view that a mixture of individual, group, and whole class teaching is the most appropriate way to teach, by heavily emphasising whole class and group teaching. A particular concern for parents has been the shift away from the traditional practice of individual reading (➡ Chapter 6, 'Listening to Children Read') that is no longer recommended as the most effective form of teaching.

It seems particularly regrettable, though not surprising, that no serious attempt has been made to evaluate what pupils thought of the project. Sainsbury et al admitted that

> The reading enjoyment findings are less easy to interpret. The survey showed that children do, on the whole, enjoy their reading, with substantial majorities of both age groups expressing favourable attitudes both before and after involvement in the project. These measures, however, did not change very much, indicating that the systematic introduction of different text types that was a feature of the project did not have any clearly apparent effect on children's enjoyment of reading these varied text types. In the absence of a control group, however, it is difficult to draw any more definite conclusions.
>
> (Sainsbury et al, 1998: 27)

If higher standards are to be achieved, it is essential to fully involve those people who arguably are going to be most affected by the changes, namely the children. Motivation is an extremely important factor in learning and is closely tied to involvement and empowerment (☞). In the twenty-first century this is not simply something to be bolted on as an afterthought, it is part of children's rights as recognised under international law (see Wyse and Hawtin, 2000). The history of curriculum reform would suggest that meaningful involvement of the children themselves does not happen. An OFSTED (1998) evaluation of the National Literacy Project illustrates this in a section on pupils' responses where 'class control' and 'behaviour' were cited as significant aspects of pupils' responses rather than a genuine attempt to assess what their views were about the project.

Evaluating the National Literacy Strategy

At the time of writing there was only one formal evaluation of The National Literacy Strategy called *An Interim Evaluation* (OFSTED, 1999). Like the other OFSTED evaluation commented on above, there are grounds for being cautious about its findings. The objectivity of OFSTED's inspections and reports has repeatedly been called into question over the last few years. This was a fact that the parliamentary select committee on education and employment recognised.

> 129. We welcome the fact that OFSTED has undertaken research on the validity (☞) and reliability (☞) of inspectors' judgements. However, we note the criticisms of this research project. It is important that there is confidence about this fundamental aspect of inspection. Full and frank research into this area must establish the level of reliability and validity of the basic elements of inspection. We wish to see research into this issue extended. It is important, to help ensure public acceptance of inspection, that such work is open to scrutiny by the academic community. Given that the OFSTED research was carried out in 1996, and the inspection system has evolved since then, it might also be timely to consider carrying out a similar exercise using a wider sample of inspectors than OFSTED's initial research.
>
> (Select Committee on Education and Employment, 1999: Section 29)

The interim evaluation found that the teaching of word- and sentence-level strands, phonics, writing, independent group activities, and teaching generally at years 3 and 4, were all weaknesses. As far as year 3 teaching is concerned it should be remembered that this is the cohort who will sit the SAT in 2002 and who will determine whether the national target is achieved or not. While we might have questions about the objectivity of the conclusions about year 3 teaching there has been a clear commitment signalled by extra money for 'booster classes' and additional support materials. As far as the teaching of writing and the organisation of independent group activities is concerned there seems to be a greater level of consensus that these are areas that need to be improved.

Since the introduction of the National Literacy Strategy Framework for

Teaching a number of criticisms have emerged. Hilton's (1998) polemical (☞) argument makes the important point that longitudinal (☞) research evidence showing the advantage of particular teaching approaches is scarce. She goes on to report two significant studies that show that economic and social disadvantage are the biggest factors in relation to literacy skills not teaching methods. She concludes that links with parents – and approaches that emphasise this community involvement – are vital. Campbell (1998) questions why there should be a literacy 'hour' and not one and a half or two hours. He also reminds us that various activities are supposed to happen outside of the hour including sustained silent reading and reading aloud to children. The idea that reading aloud to children is given such a low priority in the literacy hour is something that Graham (1998) finds extraordinary in the light of the documented benefits for such reading.

Earlier in this chapter we mentioned the important contribution of Brian Cox. Following his achievements with the English National Curriculum documents it is appropriate to conclude with his views on the National Literacy Strategy which are included in his recent book *Literacy is not Enough*; he does not mince his words: the policy on reading 'is too prescriptive, authoritarian and mechanistic', there should be 'more emphasis on motivation, on helping children to enjoy reading'(Cox, 1998: ix). Other contributors are equally critical: Margaret Meek (1998: 116) criticises the 'repeated exercises in comprehension, grammar and spelling' and Bethan Marshall (1998: 109) suggests that 'the bleak spectre of utilitarianism (☞) hangs over our schools like a pall'. The words of an inspector in 1905 quoted by Marshall should cause all concerned to think very carefully about the potential impact of the National Literacy Strategy:

> A blackboard has been produced, and hieroglyphics are drawn upon it by the teacher. At a given signal every child in the class begins calling out mysterious sounds: 'Letter A, letter A' in a sing-song voice, or 'Letter A says Ah, letter A says Ah', as the case may be. To the uninitiated I may explain that No. 1 is the beginning of the spelling, and No. 2 is the beginning of word building. Hoary-headed men will spend hours discussing whether 'c-a-t' or 'ker-ar-te' are the best means of conveying the knowledge of how to read 'cat'. I must own an indifference to the point myself, and sympathise with teachers not allowed to settle it for themselves . . . 'Wake up, Johnny; it's not time to go to sleep yet. Be a good boy and watch teacher.'
>
> (Marshall, 1998: 115)

There are a number of features of the framework that seem to break with some of the traditions of English teaching that we outlined earlier. The prescriptive nature of allocating objectives to school years and terms is unprecedented in the history of teaching English. The framework divides the objectives into word-level, sentence-level, and text-level work (this differs from the original National Literacy Project framework in that text level work appeared as the first column). The framework also spells out the 'technical vocabulary' that children are supposed to acquire: 4- and 5-year-old reception children are expected to know the terms 'phoneme', 'grapheme', 'onset', 'rime', etc. Fortunately the framework also contains a very useful glossary! There is no legal requirement for schools to adopt the framework or the prescribed hour, although the inspection system has created pressure to do so.

At the time of writing the National Literacy Strategy was very much in its infancy. A Canadian academic had been appointed to undertake an evaluation of the strategy and we look forward to that with interest. However, few people would argue with the importance of the points that make up the definition of a literate child, even if they may be unhappy with the authoritarian sounding 'Literate primary children should':

- read and write with confidence fluency and understanding;
- be interested in books, read with enjoyment and evaluate and justify preferences;
- know and understand a range of genres in fiction and poetry, and understand and be familiar with some of the ways that narratives are structured through basic literary ideas of setting, character and plot;
- understand and be able to use a range of non-fiction texts;
- be able to orchestrate a full range of reading cues (phonic, graphic, syntactic, contextual) to monitor and self-correct their own reading;
- plan draft revise and edit their own writing;
- have an interest in words and word meanings, and a growing vocabulary;
- understand the sound and spelling system and use this to read and spell accurately;
- have fluent and legible handwriting.

(DfEE, 1998: 3)

Practice points

- As a professional you should evaluate all educational initiatives critically to ensure that they reflect the needs of the children that you teach.
- You need to develop a knowledge of historical developments as a vital tool for understanding educational change.
- The National Literacy Strategy Framework for Teaching will need to be changed at some point in the future. It is important that you take an active part in that process by (1) fully understanding the Framework; (2) communicating your opinions about its effectiveness.

Glossary

Dialect – regional variations of language shown by different words and grammar.
Empowerment – full and equal involvement in societal activities.
Etymology – the origins of words.
'Harvard' method – a system for citations and references that is sometimes

called the 'author/date' system. Mainly used in the social sciences.

Line justification – ensuring that the beginnings and ends of lines of print are all lined up.

Loan words – words adopted from other languages.

Longitudinal – research carried out over extended periods of time with the same sample of participants; usually at least five years.

National Literacy Project – a three-year professional development project that was carried out with authorities and schools who wanted to raise their standards of literacy.

National Literacy Strategy – a national strategy for raising standards in literacy over a five- to ten-year period.

Phonological form – the sounds of the words.

Polemical – writing and views which are deliberately controversial.

Progressive education – teaching approaches that rejected old-fashioned rote learning methods in favour of methods that put the child's interests and needs first.

Reliability – the extent to which research findings can be replicated by the same or other methods.

School effectiveness – a movement that has used research to identify the key features that characterise effective schools.

School improvement – a movement that has recommended the actions that are necessary for schools to improve their practice based on research evidence.

Standard English – the formal language of written communication in particular. Many people call this 'correct' English.

Utilitarianism – the idea that education and learning can be reduced to crude skills and drills.

Validity – the extent to which research methods are appropriately used resulting in significant findings.

References

APU (Assessment of Performance Unit) (1988) *Language Performance in Schools: Review of APU Language Monitoring 1979–1983*. London: HMSO.

Barber, C. (1993) *The English Language: A Historical Introduction*. Cambridge: Cambridge University Press.

Beard, R. (1999) *National Literacy Strategy Review of Research and other Related Evidence*. London: DfEE.

Board of Education (1921) *The Teaching of English in England (The Newbolt Report)*. London: HMSO.

Board of Education (1931) *The Primary School (The Second Hadow Report)*. London: HMSO.

Board of Education (1933) *Infant and Nursery Schools (The Third Hadow Report)*. London: HMSO.

Bryson, B. (1990) *Mother Tongue: The English Language*. London: Penguin.

Campbell, J. 'Towards curricular subsidiarity?' Paper presented at the School Curriculum and Assessment Authority conference 'Developing the Primary School Curriculum: the Next Steps'. June 1997.

Campbell, R. (1998) 'A literacy hour is only part of the story'. *Reading*, 32 (1): 21–23.

Cauter, R. (ed.) (1990) *Knowledge about Language and the Curriculum: The LINC Reader*. London: Hodder & Stoughton.

Cox, B. (1991) *Cox on Cox: An English Curriculum for the 1990s*. London: Hodder & Stoughton.

Cox, B. (1995) *Cox on the Battle for the English Curriculum*. London: Hodder & Stoughton.

Cox, B. (1998) 'Foreword', in B. Cox (ed.) *Literacy Is Not Enough: Essays on the Importance of Reading*. Manchester: Manchester University Press and Book Trust.

Crystal, D. (1997) *The Cambridge Encyclopaedia of Language*, second edition. Cambridge: Cambridge University Press.

Department of Education and Science and The Welsh Office (DES) (1987) *National Curriculum Task Group on Assessment and Testing (The TGAT Report)*. London: DES.

Department of Education and Science and The Welsh Office (DES) (1989) *English for Ages 5–16 (The Cox Report)*. York: National Curriculum Council.

Department of Education and Science and The Welsh Office (DES) (1990) *English in the National Curriculum*. London: HMSO.

Department of Education and Science (DES) (1967) *Children and Their Primary Schools (The Plowden Report)*. London: HMSO.

Department of Education and Science (DES) (1975) *A Language for Life (The Bullock Report)*. London: HMSO.

Department of Education and Science (DES) (1988) *Report of the Committee of Inquiry into the Teaching of English Language (The Kingman Report)*. London: HMSO

Department for Education (DFE) (1995) *English in the National Curriculum*. London: HMSO.

Department for Education and Employment (DfEE) (1998) *The National Literacy Strategy Framework for Teaching*. London: DfEE.

Gordon, P., Aldrich, R. and Dean, D. (1991) *Education and Policy in England in the Twentieth Century*. London: Woburn.

Graham, J. (1998) Teaching, Learning and the National Literacy Strategy. *Changing English: Studies in Reading and Culture*, 5 (2): 115-122.

Hilton, M. (1998) Raising Literacy Standards: The True Story. *English in Education*, (3): 4-16.

Holmes E. A. G. (1922) 'The confessions and hopes of an ex-Inspector of Schools. *Hibbert Journal*, vol. 20 (no further information in secondary source). Quoted in Gordon, P., Aldrich, R. and Dean, D. (1991) *Education and Policy in England in the Twentieth Century*. London: Woburn.

Lawson, J. and Silver, H. (1973) *A Social History of Education in England*. London: Methuen

LINC (Language in the National Curriculum) (1991) *Materials for Professional Development*. No publication details.

Literacy Task Force (1997) *The Implementation of the National Literacy*

Strategy. London: DfEE.

McCourt, F. (1996) *Angela's Ashes: A Memoir of Childhood*. London: Harper Collins.

Marshall, B. (1998) 'English teachers and the third way', in B. Cox (ed.) *Literacy Is Not Enough: Essays on the Importance of Reading*. Manchester: Manchester University Press and Book Trust.

Meek, M. (1998) 'Important reading lessons', in B. Cox (ed.) *Literacy Is Not Enough: Essays on the Importance of Reading*. Manchester: Manchester University Press and Book Trust.

Office for Standards in Education (OFSTED) (1998) *The National Literacy Project: An HMI Evaluation*. London: OFSTED.

Office for Standards in Education (OFSTED) (1999) *The National Literacy Strategy: An Interim Evaluation*. London: OFSTED.

Protherough, R. and Atkinson, J. (1994) 'Shaping the image of an English teacher', in S. Brindley (ed.) *Teaching English*. London: Routledge.

Pyles, T. and Algeo, J. (1993) *The Origins and Development of the English Language,* Fourth Edition. London: Harcourt Brace Jovanovich.

Reynolds, D. (1998) 'Schooling for literacy: A review of research on teaching effectiveness and school effectiveness and its implications for contemporary educational policies', *Educational Review*, 50 (2): 147–163.

Sainsbury, M., Schagen, I., Whetton, C. with Hagues, N. and Minnis, M. (1998) *Evaluation of the National Literacy Project Cohort 1, 1996–1998*. Slough: NFER.

Select Committee on Education and Employment. *House of Commons: Education and Employment–Fourth Report*. [Online] CCTA Government Information Service. June 1999 [cited July 1999]. Available from http://www.open.gov.uk/.

Shayer, D. (1972) *The Teaching of English in Schools 1900–1970*. London: Routledge and Kegan Paul.

Wells, G. (1992) 'The centrality of talk in education', in K. Norman (ed.) *Thinking Voices The Work of the National Oracy Project*. London: Hodder & Stoughton.

Williamson, B. (1981) 'Contradictions of control: Elementary education in a mining district 1870–1900', in L. Barton and S. Walker (eds*) Schools, Teachers and Teaching*. Lewes: Falmer Press.

Wyse, D. and Hawtin, A. (2000) Children's Rights, in D. Wyse and A. Hawtin (eds) *Children: A Multi-professional Perspective*. London: Edward Arnold.

Annotated bibliography

Beard, R. (1999) *National Literacy Strategy Review of Research and other Related Evidence*. London: DfEE.
A useful overview of the research evidence that supports the NLS. This is important because it gives the official line which provides a starting point for discussion. Came out *after* the implementation of the strategy.
L3 ***

Bryson, B. (1990) *Mother Tongue: The English Language*. London: Penguin.
A light-hearted and readable account of the English language. Bryson is better known for his travel writing and he brings his sense of humour to this book. As the crime writer Ruth Rendell points out: 'anecdotal, full of revelations, and with not one dull paragraph'.
L1

Cox, B. (ed.) (1998) *Literacy Is Not Enough: Essays on the Importance of Reading*. Manchester: Manchester University Press and Book Trust.
Interesting comparison with official views of the literacy strategy. Contributors include a wide range of people whose work involves literacy.
L2 **

Crystal, D. (1997) *The Cambridge Encyclopaedia of Language,* second edition. Cambridge: Cambridge University Press.
This is a book on epic scale. It shows us that educational discussions about the teaching of English can be rather narrowly focused and that the study of language is a very wide and fascinating area of study.
L1 **

Czerniewska, P. (1992) *Learning about Writing*. Oxford: Blackwell.
Czerniewska used her experience as director of the National Writing Project to produce a thought-provoking account of the teaching of writing.
L2 **

Sainsbury, M. (1998) *Evaluation of the National Literacy Project: Summary Report*. London: DfEE.
A more readable version of the evaluation we outlined above but beware slight changes to the wording which result in subtle differences, for example the findings on children's attitudes to reading.
L1 ***

Shayer, D. (1972) *The Teaching of English in Schools 1900–1970*. London: Routledge and Kegan Paul.
The study of the history of education is something that has been neglected recently and it does not feature in Circular 4/98. As we indicated in this chapter, a knowledge of history is vital to make sense of the present. This book makes very interesting reading particularly by showing how the debates about English have progressed.
L3 ***

Ward, G. E. (ed.). *A Brief History of English Usage*. About featured link. *Webster's Dictionary Of English Usage*. Springfield (MA): Merriam-Webster 1989 [online – cited 26-6-00].
A short factual account of historical developments in English. This includes reference to the first dictionary and has references to many of the early grammar books. Available from:
http://teenwriting.about.com/teens/teenwriting/gi/dynamic/pffsite.htm?site=http://angli02.kgw.tu%2Dberlin.de/lexicography/data/B%5FHIST%5FEU.html
L1 ***

Chapter 2

Theories of learning

Theories (☞) of learning are vital because they inform effective teaching. This chapter outlines some of the important learning theories that have contributed to our understanding of how children learn. Links are made between the theories and classroom practice. We conclude with the controversial ideas of postmodernism.

A criticism that is sometimes levelled at educationists is that they emphasise theory at the expense of practice; while this is rarely accurate it is an idea that needs debate. Occasionally there are those who will suggest that 'you don't need all that theory rubbish to be a good teacher'. All teachers are naturally particularly concerned to make sure that their practice is as good as possible. However, effective practice can be enhanced through a necessary knowledge of learning theories. The advantage of clearly thought-out theories is that they can guide you through unfamiliar practical experiences by giving direction to teaching decisions. They can also contribute to successful whole school approaches by offering a shared framework.

Many people find it difficult to articulate their theories, nevertheless we all have theories which guide us through our lives. Sometimes these reveal themselves in turns of phrase: 'They've got no language these kids' (deficit models); 'She's a bright girl' (nature more than nurture); 'Boys are always naughty' (gender and stereotypes); etc. Teachers need to be consciously aware of their personal theories and be able to relate those to other published theories. This kind of self-awareness is important as it can help your ability to understand other people's points of view.

Philosophies (☞) and theories of education have existed at least since the time of the ancient Greeks. Plato felt that there should be two main foci in education: culture and athletics. Both terms were meant in the very broadest sense so that culture was to include all the arts, and athletics implied a wide range of physical activities. Plato felt that education should be mainly concerned with turning boys into gentlemen. He proposed that there should be rigid censorship over the literature and music that children were exposed to. Some particular musical harmonies were felt to be bad for children and only those that expressed courage and temperance were deemed to be suitable.

The physical training of the body was to be rigorous. If we compare these theories with modern times, it is interesting to reflect on the place of music, physical education and other foundation subjects compared with the heavy focus on maths, English, science and ICT. Also, the idea that education was to create elite groups of people (i.e. gentlemen) is one that has featured throughout the English education system: initially sustained by overt discrimination and more recently through institutionalised discrimination.

Although early philosophies are a fascinating area it is to more recent thinking that we now turn.

THEORIES OF LANGUAGE ACQUISITION

There are two main schools of thought about language acquisition: behaviourist theories and cognitive (☞) theories.

The behaviourist view of language acquisition stretches back to American writers of the 1930s who argued that all behaviours are learned, and that while language is a sophisticated process, it is merely another form of behaviour. Probably the most important text from this perspective is Skinner's *Verbal Behaviour* (1957). Skinner developed the idea that parents actively reinforce certain utterances made by children, providing (for example) a biscuit when the word 'biscuit' is spoken, thereby creating positive confirmation of the utterance which encourages the child to use the same language in future.

Behaviourists also suggested that much early learning in language comes through imitation. It was claimed that the turn-taking games seen between adults and babies help the child to acquire certain sounds and patterns of speech which evolve into an early vocabulary. All parents know that there is some truth to this suggestion, but most would equally be aware that this is not a simple transference of sound and meaning:

> ...if imitation were the governing principle, then we would expect children to produce rather different patterns in their language than in fact they do. On the other hand, we would expect them not to produce some of the patterns that in fact they come out with.
>
> (Crystal, 1976 :34).

A good example of language use producing an unexpected pattern is the way that our own children used 'why' in place of because: 'That's why I was a good boy.' The behaviourist view of language acquisition assumes that all children are motivated to speak in the same way, and that the grammatical structures of the language are not perceived by them but merely copied as learned behaviour.

Others would claim that children are not mere imitators of the language they hear around them. During the early years, children often begin to apply grammatical rules (in the *descriptive* sense; ➡ Chapter 18, 'Grammar') to the language they know. For example children often use the convention 'ed' on the end of a verb to place it in the past tense. In the majority of instances this results in a perfectly acceptable word, but occasionally the child will apply the same rule to initiate a word such as 'eated' (for 'ate'), 'goed' (for 'went') and 'throwed' (for 'threw').

The cognitive view of language acquisition is usually credited to the work of Chomsky, specifically his two books *Aspects of the Theory of Syntax* (1965) and *Language and Mind* (1968). Put simply, Chomsky proposed that language is not learned as a form of behaviour, it is acquired as a set of grammatical rules. This meant that children were able to not only understand meanings of words, but also understand the grammatical rules which governed the ways in which sentences made sense (or not). It was argued that there are universal rules of language which apply across the world, and that children acquire the skills to understand and apply these rules in order to communicate effectively. Within this context, Chomsky hypothesised that children made use of a Language Acquisition Device (LAD). This feature of the mind enabled them to create syntactically appropriate utterances prior to imitation and repetition. The examples given earlier of children developing words such as eated, goed and throwed go some way to suggest that these are indications of the LAD in operation. The child understands that there is a verb to describe the action of throwing, verbs which are placed in the past tense are usually suffixed with 'ed', so the LAD supposes that the correct past tense form of the verb 'to throw' is throwed. While the word is incorrect, the grammatical function is perfectly clear, and the child has used this knowledge of language structure in order to generate a new word to explain the concept.

As with many pure theories, these two views of language acquisition have their weaknesses, primarily because each is overly reliant on its own view to the exclusion of the other. Anyone who has been involved in caring for a child during the first few years of life will be able to find examples of language acquisition to support either position. But both the cognitive and behaviourist theories underestimate the importance of interaction, and the language environment.

The importance of social interaction in the acquisition of language formed the basis of major theories by Vygotsky (*Mind in Society*, 1978) and Bruner (*Child's Talk*, 1983). Social interactionist theories became very influential towards the end of the twentieth century as theorists and educationists began to explore the social nature of language and knowledge acquisition.

SOCIAL INTERACTIONIST THEORIES

Vygotsky's most significant contribution related to child development. Later, in the chapters on the development of reading and the development of writing, we argue that it is important that teachers have detailed understandings of children's development. Vygotsky built on Koffka's ideas about maturation and learning by suggesting the idea that the growing maturity of an organ like the brain is complemented by learning and practice. Both maturation and learning influence each other as children develop. Vygotsky emphasises that one of the most important tests of whether learning has taken place is the extent to which it can be transferred to a new context. If we take a modern example, the effective teaching of the objectives in the NLS Framework for Teaching should result in better written composition when children carry out extended writing outside of the literacy hour.

One of Vygotsky's most well-known ideas was the 'zone of proximal development'. He recognised that most psychological experiments assessed the level of mental development of children by asking them to solve problems in standardised tests. He illustrated that one problem with this was that it only measured a summative aspect of development. In the course of some experiments Vygotsky discovered that a child who had a mental age of eight as measured on a standardised test was able to solve a test for a 12-year-old child if they were given 'the first step in a solution, a leading question, or some other form of help' (Vygotsky, 1987: 187). He suggested that the difference between the child's level working alone and the child's level with some assistance should be called the zone of proximal development (ZPD). He found that those children who had the greater zone of proximal development did better at school.

There are a number of practical consequences to ZPD. Vygotsky's ideas point to the importance of appropriate interaction, collaboration and cooperation. He suggested that given minimal support the children scored much higher on the tests. All teachers must make decisions about the kind of interventions that they make. Although the tests showed the influence of appropriate support they also remind us that collaboration is an important way of learning and that in the right context there is much that children can do *without* direct instruction. Barnes (1976) argued that there was growing evidence to suggest that language development was clearly enhanced through collaborative group work which allowed for and built on talk. This had direct implications for teachers as it brought into question the whole nature of crude transmission models of teaching.

Bruner contributed a number of significant theories which have guided the teaching of language. One of these was the idea of a 'spiral curriculum' where 'an 'intuitive' grasp of an idea precedes its more formal comprehension as part of a structured set of conceptual relationships' (Bruner, 1975: 25). The idea of a spiral curriculum is important in that it suggests that knowledge and concepts need to be revisited a number of times at increasingly higher levels of sophistication. It is also important because it calls into question the notion that learning is a simple sequence, where knowledge and concepts are only addressed on one occasion.

Bruner saw a close relationship between language and the spiral curriculum. He suggested that the spiral curriculum was supported by some essential elements in the learning process. Language learning occurs in the context of 'use and interaction – use implying an operation of the child upon objects' (1975: 25). In other words it is important that children have first-hand experience of relevant 'objects' (including their local environment) to support their learning. In terms of English this suggests that the writing of texts should be supported by real purposes and that the reading of texts should first and foremost be about experiencing whole texts and secondly about analysis. There are many teaching strategies which encourage the direct use of objects and the environment to stimulate talking, reading and writing. Bruner argued that this kind of language learning was 'contextualised' and should be supported by people who were expert, like the teacher.

Bruner also had views about Chomsky's LAD. He felt that it correctly identified the child's capacity to understand the intricacies of a language's grammatical structure, but argued that this was only part of the process of language acquisition:

> ...the infant's Language Acquisition Device could not function without the aid given by an adult who enters with him (sic) into a transactional format. That format, initially under the control of the adult, provides a Language Acquisition Support System (LASS). It frames or structures the input of language and interaction to the child's Language Acquisition Device in a manner to 'make the system function'. In a word, it is the interaction between the LAD and the LASS that makes it possible for the infant to enter the linguistic community – and, at the same time, the culture to which the language gives access.
>
> (Bruner, 1983 :19)

Although restrictions of space do not allow a lengthy focus, it would be remiss at this stage not to refer in passing to the work of Jean Piaget which has been influential in building theoretical models of cognitive and linguistic development. In addition, it is interesting to read the criticisms of Piaget's work in relation to his understanding of language in use.

CHILD-CENTRED LEARNING

The idea of child-centred education has a long history which has been attributed to the philosopher Jean-Jacques Rousseau. Later, other philosophers such as John Dewey built on Rousseau's ideas. Dewey's emphasis on spontaneity and problem solving contributed to the phenomenon of 'topic' work in primary schools (Kerry and Eggleston, 1994). This is the practice of organising learning activities around cross-curricular (☞) themes such as 'water', 'ourselves', 'vehicles'. The rationale for these links is that children's understanding of the world tends not to be organised around 'subjects'; their thinking often proceeds by association from one related idea to the next. Ideas such as topic work, problem solving, discovery learning, teachers as facilitators, etc., became linked to the philosophy of 'child-centred education' which was one of the rare attempts by a small number of educators to genuinely involve children in their curriculum. Examples of the practice included building on the children's interests, involving them in the planning of work, reacting spontaneously to issues of interest, offering choices, engaging in discussion and decision making, and encouraging independent learning strategies.

The current educational climate has a subject-based curriculum pre-scribed by government that must be followed by all children. The idea of a national curriculum was based on the idea that *parents* should be able to guarantee an entitlement to a basic curriculum for their children. This would allow them to select the best schools and be reassured that their child would not miss important aspects of knowledge. We need to ask our-selves how satisfactory such entitlement is in the eyes of children. We would argue that true entitlement is closely tied in with the power and rights of children, not a simple access to uniformity. In spite of the many problems with centralised curricula (the third National Curriculum since 1988 was published in 1999 for implementation in September 2000) the trend as we begin the twenty-first century is for more government interven-tion in an area that historically has been part of teachers' professional decision making.

The Plowden Report (DES, 1967) is a pivotal document in relation to the modern debate about child-centred education, and its recommended methods have come under intense criticism. The attacks follow similar lines to other criticisms of progressive practice (☞) and are based on the principle that such practice has been widely adopted. Research evidence has frequently shown that progressive ideas are rarely particularly popular. The current fashion for centralised and prescriptive curricular is a far cry from the Plowden report which stated that:

> The tendency is spreading to junior schools. Children may plan when to do the work assigned to them and also have time in which to follow per-sonal or group interest of their own choice. In a few infant and junior schools the day is still divided into a succession of short periods. In the great majority, we are glad to say, there are longer periods and these can be adjusted at the teacher's discretion.
>
> (DES, 1967: 197)

The idea that children are able to follow their own interests or even to plan when to do work assigned to them is quite alien to the current climate. Similarly the notion of the teacher as a professional with discretion to adjust the timetable to suit the children's needs and interests runs counter to the insistence on detailed subject timetabling. Most primary schools currently run secondary style timetables with the practice of children moving to other class-rooms in ability groups (or sets) for certain subjects not uncommon. The comparison between current political opinion on education and the Plowden report is startling:

> The idea of flexibility has found expression in a number of practices, all of them designed to make good use of the interest and curiosity of children, to minimise the notion of subject matter being rigidly compartmental, and to allow the teacher to adopt a consultative, guiding, stimulating role rather than a purely didactic one...The topic cuts across boundaries of subjects and is treated as its nature requires without reference to subjects as such.

At its best the method leads to the use of books of reference, to individual work and to active participation in learning.

(DES, 1967: 199)

Unfortunately for current teacher education students and newly qualified teachers there can almost be disbelief that such practice is even possible.

Self-fulfilling prophecy

Another theoretical strand to child-centred education is the notion that high expectations of children's capabilities lead to higher standards of learning. The idea of the 'self-fulfilling prophecy' was investigated in a famous study by Rosenthal and Jacobson (1968). The study used a test called the 'Harvard Test of Inflected Acquisition' which purported to be a predictor of academic success or 'blooming/spurting'. This particular test was used because the teachers in the study were unlikely to have seen it before and because in a school with significant numbers of bilingual children it was deemed to show basic learning ability and did not rely on a high level of skill in literacy or numeracy. Although its approach was predominantly scientific the study also used qualitative techniques to develop a welcome methodological eclecticism (☞). One section of their book 'a magic dozen' includes a series of twelve (admittedly limited) portraits of the children. Also the use of Bernard Shaw's play (the book where the research is reported is called *Pygmalion in the Classroom*) as a means to enhance the narrative (☞) predates the current interest in genre (☞) and the writing of research.

The 500 or so children were tested and the teachers were informed about the children who the researchers deemed to be intellectually 'blooming'. However, the children concerned were not chosen on the basis of the tests but at random. When the children were re-tested, the younger children (American first and second grades) who had randomly been designated as bloomers had made statistically significant gains on the test. This was attributed to the teachers' change in expectations.

SOCIOLINGUISTIC THEORY

The theory of self-fulfilling prophecy is perhaps one of the most important influences on effective primary teachers' belief that it is vital to look for positive factors in the teaching and learning context. Unfortunately there are many examples of negative factors or 'deficit theories' playing a part in educational theory. One of the memorable metaphors illustrating deficit models was the idea of pre-school children being 'empty vessels' waiting to be filled with knowledge by their schools and teachers. This image of course failed to reflect the learning that goes on before school.

Basil Bernstein spent much of his career trying to argue that working-class children had inferior language compared to middle-class children: 'one of the effects of the class system is to limit access to elaborated codes' (Bernstein, 1972:

105). Fortunately there were more enlightened thinkers also working on these issues. William Labov argued that non-standard forms of English were just as logical and meaningful as standard forms. In a particularly powerful piece of analysis he compared the speech of a 15-year-old black New York gang member – about whom Labov (1974: 203) said 'it is probable that you would not like him any more than his teachers do' – with an upper-middle-class college educated black American. The two speakers were both asked to comment on life after death and Labov's analysis found that if he looked below the surface features of the language, the gang member's argument on life after death was logically superior to the middle-class man. The gang member's points were also quick and decisive, and he used the minimum words necessary for them. This contrasted with the middle-class speaker who made fewer and weaker points and who added many unnecessary words. Many of today's teachers continue to make negative assumptions about children because of their theories about links between socio-economic status (☞), language and intelligence.

Race has also been used as the basis for deficit theories. It has often been suggested that multilingual children should only use English in the school and that the use of their community language in the home is a disadvantage. Most modern research and theory would suggest that this is untrue. On the contrary, multilingual children should be at an advantage over their monolingual peers in that they have better insights into language as they compare their use of two or more languages. Skutnabb-Kangas (1981) illustrates the importance of sustaining all the child's languages through her image of a lily (see Figure 2.1). She shows that inappropriate emphasis on an additional language (e.g. English) can be a threat to the community language. So if, for example, a school had a policy of insisting that its pupils only used English in the classroom and encouraged the children to use only English at home this could damage the other language(s). In the worst cases this might lead to weaknesses in both languages, something she calls 'double semilingualism' (1981: 53).

POSTMODERNISM

It is a hopeless task to try to give *any* clue about post modernism in the short space that is now available in this section. However, postmodern theories continue to be important at the present time. We cannot even satisfactorily define post-modernism as it is 'an impossible object – both asserting the need for, and failing to provide, coherent rationales for definition, boundary, specific meaning, and generalisation' (Hodkinson, 1998: 38).

Chomsky once appeared on a television programme with Michel Foucault who is an important influence on postmodern thinking. When asked about human nature, Chomsky referred to his research and suggested that there are innate governing principles leading to a unified language. Foucault's response was to ask some further questions about conceptualisation of human nature, and how history can be re-examined in order to question universal beliefs (Rabinow, 1984). In so doing his answer illustrated an aspect of postmodern

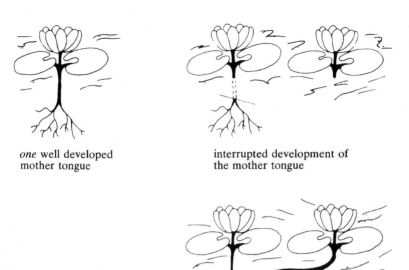

one well developed
mother tongue

interrupted development of
the mother tongue

well developed bilingualism

Figure 2.1 Skutnabb-Kanges' image of a lily. (Reproduced from T. Skuttnab-Kangas
(1981) *Bilingualism or Not*. Cleveland: Multilingual Matters. Used with
permission)

thought. One of postmodernism's important contributions has been to dis-
rupt simple binary (☞) 'truths' and 'standpoints': e.g. question/answer;
black/white; conservative/socialist; progressive/traditional. Postmodern thinking often leads to 'messy' and 'playful' descriptions of society.

One of the interesting aspects of postmodern educational theory is that it
often examines the nature of power in society. Tony Blair's rallying call for
'education, education, education' clearly signalled a more direct link between
politics and education. Politics is concerned with power, and education is
linked to politics therefore it is necessary for educational theory to address
power in society. Foucault is one of many postmodern thinkers who directly
address power in their writing, something that even the most confident govern-
ments can be uncomfortable with. In this context it is perhaps not surprising
that an OFSTED report on educational research (Tooley and Darby, 1998)
concluded that there was too much 'adulation of great thinkers' like Foucault.

PHILOSOPHY AND THE NATIONAL LITERACY
STRATEGY

The most striking thing about the NLS is that it is not based on theories or
philosophies of *learning*. The theories that have been reviewed in this section

have mainly concerned themselves with the ways in which people learn but as far as the NLS is concerned there are different influences. The first influence concerns competitiveness in the global market place. This has been expressed as a desire to develop a 'world-class education system' which will be measured by international comparisons of educational achievement. Underlying this is the political belief that the country's prosperity will be improved by higher standards of education. The second influence has been the idea that school effectiveness and school improvement research provides the most important evidence for improving the standards of education in England.

An important question for teachers to ask themselves concerns whether global competition and school effectiveness are sufficient to replace other philosophies and theories of teaching and learning. In reality many philosophies and theories are constantly at work in the education system. As we said at the beginning of this chapter everyone has personal theories of learning and teaching. Local authorities' theories have an influence on headteachers, headteachers' theories have a strong influence on schools and teachers' theories have a strong influence on their children. Although common approaches and theories are important to ensure continuity there must also be a place for diverse thinking. From the child's point of view this may offer variety and the opportunity to benefit from a range of teaching and learning styles.

Practice points

- Identify the theories of learning that you think are important and use them to inform your teaching.
- Remember that to help children learn you need to take account of social factors (like motivation) as well as cognitive ones.
- The ability to use focused positive feedback with children is one of your most important skills.

Glossary

Binary – in this context refers to the summary of issues in only two possible positions, e.g. either/or.

Cognitive – pertaining to the perceptions, knowledge and learning of the brain.

Cross-curricular – activities and lessons that address more than one subject.

Genre – forms of writing (➡ Chapter 14, 'Genre and the process of writing').

Methodological eclecticism – using a range of research methods.

Narrative – a text which retells events often in chronological sequence.

Philosophies – ideas about the nature of knowledge and human existence.

Progressive practice – new ideas about teaching at the forefront of current knowledge.

Socio-economic status – the links between people's class, wealth, and their place in society.

Theory – a principle or a set of principles that form the basis for action.

References

Barnes, D. (1976) *From Communication to Curriculum* Harmondsworth: Penguin.

Bernstein, B. (1972) 'Social class, language and socialization', in A. Cashdan and E. Grugeon (eds) *Language in Education: A Source Book*. London: Routledge and Kegan Paul.

Bruner, J. S. (1975) *Entry into Early Language: A Spiral Curriculum*. Swansea: University College of Swansea.

Bruner, J. S. (1983) *Child's Talk: Learning to Use Language* Oxford: Oxford University Press.

Chomsky, N. (1965) *Aspects of the Theory of Syntax*. Cambridge, MA: M.I.T. Press.

Chomsky, N. (1968) *Language and Mind*. London: Harcourt Brace Jovanovich.

Crystal, D (1976) *Child Language, Learning and Linguistics*. London: Arnold.

Department of Education and Science (DES) (1967) *Children and Their Primary Schools (The Plowden Report)*. London: HMSO.

Hodkinson, P. (ed.) (1998) *The Nature of Educational Research: Realism, Relativism or Post-Modernism?* Crewe School of Education: Manchester Metropolitan University.

Kerry, T. and Eggleston, J. (1994) The Evolution of the Topic, in A. Pollard and J. Bourne (eds) *Teaching and Learning in the Primary School*. London: Routledge.

Labov, W. (1974) 'The logic of nonstandard English', in A. Cashdan and E. Grugeon (eds) *Language in Education: A Source Book*. London: Routledge and Kegan Paul.

Rabinow, P. (ed.) (1984) *The Foucault Reader*. London: Penguin Books.

Rosenthal, R. and Jacobson, L. (1968) *Pygmalian in the Classroom*. New York: Holt, Rinehart and Winston.

Skinner, B. F. (1957) *Verbal Behaviour*. Englewood Cliffs, NJ: Prentice Hall.

Skutnabb-Kangas, T. (1981) *Bilingualism or Not: The Education of Minorities*. Cleveden: Multilingual Matters.

Tooley, J. with Darby, D. (1998) *Educational Research: A Critique*. London: OFSTED.

Vygotsky, L. S. (1978) *Mind in Society: The Development of Higher Psychological Processes*. Cambridge, Mass: Harvard University Press.

Vygotsky, L. S. (1987) *Thought and Language*. Cambridge, MA: Harvard University Press.

Annotated bibliography

Donaldson, M. (1978) *Children's Minds*. Glasgow: Fontana Press.
A very important book that looked at children's development. One of its important contributions was to rethink the implications of some of Piaget's experiments, particularly in relation to the language used by the researcher.
L2 ***

Gould, S. J. (1996) *The Mismeasure of Man* (revised and expanded edition). London: Penguin Books.

A fascinating and provocative attack on simplistic ideas about intelligence. Destroys the myth that black races are less intelligent than white races.
L2 ***

Vygotsky, L. S. (1987) *Thought and Language*. Cambridge, MA: Harvard University Press.

Probably Vygotsky's most well-known book. Includes the description of the zone of proximal development.
L3 ***

Wyse, D. and Hawtin, A. (2000) *Children: A Multi-professional Perspective*. London: Arnold.

An important reminder that education is not the only aspect of children's complex lives. Education can be too much about the things that teachers must do rather than about supporting children in line with *their* interests and needs.
L2 **

Part II

Reading

Chapter 3

The development of reading

Helping children learn to read is one of the most important roles that primary teachers carry out. In order to support children effectively it is necessary to be aware of the ways children might develop. Detailed pictures of individual children's development are presented in this chapter. These are followed by reflections on how this knowledge might affect pedagogy (☞). The research on the teaching of reading is reviewed and conclusions are drawn about reading in the National Literacy Strategy.

It is important to understand the typical stages of development that children pass through in their reading. This knowledge helps you to pitch your planning and interaction at an appropriate level for the children you are teaching. People who have already experienced such development as teachers and parents are in an advantageous position. However, teachers who are inexperienced need to grasp the fundamental aspects of such development. One of the reasons for this is that it heightens their awareness of what to look for when they do have the opportunity to interact with developing readers.

Fortunately there are a number of in-depth case-studies of individual children that can help in acquiring knowledge about children's development. Studies of individual children do not act as a blueprint for all children: one of the important things that such case studies show us is that children's experiences vary greatly. However, if we focus on certain key concepts and significant milestones these can be applied to larger groups of children. These milestones are likely to happen at roughly the same age for many children, but there will be significant numbers of children whose development is different.

The first part of this chapter looks at children's reading development from age 3 to 10. We use three research studies that feature detailed accounts of individual children to draw out significant concepts and milestones. Payton (1984) documented her daughter Cecilia's developing awareness of print and literacy. Minns (1997) charted the emergent literacy learning of five 4-year-old children, one of whom we look at both at age 4 and at age 10. But the most influential study we use is the seminal work (☞) by Bissex (1980) which was called 'GNYS AT WRK' (Genius at Work) based on a sign that her son Paul hung on his door.

It is important to make clear that although we have indicated ages of development and have associated certain kinds of reading behaviour with those ages, we are aware that learning does not proceed in a simple linear or step-by-step fashion. The fact that a certain concept is revealed at age 3 does not imply that it does not feature in later ages. For example, the three-year-old who relates their own visit to a fair to Ted Hughes' picture book *Shaggy and Spotty* is not so different to the adult who, for example, responds to *The Diary of Bridget Jones* by recognising insecurities about their own lives. Both instances involve linking personal experience with a text.

CHILDREN'S READING DEVELOPMENT

Age 3 to 4 – Cecilia at Home

At this age one of the important early realisations is that text and pictures serve different functions. This knowledge is acquired slowly, and fundamentally requires the child to recognise that text carries specific meanings. Cecilia demonstrated this knowledge at 3 years and 5 months when she asked her mother 'Does this say Smarties?' and pointed at the word on the box. There is strong evidence to suggest that in the early stages, print in the environment is an important factor in supporting the child's discovery of this concept. Initially children find it difficult to understand print words and logos without their familiar context, i.e. decontextualised (☞). But sometimes, even before the age of three, they might see a letter 'm' without its familiar yellow colour and distinctive font and say 'That's for McDonald's'.

Once the child has understood the fact that text carries meaning they tirelessly use this assumption to try to make sense out of all text that they see. Sometimes this results in confusion. Cecilia (3.7) was listening to a story with her mother when she heard the phrase 'hot cinder'. She did not understand the word and decided that it might be like Cinderella; an appropriate guess in the light of her knowledge of stories.

At 3 years 9 months Cecilia decided to write a shopping list. When her mother asked if she wanted sweets on the list she replied that she did not because she would not forget them. This showed her developing knowledge of texts. She realised that a shopping list has a specific function as an *aide mémoire* and that this function was different from a range of other texts. For example, on another occasion, when her mother was writing a note to the milkman, Cecilia assumed that it was a thank you letter to her grandma. Although she wasn't aware of the audience she did know that letters convey messages.

Age 4 to 5 – Gurdeep at nursery

Play is fundamental to all early learning, and reading is no exception. At 4 years and 4 months Gurdeep would flick through his personal photo album daily. This contained pictures of him growing up and he would provide his own audible narrative as he flicked through the pages. This compared well with the occasions when he would re-enact stories with his friends in the nursery. This 'pretending' to read included the use of 'book language': this is language that you would normally only find in books, such as 'a dark dark moor', or 'ogre' or 'they gnashed their terrible teeth'. The memorisation of such language is an important part of the later recognition of the language as printed words.

As can be seen from this emerging picture of development it is impossible to separate development from the social context in which it occurs. It is important for the teacher to reflect on these social factors when they are thinking about development. For Gurdeep the world of print was very much a bilingual one. As a Sikh he often went to the temple to learn about the teachings of his religion. The Sikh holy book is called the Guru Granth Saheb, and Gurdeep heard this at the temple and in his home. Over the years a strong body of research has shown that although bilingual children may be slow to develop English language skills initially, as they progress they use all their languages to reflect on their learning of English and this usually gives them greater insight than monolingual children. It should also be remembered that their needs differ greatly according to how long they have been in the country (➡ Chapter 29, 'Supporting black and multilingual children').

At 4 years 4 months Gurdeep had developed a strong interest in particular favourite stories, for example *Goldilocks and the Three Bears*. Although the ability to identify favourite books is something that happens at all ages, in the early stages it requires the child to be familiar with the purpose of books, to know and remember a selection, and to identify at some level why they prefer some books to others. At this age Gurdeep also showed his ability to read between the lines when he was questioned about aspects of 'Where the Wild Things Are'.

Age 5 to 10 – Paul at home

Working on reading

- *Age 5*

At age 5 years and 1 month Paul recognised his first words and was consolidating his understanding of the concept of 'word'. An important understanding at this stage was that of the spaces between words. Word spaces are unique to written text as when we are speaking the meaning is composed of continuous sounds with pauses mainly for breathing or interruptions. The understanding of the concept of words may seem rather obvious to skilled readers but this stage can be demanding for beginning readers.

A recurring theme for Bissex was the balance of cueing strategies that Paul used at different stages in his development. At 5 years and 3 months there was evidence that Paul was using both semantic (☞) and graphophonic (☞) cues to work out texts. Signs, labels and captions were of more interest to

Paul than continuous text and he tended to concentrate on whole words when he was reading but sounds when he was writing. At 5 years 6 months for the first time Paul was able to decode words out of context, such as: baby, stop, yes, duck, join. These were on cards for a reading game that he played with his mother. Significantly at this stage he temporarily abandoned semantic and syntactic cueing (☞) in order to concentrate on the sounds and this reflected the demands of trying to work out the complicated sound symbol links that exist for English text. Occasionally his decoding included reading letter strings backwards.

During a time when mum was reading *Dr Doolittle* Paul stopped her and reread the sentence himself. It seemed that he suddenly became aware that he could follow the text. At 5 years 7 months he read most of his first whole book and three months later he completed his first whole book (apart from one word). He began to realise the limitations of the 'one-letter-makes-one-sound-method' (OLMOSM) and this resulted in more attempts at unfamiliar words. For example when he came across 'Huckleberry Finn' he tried 'fun', 'fin' (which he rejected because he wasn't familiar with the name) and 'fain'.

Enjoying reading

● Age 6

Paul was beginning to read silently at 5 years and 11 months and this coincided with a change in his attitude to reading. Reading was becoming much less hard work and he was enjoying it much more. He was also reading with appropriate expression that Bissex presumed had been supported by the regular story reading that the parents did, and their use of expression during these times. At 6 years and 3 months Paul no longer needed to use his finger to point at words. Using the finger to point to the words is something that usually happens when children first start decoding. Unknown texts were read with less expression than known texts at this stage.

When Paul was 6 years and six months he was gaining confidence and attempting harder texts and a greater range of texts. His purposes for reading were changing and he was moving away from learning to read to reading to learn: his purposes included easy texts, hard texts, speed reading, sounds of poetry and rereading his favourites. Unlike the reading scheme books at school his choice of reading material at home did not represent a neat progression of text level and difficulty. As Paul attempted harder texts his reading was characterised by more substitution errors. This was partly because he was meeting many more new words including polysyllabic ones. He also struggled with knowing how certain words should be pronounced particularly in relation to the appropriate stresses. This understanding was one of the last that he achieved.

By 6 years and 11 months most of Paul's' reading was silent. The school had moved him up the reading scheme but he wasn't particularly motivated by the literacy experiences at school. He no longer asked his parents to read aloud and he had advanced to short novels. Names were the main source of his reading miscues and he was getting interested in informational reading.

Working on vocabulary

- Age 7 to 9

The remaining minor difficulties that Paul faced with words were to do with definitions and multiple meaning. He became interested in the derivations of words and would frequently ask questions about unfamiliar words. He could read many difficult words in context but sometimes found it hard to define them out of context. At 7 years and 8 months he was able to segment words into prefixes (☞), roots (☞) and suffixes (☞) and to think about the meanings of the different segments. At 8 years and 3 months Paul invented names for new chemicals as a result of playing with a chemistry set. His interest in definitions resulted in much exploration of dictionaries. By 9 years he had developed awareness of puns and multiple meanings.

Diversified reading

- Age 9 to 10

Paul was now interested in acquiring information on a wide range of subjects. He enjoyed using encyclopaedias and he developed skimming and scanning skills. At 9 years and 8 months he read his first adult novel: *Star Wars* (part 4). This sparked his imagination resulting in the design of Star Wars quizzes and the taped recordings of excerpts from the book. One month later he reread *Star Wars* and was amazed at how much he had missed the first time. The range and amount of his reading was now wide and this included literature, non-fiction, comics, and the rereading of favourites such as *Danny Champion of the World*.

Age 10 – Gurdeep at School

Minns spoke to Gurdeep again when he was 10 and this was reported in Barrs and Pidgeon (1993). By the age of 10 Gurdeep had developed his interest in narrative. He liked some story books, particularly funny ones, but his main interest was in texts with a strong visual content such as comics, graphic novels and books that were influenced by computer technology. He was not particularly interested in information books, but did enjoy looking at dictionaries. One of the things he liked to do was learn new words in Punjabi and then translate them into English.

Out of school he was now learning to play the tabla (Indian drum) at the temple and this involved the reading of musical rhythms. His mother thought that he was less interested in reading because of the enjoyment he found through other things such as his bike and the television. He was interested in reading comics at home, but was dissuaded by his parents because they felt they contained 'slang'. He would sometimes read newspapers. In the local free paper he liked to look for things for sale and in the *Daily Mail* he would read the headlines or look at the sport section.

Having looked at three children in detail it is possible to compare their development with other sources such as the Centre for Language in Primary Education (CLPE) reading scales (CLPE, 1991) and our own experience teaching young readers. This enables us to be aware of some of the main signs of development which we have organised into four stages.

1 **Beginning reading**
   - Understands the differences between text and pictures
   - Can read words/logos which are part of environmental print
   - Understands that text carries meaning and conveys messages
   - Understands that text is an aid to memory
   - Understands that the meaning of text does not change
   - Enjoys playing at reading including re-enacting known stories
   - Uses 'book language' during retelling of stories
   - Understands that there are many languages
   - Can tell people about favourite texts.

2 **Learning to decode**
   - Knowledge of favourite texts supports decoding of reading scheme texts
   - Needs help with concepts of words and spaces
   - Uses finger pointing to show level of 1–1 correspondence
   - Begins to be able to read words out of context
   - Temporarily a strong emphasis on graphophonics
   - Independent reading starts for first time
   - Beginning to realise the limits of the One Letter Makes One Sound Method (OLMOSM).

3 **Silent reading**
   - Silent reading starts for first time
   - Wider reading of unknown texts
   - Greater fluency and appropriate expression when reading aloud
   - No need for finger pointing
   - Choosing to read a greater range of texts
   - Temporarily a return to a larger number of substitutions (☞)
   - Pronunciation and word-stress problems are main area of difficulty.

4 **Wide range reading**
   - Silent reading is preferred
   - Enjoys short novels
   - Likes to re-read favourite books sometimes
   - Finds difficulties with unfamiliar proper nouns
   - Enjoys a wider range of reading including information texts

- Shows interest in word definitions out of context (like dictionaries)
- Shows ability to segment words
- Enjoys word play
- Uses reading to learn
- Occasionally may enjoy adult level texts
- Interested in foreign languages and translations.

At the beginning of this chapter we suggested that knowledge about children's development was important because it should influence the way we teach our children. This influence means that our pedagogy (☞) is related to what we know about how children develop. Let us give an example. Data from the study above of Paul Bissex revealed that he had choice over the texts that he read at home and that these were not organised into a hierarchical sequence. It was also clear that Paul developed as an enthusiastic and successful reader. We might draw the conclusion from this that the use of reading schemes in schools, where the texts are hierarchically organised, is inappropriate because this does not reflect 'natural' development. However, one of the problems with this conclusion is that Paul *was* using reading scheme books (what the Americans call 'basal readers') at school and the research cannot indicate which aspect of his reading materials were most beneficial or the different influences that they had. We would suggest that it is probable that both types of material had important influences on his reading development but we remain concerned about the lack of motivation he had for reading at school.

None of the questions about reading development and reading teaching have simple answers and it is for this reason that reading pedagogy has attracted such fierce debate. In the remaining part of this chapter we look at the debate that has taken place in relation to approaches to the teaching of reading.

THE TEACHING OF READING

Rxxl bxxks dxbxtx xs pxxntlxxs

Whxn wxll thx rxxl bxxks xrgxxmxnt xnd? Sxrxly xt mxst bx clxxr thxt chxldrxn usx a vxrxxty of strxtxgxxs tx rxxd prxnt xnd thxt xn xndxrstxndxng xf thx rxlxtxxnshxp bxtwxxn lxttxrs xnd sxxnd xs xnly xne xf thx strxtxgxxs.

It muts be fairyl obvoius to aynone raeding thsi lettre that raedres draw on thier konwledeg of how lagnuaeg wroks, thier abitily to recgonise wrods on sihgt and theri capacity to ues contextaul cleus to enabel them to maek senes of what has goen befoer and perdict what is cmoing next.

if Kenne- Cl- and Ma- Th- can re- th- let- they mu- agr- tha- a mix- appro- is nec-. If the- ar- no- abl- to re- thi- let- the- mu- be stu- or cra-,

Peter Donnely
General advisory teacher

This letter written to the *Times Educational Supplement* is interesting in that it is an eye-catching summary of some of the main issues that we cover in this chapter. The history of the debates about approaches to the teaching of reading has repeatedly hinged on fundamental disagreements related to models of learning to read. The seminal text in the debate is Jean Chall's (1983) book *Learning to Read: The Great Debate* which was first published in the 1960s. In it she defines the differences between two models:

> The top-down models relate . . . to the meaning-emphasis approaches of beginning reading and stress the first importance of language and meaning for reading comprehension and also for word recognition . . . The reader theoretically samples the text in order to confirm and modify initial hypotheses.
>
> The bottom-up models – those that view the reading process as developing from perception of letters, spelling patterns, and words, to sentence and paragraph meaning, resemble the code-emphasis, beginning reading approaches.
>
> (Chall, 1983: 28–9)

The classic example of a top-down approach to reading would be the 'real book approach' or the 'whole language approach' and the contrasting bottom-up approach would be 'phonics'; we talk more about these later. Since Chall defined 'bottom-up' and 'top-down', new models have emerged which unite both theory and practice. Wray suggests that proposals for 'interactive' and 'transactional' models of the reading process have moved us 'towards a synthesising theory' (1995: 58). The practical outcome to the synthesis of top-down and bottom-up theories suggests that teachers need to find a balanced approach to the teaching of reading. Our combined professional experience in a range of schools and local education authorities leads us to believe that the vast majority of teachers have implemented a balanced approach to the teaching of reading for at least the last 10 years. Since the introduction of the National Literacy Strategy it has been argued that the 'searchlight' model of reading and the objectives in the Framework for Teaching also reflect this balanced approach. We examine the national approach to reading towards the end of this section.

Psychological research on reading

There is a large body of research which shows that phonological awareness and phonics teaching in the early years of school are beneficial in helping children learn to decode text. A special edition of the *Journal of Research in Reading* (Oakhill et al, 1995) from the United Kingdom Reading Association put forward a convincing case that this evidence exists. One of the key articles in the edition was by Stanovich and Stanovich (1995) who raised some serious issues about theories of reading teaching. The aim of their paper was to resolve or to take forward the debate and they suggested that there are in fact areas of *agreement* between the top-down and bottom-up camps. Two of the most important being that nobody seriously recommends teaching only phonics in isolation and that all are agreed that children must be exposed to a range of high-quality texts.

Another issue that they raise is the question of how 'natural' reading acquisition is and this requires a brief digression. Frank Smith (1978) made strong claims that learning to read was just like learning to talk: a natural process that given the right support and encouragement from experienced language users most children would learn how to read. This idea is challenged by many psychological researchers including Stanovich and Stanovich. The sheer effort involved in learning to decode and the physical tiredness that often occurs is testament to the fact that learning to read and learning to talk have significant differences. However, there is undoubtedly a link between the two modes as communicating meaning using the same language is common to both: the exact nature of such links is perhaps an area for further research.

In the 1970s it was claimed by whole language enthusiasts that studies that had used computers to monitor the eye movements of fluent readers had showed that we do not read every letter or every word. This led to the conclusion that the focus of reading instruction should perhaps be the larger units of text that the eyes seemed to focus on. This theory seemed to make sense when people reflected on their own reading and realised that they were aware of omitting letters and words when they read. The following exercise from a student rag-mag is interesting in that respect:

> 1. Read the following passage once only. When the passage is covered up can you remember how many 'F's there were? 2. Count the number of 'F's; you have 30 seconds. 3. Repeat step 2 until you think you have counted them all.
>
> FINISHED FILES ARE THE RE-
> SULT OF YEARS OF SCIENTIFIC STUDY COMBINED WITH
> THE EXPERIENCE OF YEARS

(Did you spot all six?!)

Since then it has been claimed that further study has shown that we do in fact attend to nearly every letter of every word when we read. The point is important because it is argued that if we do attend to the meaning of every letter it makes sense to teach children letters and sounds as a priority. The work of Marilyn Jager Adams is important in this respect.

Adams's (1990) work is characterised by a rigorous approach to the subject that results in a complex picture of the reading process: for example she recognised that skilful readers use a variety of strategies for decoding print. However, her reading of the research literature led her to the conclusion that 'skilful readers visually process virtually every individual letter of every word as they read' (Adams, 1990b: 18). Adams supported this idea with reference to a chapter by McConkie and Zola (1981). Unfortunately their chapter does not present the convenient water-tight picture that we might be lead to believe from Adams's statements.

McConkie and Zola's chapter is broad in its review of research evidence that was available at the time: the stated aim of the chapter was to address 'whether contextual information produces changes in what visual information is acquired and used for reading during a fixation – that is, whether contextual information influences the functional stimulus' (McConkie and Zola, 1981: 156). In other words they were interested in the ways that contextual information might have an impact on the things the eyes focus on when people read. This is an important question because there are those who believe that fluent readers use less visual information, particularly in terms of individual letters, and that if this is the case our teaching should encourage whole word, sentence- and text-level reading strategies as opposed to concentrating on letters and sounds.

It is quite difficult to see how Adams was able to make such definitive statements about the perception of letters in the light of the complex analysis that McConkie and Zola put forward and particularly in the light of their tentative conclusions. One study that was reviewed in their chapter did suggest that skilled readers do not use visual information more than four letter positions to the left of the fixation point. However, McConkie and Zola went on to review a large number of interesting research studies that problematised this finding and indicated that knowledge about amount of visual information and the links with understanding of the text were still poorly understood. The overall conclusion was that 'the studies conducted to date that investigate perception during reading are not definitive on these issues' (McConkie and Zola, 1981: 173).

In contrast to the certainties about eye movement studies expressed by some researchers Perfetti (1995) offers more realistic conclusions. He confirms the fact that the eyes can only make out the letters of a target word within a degree or two from the central visual angle. However, he also suggests that readers' eyes fixate on only between 50% and 80% of words depending on the purpose of the reading and the type of word. Perfetti (1995: 108) maintains that

> the disagreement [in the research] concerns whether phonology mediates all written word identification: when phonology is observed is it 'pre-lexical' (mediating identification) or is it 'post-lexical' (resulting from identification)? This question has received differing answers from well-conceived research.
>
> (Perfetti, 1995: 108)

We can now return to another of Stanovich and Stanovich's (1995) assumptions. Like other contributors to the special edition of the *Journal of Research in Reading* they portray the USA-based academics Frank Smith and Kenneth Goodman as the main figures of the whole language movement and claim that whole language teaching involves 'simple immersion in print and writing activities' (Stanovich and Stanovich, 1995: 88) As we said earlier, in the UK the real books approach has been the most influential whole language teaching method. This has been described recently by writers such as Wade (1990), Campbell (1992), Harrison and Coles (1992) and Wyse (1998), and schools and teachers using the approach continue to modify the theory and practice. As can be seen from reading such authors it is quite erroneous to suggest that this whole language approach to reading involves 'simple immersion in print and writing activities'.

Another common claim about whole language approaches is that they have been widely practised in the UK and that this has resulted in lower standards of reading. The research evidence strongly opposes the view that whole language approaches to reading have dominated primary teaching in the UK. In a survey of 110 randomly selected schools in Northern Ireland, Gray (1983:30) revealed that 'a large rural school was the only school in the sample in which beginners were taught to read through the use of "Breakthrough" materials alone'. It is possible that there were schools who used the real book approach and that the questionnaire did not allow them to record this evidence, however, this is unlikely. Assuming that the language experience approach represented by 'Breakthrough' was the closest that schools got to the real book approach this study provides clear evidence of minimal use of a whole language approach. Similarly, Rice (1987) surveyed all the primary schools in 'a large northern industrial city': 196 of the 199 schools returned the questionnaire and only two of the schools claimed *not* to use a reading scheme.

Kirklees Local Education Authority's (LEA) survey of 27 schools found that 'in only one school was a deliberate move being made towards using no scheme material at all' (Kirklees LEA, 1993: 18). Similar evidence of minimal use of the real book approach was recorded by Cato et al (1992). Their study was titled *The Teaching of Initial Literacy: How Do Teachers Do It?* and consisted of 234 randomly selected schools across England and Wales. A total of 122 headteachers completed a questionnaire that asked for information on the range of methods used by year 2 teachers. A smaller sub-section of schools were visited to add to the data provided by the questionnaires. On the teaching of reading the authors commented that:

> In view of the recurrent debate about the use of 'real books', it must first of all be pointed out that only four percent of headteachers taking part in the survey claimed their schools exclusively used 'real books' in teaching reading. This replicates the findings of Her Majesty's Inspectorate (DES 1990).
>
> (Cato et al, 1992:22)

The idea that whole language approaches have had a profound impact on schools in the UK is a myth. The reason for this lack of impact is possibly that primary schools are often conservative in their approach to the curriculum as major national studies such as those by Galton (1989) and Bennett et al (1984) have found. Alexander (1995) summarised a series of in-depth studies of primary education over a 10-year period and concluded that in spite of the introduction of the National Curriculum in 1988, primary teaching had undergone 'a change in the collective culture of schools [but] against a backdrop of relative continuity in pedagogy'.

Educational research on reading

The dominant view from psychologists and many other people is that phonics has been neglected and therefore should be prioritised. However, too often research from other disciplines and paradigms (☞) is ignored. At its crudest level there are those who seem completely unaware of a powerful body of *qualitative research* (☞):

> Some educational 'research' consists of observing children in classrooms and forming subjective opinions about this experience.
>   None of these activities qualify as **scientific** research. Science can only work when things can be measured and recorded in numbers. If you want to find out if a particular teaching method is good or bad **ask to see the data** from research on the method. The data should be reported in comparisons of test scores on standardized tests. Statements such as 'the children really like it', or 'Research in Liverpool showed that the teachers and parents report that children are reading "better" using this method' don't count.
>
> (McGuinness, 1998: 127. Emphasis as in original)

Although this represents a very worrying level of knowledge for someone reviewing the research on reading it probably does represent a wider held view about types of research. Although this book is not the right place to raise some of the methodological issues that this quote ignores there are a few points that need to be made. There is a wealth of qualitative observational research that has had a significant impact on teaching and learning. Even within the discipline of psychology itself there is a growing realisation that qualitative methods have an important contribution to make (Richardson, 1996).

An inter-disciplinary review of research evidence provides a much richer view of the reading process. One of the underlying rationales of the research is that the reading process needs to be thought about as something that involves 'people' learning to read in a social 'context' and that reading is part of an inter-connected process that includes the learning of writing, talking and language. The following is a snapshot of other research that has influenced the teaching of reading.

As you saw at the beginning of the chapter, in-depth case studies of individual children and families have offered detailed accounts of learning to read (Bissex, 1980; Payton, 1984; Laycock, 1990; Browne, 1993; Minns, 1997.

These have caused some educators to question the pedagogic assumptions of traditional systematic teaching approaches such as phonics. Ferreiro and Teberosky (1982), Harste et al (1984), Tizard and Hughes (1984), Wells (1986) carried out research with larger groups of young children and also questioned such assumptions. Learner motivation remains an essential element of any teaching approach with gender differences an important aspect of this (Pidgeon, 1993; Barrs and Pidgeon, 1998) and related to learner motivation is the importance of particular text genres and authors (Children's Literature Research Centre, 1996). Chapman's (1987) research found that cohesion and genre were important elements in the reading process and that standardised reading age tests or reading quotients were problematic as indicators of reading success. Clark (1976) found that the early experiences of young fluent readers were characterised by a wide range of meaningful supported text experiences and that 'only a few parents had made a conscious and systematic attempt to teach their children to read with the aid of graded readers of the kind used in school reading instruction or of flash cards' (1976: 49). Southgate et al (1981) in the study *Extending Beginning Reading* found that the 7-year-old children in their study 'were no longer much hampered by difficulties at the phonic level [and that] many had not learned to use the context well or to look across the text for clues' (1981: 284). More recently Moustafa (1997) reviews a range of studies that support this broad picture of the reading process including evidence that children use their knowledge of the world and their knowledge about reading in order to read.

Our review of the research evidence reveals that the implications for classroom practice are at times contradictory and that there are no simple and straightforward answers. It is arguable that the significant body of psychological research has not had the attention from some educators that it deserves. However, as has been indicated, this has tended to dominate thinking in the minds of others. Overall there is strong evidence that pedagogy should include foci on semantic, syntactic and graphophonic reading strategies and that these need to be carefully balanced according to age, development, individual characteristics, and so on.

National policy on the teaching of reading

In 1991 Her Majesty's Inspectorate (HMI) commented on the teaching of English in a report on the first year of the National Curriculum:

> 9. In the best reading practice (AT2), children frequently heard well-chosen stories, and they then explored them through retelling and reenactment as well as in shared enjoyment and discussion. Such work laid a foundation for reading with pleasure and discrimination. Children chose books to take home from attractive and well-displayed collections and talked about the language of books with adults. Being encouraged to notice and reflect on sounds in context directly related to the knowledge about language strands of the National Curriculum; [sic] it also played an important part in the early stages of learning to read. The repeated sounds of jingles and rhymes formed a basis for the linguistic concepts involved in the explicit teaching of phonics.
>
> (HMI, 1991: 16)

Her Majesty's Inspectorate were generally respected for the measured and constructive language that they used in such reports. You will notice that there is an emphasis on whole texts and the importance of motivation is signalled. Reference to the explicit teaching of phonics comes last and is linked with activities that children enjoy. If we compare this to 'The teaching of Reading in 45 Inner London Primary Schools' a report by OFSTED/HMI that came some five years later there is a striking change in the emphasis. The first clear difference is the change of language: the report has a much more negative tone. It could be argued that this was inevitable as the authorities who 'collaborated' with HMI inspectors had recognised that there were some difficulties in developing reading in their schools. However, the other possibility is that political agendas were in part behind the reporting. The report mentions phonics in 10 paragraphs – 15, 16, 17, 28, 34, 35, 38, 44, 48, 97. Although the report comments on a range of what it considers to be poor practice, phonics is given a high priority: 'in particular, insufficient attention was paid to phonic work' (OFSTED, 1996: S15, 8); and 'A significant omission in much of the work was the systematic teaching of an effective programme of phonic knowledge and skills.' (1996: S16, 8). There is no doubt that the report was extremely important and in spite of damning criticism from a range of sources (e.g. Mortimore and Goldstein, 1996) it was the beginning of a trend towards a heavier emphasis on phonics teaching in England.

Evidence for this change in emphasis comes from a range of government publications. Circular 4/98 (DfEE, 1998a), a national curriculum for teacher training, places great emphasis on phonics by locating graphophonic strategies first in the relevant sections and with a more explicit treatment than for whole text, semantic and/or syntactic references (1998a: S3. b, c, d; 6. a.i, ii, b.i.; 12. b.i.) The methodology of the OFSTED (1997a) Primary Follow-up Survey (PFUS) – an inspection of teacher training – made explicit reference to the teaching of phonics consistent with its emphasis on the 'basics' although it is interesting to note that these differed in some respects from the emphasis given by the DfEE in the circular. Stannard (1998) announced that the final draft of the National Literacy Strategy Framework for Teaching would reverse the order of the three columns of teaching objectives so that phonics, spelling and vocabulary appear first. The flagship OFSTED video 'Literacy Matters' (OFSTED, 1997b), which was designed to show good practice, has a very heavy emphasis on phonics, unfortunately as Davies (1997) illustrates in his critique, the knowledge of phonics demonstrated by the participants – and by implication the producers of the video – is sometimes inaccurate. Thomas (1997) also makes the important observation that the video has a very narrow view of the language/English curriculum.

The move towards the greater emphasis on phonics reached a new height with the National Curriculum 2000 and the Framework for Teaching. The difference between the 1995 and 2000 National Curriculum documents is dramatic. In the 1995 curriculum there was one section within 'Key skills' at

Key Stage 1 that identified phonics knowledge but this came after the first paragraph that emphasised purposes for reading and motivation. At Key Stage 2 a mere three lines was devoted to graphophonic skills. The 2000 curriculum in common with other documentation that we have reviewed reverses the order of reading strategies and places 'phonemic awareness and phonic knowledge' first and 'contextual understanding' last for both Key Stage 1 and Key Stage 2. These are to be taught through the Framework for Teaching where we find more than 80 objectives explicitly dealing with phonics and a strong emphasis in the introductory material. Although the text-level objectives are equally numerous there is not a corresponding emphasis on semantic and syntactic strategies at word level. If the research evidence is not the rationale for the change in emphasis, we must look critically at a potential political influence. The prime minister and the secretary of state for education had not disguised their enthusiasm for phonics teaching:

> Young people must learn how to read effectively from the start. That means a structured approach based on phonics.
>
> (Blunkett, 1998: 22)

You should question the kind of detailed knowledge that politicians can be expected to have in the specialised area of reading compared to that of teachers and people who research the teaching of reading.

Conclusion

The research evidence supporting the explicit teaching of phonics is far from conclusive. It is very difficult to extrapolate the findings reliably and apply these directly to national educational policy. There is evidence to suggest that the teaching of phonics particularly in years 1 and 2 does improve ability to decode. However, much of this evidence has been collected in the context of struggling readers. There is significant evidence that individual children differ in their pedagogic needs and that some children acquire the necessary phonological understanding prior to starting formal education. There are serious questions still being asked about the nature of the systematic teaching of phonics and the extent to which it is beneficial. For example, as Scholes points out, phonetic segment awareness research has not shown that it 'improves/enhances/predicts a child's ability to *understand* a written text' (1998: 185). Evidence to support the decision that explicit teaching of phonics should be prescribed from reception to year 4 as a series of 80+ objectives is extremely weak. There is also no evidence to support the idea that all children, irrespective of their pre-school development, should be subjected to the same programme of phonics teaching.

If the evidence to support the phonics emphasis in the Framework for Teaching is weak this necessitates changes to the framework that would more accurately reflect empirical evidence. Weaver points out that 'among reading researchers and educators, almost all who advocate the direct and systematic teaching of phonics also insist that such teaching nevertheless be relatively simple and brief (e.g. Stahl, 1992)' (1994: 302). This is a position that can usefully be linked with Beard and McKay's (1998) views on the best use of reading scheme texts with controlled vocabularies. Beard and McKay draw on Chall's (1983) less well-known work on reading *development* and suggest that the highly structured controlled vocabularies of reading scheme texts should be exploited between the ages of 5 and 7 and then 'jettisoned' quickly. This may also be the appropriate time for a carefully controlled programme of phonics teaching that was sensitive to individual children's development and learning styles. This teaching should perhaps take place much more during small group activities as this would facilitate appropriate differentiation for those children who are proficient at decoding. The implications are that the Framework for Teaching needs rewriting in particular to remove the phonics objectives from years 3 and 4; to change the objectives in the early years and to change the emphasis of the introductory material in recognition of the necessity for a more balanced approach to the teaching of reading.

Practice points

- A truly objective and balanced approach to the teaching of reading is vital.
- Work on your observation skills and extend your understanding of children's reading development.
- Phonics teaching should be regular, brief and as enjoyable as possible.

Glossary

Decontextualised – something removed from its normal context. For example single words written on cards.

Fixations – the moment when the eye stops moving and looks at a particular part of the text.

Graphophonic cueing – using sounds and visual features to work words out when reading.

Paradigm – in this context used to mean a broad category of research/theory.

Pedagogy – approaches to teaching.

Prefixes – an addition to the beginning of a root word which modifies its meaning: e.g. *in*-finite.

Qualitative research – uses text (e.g. interview transcripts; field notes) as main basis for findings.

Quantitative research – uses numbers and statistics as main basis for findings.

Root – a word to which prefixes and suffixes can be added.

Saccards – The moments when the eyes are moving to different points in the text between fixations.

Semantic cueing – using meaning to work words out when reading.

Seminal work – classic (often old) academic work this continues to be referenced by large numbers of writers.

Substitutions – words suggested when guessing unfamiliar words.

Syntactic cueing – using grammar to work words out when reading.

Suffix – an addition to the end of a root word which modifies its meaning: e.g. infinite-*ly*.

References

Adams, M. J. (1990a) *Beginning to Read. Thinking and Learning about Print*. London: MIT Press.

Adams, M. J. (1990b) *Beginning to Read. The New Phonics in Context. A Précis of the Classic Text*. London: Heinemann.

Alexander, R. (1995) *Versions of Primary Education*. London: Routledge.

Barrs, M. and Pidgeon, S.(eds) (1998) *Boys and Reading*. London: Centre for Language in Education.

Beard, R. and McKay, M.(1998) An Unfortunate Distraction: The Real Books Debate, 10 Years On. *Educational Studies*, 24(1): 69–82.

Bennett, N., Desforges, C., Cockburn, A. and Wilkinson, B. (1984) *The Quality of Pupil Learning Experiences*. London: Lawrence Erlbaum Associates.

Bissex, G. L. (1980) *GNYS AT WRK: A Child Learns to Write and Read*. Cambridge, MA: Harvard University Press.

Blunkett, D. (1998) 'Total commitment'. *Times Educational Supplement*, 16 January.

Browne, N. (1993) 'From birth to sixteen months', in M. Barrs and S. Pidgeon (eds) *Reading the Difference*. London: Centre for Language in Primary Education.

Campbell, R. (1992) *Reading Real Books*. Buckingham: Open University Press.

Castle, J. M., Riach, J., and Nicholson, T. (1994) 'Getting off to a better start in reading and spelling: The effects of phonemic awareness instruction within a whole language program'. *Journal of Educational Psychology*, 86 (3): 350–359.

Cato, V., Fernandes, C., Gorman, T., Kispal, A. with White, J. (1992) *The Teaching of Initial Literacy: How Do Teachers Do It?* Slough: NFER.

Centre for Language in Primary Education (CLPE) (1989) *The Primary Language Record: Handbook for Teachers*. London: Inner London Education Authority (ILEA)/CLPE.

Chall, J. S. (1983) *Learning to Read: The Great Debate* (updated edition). New York: McGraw-Hill.

Chapman, L. J. (1987) *Reading: From 5–11 years*. Milton Keynes: Open University Press.

Children's Literature Research Centre (1996) *Young People's Reading at the End of the Century*. London: Roehampton Institute.

Clark, M. M. (1976) *Young Fluent Readers*. London: Heinemann Educational Books.

Davies, A. (1997) 'Sounding out'. *Literacy and Learning*, Autumn, Issue 1: 13–14.

Department for Education and Employment (DfEE) (1998a) *Teaching: High Status, High Standards. Requirements for Courses of Initial Teacher*

Training. London: DfEE.

Department for Education and Employment (DfEE) (1998b) *The National Literacy Strategy Framework for Teaching*. London: DfEE.

Ferreiro, E. and Teberosky, A. (1982) *Literacy Before Schooling*. Portsmouth, NH: Heinemann Educational Books.

Galton, M. (1989) *Teaching in the Primary School*. London: David Fulton.

Gray, B. (1983) 'A survey of books used in Northern Ireland to teach Beginners to read'. *The Northern Teacher*, 14 (1): 28–32.

Harrison, C. and Coles, M.(1992) (eds) *The Reading for Real Handbook*. London: Routledge.

Harste, J. C., Woodward, V. A. and Burke, C. L. (1984) *Language Stories and Literacy Lessons*. Portsmouth, NH: Heinemann Educational Books.

Her Majesty's Inspectorate (HMI) (1991) *English Key Stage 1: A Report by H M Inspectorate on the First Year, 1989–90*. London: HMSO.

Kirklees LEA (1993) 'First I Have to Read it in my Head. A Survey of Reading in Kirklees Primary Schools'. Huddersfield: Kirklees LEA.

Laycock, E. (1990) 'Fifteen months in the life of a writer (teacher inquiry in the classroom)'. *Language Arts*, 67 (2):206–217.

McConkie, G. W. and Zola, D. (1981) 'Language constraints and the functional stimulus in reading', in A. M. Lesgold and C. A. Perfetti (eds) *Interactive Processes in Reading*. Hillsdale, NJ: Erlbaum Associates.

McGuinness, D. (1998) *Why Children Can't Read and What We Can Do About It*. London: Penguin Books.

Minns, H. (1997) *Read It To Me Now! Learning at Home and at School*, (second edition). Buckingham: Open University Press.

Mortimore, P. and Goldstein, H. (1996) *The Teaching of Reading in 45 Inner London Primary Schools: A Critical Examination of OFSTED Research*. London, Institute of Education: University of London.

Moustafa, M. (1997) *Beyond Traditional Phonics: Research Discoveries and Reading Instruction*. Portsmouth, NH: Heinemann Educational Books.

Oakhill, J., Beard, R. and Vincent, D.(eds) (1995) 'The contribution of psychological research'. *Journal of Research in Reading*, 18 (2).

Office for Standards in Education (OFSTED) (1996) *The Teaching of Reading in 45 Inner London Primary Schools. A Report by Her Majesty's Inspectors in Collaboration with the LEAs of Islington, Southwark and Tower Hamlets*. London: OFSTED Publications.

Office for Standards in Education (OFSTED) (1997a) *PFUS Guidance Methodology and Forms*. London: OFSTED.

Office for Standards in Education (OFSTED) (1997b) *Literacy Matters*. 56 minutes. Videocassette.

Payton, S. (1984) *Developing Awareness of Print: A Young Child's First Steps Towards Literacy*. University of Birmingham: Educational Review.

Perfetti, C. A. (1995) 'Cognitive research can inform reading education'. *Journal of Research in Reading*, 18 (2): 106–115.

Pidgeon, S. (1993) 'Learning reading and learning gender', in M. Barrs and S. Pidgeon (eds) *Reading the Difference*. London: Centre for Language in Primary Education.

Questions Publishing (1997) *Literacy and Learning.* Autumn, Issue 1.

Rice, I. (1987) 'Racism and Reading Schemes, the Current Situation'. *Reading*, 21 (2): 92–97.

Richardson, J. T. E. (1996) *Handbook of Qualitative Research Methods for Psychology and the Social Sciences.* Leicester: The British Psychological Society.

Scholes, R. (1998) 'The case against phonemic awareness'. *Journal of Research in Reading*, 21 (3): 177–188.

Smith, F. (1978) *Reading* (second edition). Cambridge: Cambridge University Press.

Southgate, V., Arnold, H. and Johnson, S. (1981) *Extending Beginning Reading.* London: Heinemann Educational Books for the Schools Council.

Stannard, J. (1998) 'National Literacy Strategy implementation details'. Presentation at National Literacy Strategy Conference for Teacher Educators, 8–9 February at Bishop Grosseteste University College.

Stanovich, K. E. and Stanovich, P. J. (1995) 'How research might inform the debate about early reading acquisition'. *Journal of Research in Reading*, 18 (2): 146–153.

Taylor, D. (1993) *From the Child's Point of View.* Portsmouth, NH: Heinemann.

Thomas, H., (1997) 'Sounding out'. *Literacy and Learning*, Autumn, Issue 1: 15–16.

Tizard, B. and Hughes, M. (1984) *Young Children Learning.* London: Fontana.

Wade, B. (1990) *Reading for Real.* Milton Keynes: Open University Press.

Weaver, C. (1994) *Reading Process and Practice From Socio-psycholinguistics to Whole Language*, second edition. Portsmouth, NH: Heinemann.

Wells, G. (1986) *The Meaning Makers: Children Learning Language and Using Language to Learn.* Sevenoaks: Hodder & Stoughton.

Wray, D. (1995) 'Reviewing the reading debate', in D. Wray and J. Medwell (eds) *Teaching Primary English: The State of the Art.* London: Routledge.

Wyse, D. (1998) *Primary Writing.* Buckingham: Open University Press.

Annotated bibliography

Adams, M. J. (1990) *Beginning to Read: Thinking and Learning About Print.* Cambridge, MA: MIT Press.
Has become a very important text in relation to the teaching of reading. Although it is often used to defend phonics teaching it covers a wide range of issues.
L3 ***

Beard, R. (1993) *Teaching Literacy Balancing Perspectives.* London: Hodder and Stoughton.
One of the first texts in the UK to raise serious questions about the direction of reading teaching at the time. Has an emphasis on cognitive psychology but this is related to the primary classroom.
L3 ***

Lemann, N. The Reading Wars. [online] *Atlantic Monthly*, November 1997 [cited 26-6-00]. Available from:
   http://www.theatlantic.com/issues/97nov/read.htm
Interesting overview of the political debate concerning methods of teaching in America.
L1 *

Moustafa, M. (1997) *Beyond Traditional Phonics: Research Discoveries and Reading Instruction*. Portsmouth, NH: Heinemann.
A welcome response to the heavy emphasis on phonics in many English-speaking countries. A reminder that there is research to support top-down theories.
L2 **

Smith, F. (1978) *Reading*, second edition. Cambridge: Cambridge University Press.
Controversial but readable and important text. Very interesting insights on some of the theories that were prevalent in the 1970s and early 1980s.
L1 **

Wyse, D. (2000) 'Phonics: The whole story?: A critical review of empirical evidence'. *Educational Studies*, 26(3): 355–64.
This article goes into more detail about the research on reading that relates to many of the issues that have been raised in this section.
L3 ***

Chapter 4

Texts for children

The teaching of English, language and literacy involves extensive use of texts. We explore some of the issues related to the selection and use of texts in the classroom. Picture fiction and longer fiction are followed by a look at the use of non-fiction.

> Willy didn't seem to be any good at anything. He liked to read . . . and listen to music . . . and walk in the park with his friend, Millie.
>
> (Brown, 1985:1-3)

Margaret Meek has spent her professional life arguing forcefully and logically that the specific texts that children experience are the most important ingredient in their learning to read. If this is the case, it follows that all teachers must be knowledgeable about texts and the particular ways that different texts support reading.

FICTION

There has been an explosion in the range and quality of children's picture fiction over the last 20 years; there also continues to be much picture fiction that is poor quality. The issue of quality is an important and problematic one. People who work with children clearly want them to get the maximum benefit from the texts that they are exposed to. Too often the quality of picture books (☞) on offer is of questionable quality: an examination of the books in most supermarkets, many book shops, some nurseries and schools highlights this view. Children themselves reveal their preferences through their enjoyment of particular texts and this is one important measure of quality. However, there are a number of dilemmas that exist when using children's judgements. Sometimes their judgements can be incomplete if they have not had the opportunity to read a wide range of texts and actively comment on their quality. The same is true of teachers: if you have not read widely and analytically it is impossible to form appropriate judgements about the quality of texts.

Picture books offer children a unique opportunity to connect with the author's imaginary world. Often this can be a particularly personal and intense experience. The features of books that generate such experiences include a stimulating text and brilliant illustrations. However, although the best picture books offer artistically effective illustrations which themselves often contain a number of sub-plots (☞) (for example, when Lily takes a seemingly peaceful walk but her dog is subjected to a range of nightmare visions conjured by ordinary features of the urban landscape: Kitamura, 1987) it is possible to exaggerate the importance of the pictures over and above the special meanings that text can create.

High-quality texts operate on a number of semantic levels (☞). First and foremost the texts should appeal directly and powerfully to children. But adults should also find aspects that engage their curiosity and analytic skills. Such books are usually characterised by the different layers of meaning they contain that only reveal themselves through rereading and analysis. Books like this also stand the test of time and become 'classics' (☞). *The Very Hungry Caterpillar* is a wonderful example that has been 'translated into over 25 languages, and has sold 15 million copies. 'So much from so little, as one of my friends once put it!' says [the author Eric] Carle merrily, (Carey, 1999: 13).

Authors of children's fiction find a variety of ways of rooting their work in children's culture. Janet and Alan Ahlberg's most important contribution is in the ways that they weave children's stories and nursery rhymes within one text (sometimes called 'intertextuality'), a good example of this is *Each Peach Pear Plum*. The text is structured in rhyming couplets with each double page having one couplet and an accompanying illustration. The rhythm and rhyme appeals to young children and aids their memory of the text. The book also draws on the game 'I spy' as each couplet includes the words from the game: for example, 'Baby Bunting fast asleep I spy Bo-Peep'. As you have probably guessed a whole range of nursery rhyme characters populate the story culminating in a picnic which includes plum pie:

> Three Bears still hunting
> THEY spy Baby Bunting
> Baby Bunting safe and dry
> I spy Plum Pie
> Plum Pie in the sun
> I spy . . .
> . . . EVERYONE!
>   (Ahlberg and Ahlberg, 1978: 24-31)

Anthony Browne's work is notable because of the way that his books often focus on important issues while maintaining genuinely interesting stories. Examples of such issues include: sexism – *Piggybook*; self-esteem and bullying – *Willy the Champ*; one-parent families – *Gorilla*; class – *A Walk in the Park*; gender and sibling rivalry – *The Tunnel*. All his books are accompanied by mesmeric illustrations that seem to derive from surrealist (☞) art.

The final picture fiction author we examine is Trish Cooke. Her book *So Much* is more recent than some of the previous examples as it was published in 1996. Although prizes are a notoriously unreliable way of judging books, on this occasion the awards of the Smarties Book Prize, the Kurt Maschler Award and the *She*/W H Smith awards were justified. Indeed Anthony Browne is quoted on the back of the book: 'It is always a delight to see an established artist taking risks, breaking new ground and succeeding brilliantly'. *So Much* explores an aspect of Black British children's culture and like many children's books has a *naturally* repetitive structure:

> They weren't doing anything
> Mum and the baby
> nothing really . . .
> Then,
> DING DONG!
> 'Oooooooh!'
> Mum looked at the door,
> the baby looked at Mum.
> It was . . .
> (Cooke, 1994: 7)

As can be seen from the extract the text encourages children to predict what will happen next; this helps to develop an important reading strategy and recognises their enthusiasm for guessing and problem solving. The illustrations show accurate and positive images of a British Afro-Caribbean extended family and as each character arrives at the house they first want to do something with the baby, such as squeeze him (Auntie Bibba), kiss him (Uncle Didi), eat him (Nanny and Gran-Gran), fight him (Cousin Kay Kay and Big Cousin Ross):

> And they wrestle
> and they wrestle.
> He push the baby first,
> the baby hit him back.
> He gave the baby pinch,
> the baby gave him slap.
> And then they laugh
> and laugh and laugh.
> 'Huh huh huh!'
> (Cooke, 1994: 28)

The language of the book brilliantly uses some of the rhythms and repetitions of African English which links it with other writers such as the Ghanaian poet John Agard. Once again one of the core features of the book reflected in the title is based on a common childhood experience; the adult and child game: 'How big's baby?' or 'How much do we love you?'.

Longer fiction

One of the challenges for teachers of Key Stage 2 children is having a knowledge of longer texts and how they can be used in the classroom. This means that if you are a Key Stage 2 teacher you need to read children's novels in order to assess their usefulness for the classroom. The 'class reader', a book that you read to the whole class daily over an extended period, gives the opportunity to extend your own knowledge and the knowledge of the children about such texts.

In order to help you make decisions about which books to read there are a range of sources of information that include reviews of books and their potential use in the classroom. The internet has become a very powerful resource which can help you to find out more about longer fiction. We have just done a quick search starting at 'English Teaching in the United Kingdom' (http://www.gosford-hill.oxon.sch.uk/etuk/etuk.htm), a site maintained by an English teacher. Here we found many impressive American sites that tend to focus on American books and authors. One fascinating site included some 30 versions of *Little Red Riding Hood* including photos of the original pages and with the option to compare two different versions on screen (➡ Chapter 5, 'Analysing texts).

The Virtual Teacher's Centre – part of the National Grid for Learning site – includes 'Literacy Time' which has a section devoted to 'featured texts'. This offers reviews, author profiles and suggested activities. Here is an extract from the review about one of the most popular series of books for children in recent years.

Featured work
Key Stage 2
Goosebumps
By RL Stine
When we ask groups of Key Stage 2 children, 'What are your favourite books?' we often get the reply . . . 'Goosebumps!' Many children are avid readers of these books and they cannot wait to get on to the next one.

A number of teachers have said they are impressed with the way this series captures the interest and imagination of even the most reluctant readers. Children have described the stories as 'funny and scary at the same time'.

The books described below are a small selection from the series.

Deep Trouble
By RL Stine
Don't go in the water!

Billy and his sister, Sheena, are staying with their uncle Dr. Deep on a small island in the Caribbean. It seems the perfect spot for Billy to practise his diving skills and he is looking forward to an adventure.

Billy's uncle gave him just one rule to remember: 'Don't go near the coral reefs!' But the reefs look so beautiful and peaceful, Billy can't resist diving there. What Billy doesn't know is that he's not alone in the water. There is something else lurking there deep below the waves. It is dark and scaly, half-human, half-fish . . .

(http://vtc.ngfl.gov.uk/resource/literacy/featured/four/ks2f.html)

PUBLISHED SCHEMES

In the past there has been much debate about the merits of reading scheme books (or *basal* readers as they say in the USA) versus 'real' books (➡ Chapter 3, 'The development of reading'). The typical reading provision for most schools consisted of one or more reading schemes arranged into levels of difficulty. Usually this consisted of a core scheme of the school's choice supplemented by examples from other reading schemes and selections of real books. Children worked through the scheme individually and had to read all the books in the sequence until they were allowed to choose their own reading books. Unfortunately in some schools this practice continued as far as year 5 or even year 6 with children having little opportunity to choose their own books and develop preferences and interests. Here is an example of a text from one of the most popular reading schemes (GINN 360):

> Help!
> Where is Dad?
> Dad, can you help?
> I can help.
> Here it is.
> Dad, come here.
> Can you help?
> Yes, I can help.
> Come in here.
> Look, here it is.
> No, stop!
> Not in here.
> Help! Where is Dad?
> (Oakley, 1988)

Many people have commented on the disjointed flow that such books have because of the controlled vocabulary that they use. You may also have noticed that there are no speech marks; presumably it is felt that young children will be confused by such things. Although you will be able to find some shocking and sometimes amusing examples of old-fashioned reading scheme texts, in recent years the publishers have brought out newer reading schemes that address some of the early problems. For example, 'Collins Pathways' offers children choice within a graded band of books. Real authors, as opposed to consultants, have written the books and the language is very close to that of real books:

> Leon was given six chocolate dinosaurs for his birthday.
> They were wrapped in silver paper.
> Leon stood the dinosaurs in a long line in his bedroom.
> 'One, two, three, four, five, six!'
> Just then his mum called him.
> He ran downstairs to the kitchen, and while he was away who should
>   spot the dinosaurs but Davina.
> She was Leon's little sister.
> (Magee, 1994: 2–7)

The advent of the literacy hour predictably has resulted in publishers writing new kinds of schemes. One of the challenges that the literacy hour has presented is that individualised reading is no longer regarded as good practice, although there are many parents and teachers who would question that idea. The emphasis now is firmly on whole class and group reading of the same text. The newest schemes try to reflect the changes to the teaching of reading but you should use schemes with caution because they often you often find that:

1   They cannot be flexible enough to reflect the changing needs of your particular class.
2   They are usually written by consultants who are put under commercial time pressures which can result in less than best educational practice.
3   They tend to be individualised and neglect collaborative learning.
4   The objectives are set by the scheme not by the teacher and this can result in lack of clear classroom focus.
5   They minimise the importance of oracy.
6   They tend to involve passive learning.
7   The convenience that they offer has often resulted in them being the *main* strategy for delivering teaching objectives.

NON-FICTION

Before the recent developments in the internet, the publisher Dorling Kindersley extended the range and quality of information books for children. In particular it set new standards in the visual images and presentation of its books. Some of its best texts were aimed at young children who in the past had very little choice as far as non-fiction was concerned. One example comes from the 'See How They Grow' series. The front cover contains the kind of vivid photography that is found throughout the book. The inside cover has lines of hand-drawn plants and pond-life that encourage counting, and these continue throughout the book as lively page borders. The text is cleverly written and most importantly is as effective as the visual aspects of the book. Each double-page spread has two levels of text: a heading and some information.

> **Just hatched**
> After two weeks I am ready to hatch.
> Look at my long feathery gills. They let me breathe underwater.
> I push my way through the frogspawn and swim away.
>   (Royston, 1991: 3–4)

The use of first-person grammar is a recognition of the way that young children respond to texts. The early importance of story is reflected in the way that the tadpole is portrayed as a character who seems to be telling the reader about its thoughts. The text also draws children's attention to important features such as 'gills' and uses the appropriate scientific language in recognition of all children's remarkable ability to learn new vocabulary.

The internet has genuinely added to the nature and use of non-fiction texts. Now, in addition to high-quality images and meaningful texts there are opportunities for interactive learning. In one-tenth of the time it would take you to reach the school library and browse through the books you could be online at the 'Natural History Museum' site (http://www.nhm.ac.uk/index.htm). In the interactive learning area there are various activities including 'Questioning, Understanding and Exploring Simulated Things; QUEST is an exciting interactive investigation'. Here it is possible to select one of a number of photographs and explore them in various ways including: look at different views; find out how old it is; find out how much it weighs; measure how big it is; find out what it feels like to touch; find out more about it; make notes and read what other people have said; ask a scientist about the object; look at it close up. One of the many interesting aspects of this site is the chance to read other people's comments about the objects; you also get the option to send them an e-mail. 'Ask a scientist' was a little disappointing in that a picture of a scientist appeared with a speech bubble which simply asked three more questions. The option to e-mail would have been ideal, but failing that some straightforward information to read would have been interesting.

Practice points

- Your knowledge of *all* the texts that you use with children needs to constantly improve throughout your teaching career.
- Use published schemes with caution and read them carefully before you use them.
- Enjoy the ever increasing range of texts that are available including those on the internet.

Glossary

Classic – books that remain of interest to significant numbers of people long after their initial publication date. They are also regarded to be of special significance.

Picture books – books for children where the pictures are equally as important as the text. Larger than A5 children's novels with full-colour artistic illustrations.

Semantic levels – the different meanings or interpretations that are possible: from basic to complex.

Sub-plots – story lines that are additional to the main one.

Surrealist – art particularly linked with the work of Salvador Dali. The paintings contain bizarre dreamlike images such as melting clocks drooped over tree branches.

References

Ahlberg, A. and Ahlberg, J. (1978) *Each Peach Pear Plum*. London: Penguin.
Browne, A. (1977) *A Walk in the Park*. London: Macmillan.
Browne, A. (1983) *Gorilla*. London: Random Century.

Browne, A. (1985) *Willy The Champ*. London: Little Mammoth.
Browne, A. (1989) *Piggybook*. London: Reed Consumer Books.
Browne, A. (1992) *The Tunnel*. London: Walker Books.
Carey, J. (1999) 'The very busy author'. *Guardian*, November 23.
Carle, E. (1970) *The Very Hungry Caterpillar*. London: Penguin Books.
Cooke, T. (1994) *So Much!* London: Walker Books.
Kitamura, S. (1987) *Lily Takes a Walk*. London: Picture Corgi.
Magee, W. (1994) *Davina and the Dinosaurs*. London: Collins Educational.
Oakley, H. (1988) *On my Bike*. Aylesbury: Ginn.
Royston, A. (1991) *Frog*. London: Dorling Kindersley.

Extracts from *So Much!* reproduced by permission of the publisher, Walker Books Ltd, London. Text © 1994 Trishe Cooke, illustrated by Helen Oxenbury.

Annotated bibliography

BBC ONLINE. Education: Schools Online. Look and Read: Spywatch. [online – cited 26-6-00]. Available from:
  http://www.bbc.co.uk/education/lookandread/lar/index.htm
  Another example of the excellent interactive educational sites provided by the BBC. Acting as a spy the young reader has to find clues and solve problems.
  L1
Graham, J. (1997) *Cracking Good Books: Teaching Literature at Key Stage 2*. Sheffield: National Association of Teachers of English (NATE).
  Similar to the Merchant and Thomas text in that this offers practical suggestions for using texts in the classroom. The emphasis is on children's novels rather than picture books and the book was written before the introduction of the National Literacy Strategy.
  L1 *
Meek, M. (1988) *How Texts Teach What Readers Learn*. Stroud: The Thimble Press.
  Argues strongly for the importance of specific high quality texts as one of the main things that will help children learn to read.
  L2 **
Merchant, G. and Thomas, H. (1999) *Picture Books for the Literacy Hour*. London: David Fulton.
  A practical guide to using high-quality picture books in the literacy hour. Each section features a particular book which is illustrated under various headings: The introduction hints at some of the difficulties that teachers face when trying to develop children's understanding of literature under the constraints of the hour.
  L1 *
Wray, D. and Lewis, M. (1997) *Extending Literacy: Children Reading and Writing Non-fiction*. London: Routledge.
  This book is based on the Exeter University Extending Literacy Project which has been influential. Practical examples are given that show how children can be encouraged to engage with non-fiction texts.
  L2 **

Chapter 5

Analysing texts

The teaching of English is centrally concerned with reading, writing and talking about texts. We open the door on some of the key ideas about the analysis of texts. Narrative (☞) structure is followed by a look at inference (☞). We conclude with 'The Thought-Fox' and views on using poetry as a resource for enjoyment and analysis.

It is important to remember that the 'analysis' of texts should not replace enjoyment and personal response. Many readers cite occasions when they felt they could have enjoyed a particular book but it was 'done to death' at school. Some people despised this kind of process so much that they never recovered a love of reading. Instead, textual analysis should be seen as a series of understandings, each offering the reader greater insight, greater pleasure and greater mastery over the written word:

> In a book written for children, as in any other, we are primarily concerned with making sense of the text and the enjoyment and pleasure that doing so will give us. A good children's book may convey layers of meaning, some of them beyond those immediately accessible to very young readers . . .
>
> (Wilson, 1999: 102)

Text-level work is quite different in nature to work at word level, and teachers need to be familiar with different concepts. Knowledge of cohesion (☞), layout and textual organisation can help us to understand texts in different ways and to teach text-level work more effectively.

One of the most commonly cited ideas about the organisation of texts is related to story structure: the ideas that stories have a beginning, middle and end (or as Philip Larkin mischievously suggested a beginning, *muddle* and end). Martin et al (1987) developed this simple idea about structure and suggested further categories: Abstract; Orientation; Complication; Evaluation; Resolution and Coda as stages in stories. Wray and Medwell (1997) modify the structure and relate it to *Little Red Riding Hood* as shown in Box 5.1.

This structure gives you the opportunity to explore the ways in which other stories may fit the model. At text level, structures like this are one way that writing maintains cohesion. Each stage requires the one before it if the

Martin et al (1987)	Wray and Medwell (1997)	
Abstract	Title of the story and introductory ideas	*Little Red Riding Hood*
Orientation	Setting of the story including characters	A forest and the two cottages.
Complication	The main event	Red Riding Hood meets the wolf dressed as her grandmother
Evaluation	The impact of the main event on the characters	She runs away and finds the woodcutter
Resolution	The final implications of the main event	The woodcutter kills the wolf
Coda	Ending the story	The moral

Box 5.1

text is to make sense. Of course one of the interesting things about any kind of model like this is the way that so many texts do not simply conform. Traditional tales such as *Little Red Riding Hood* are often used as illustrations to show how such structures work. However, narrative is a wildly diverse form which resists simple classification. How well would this structure apply to some of the following: the script of the film *Pulp Fiction* which contains three linked stories; multi-author internet texts; choose your own adventure texts; or *Bridget Jones' Diary*? You will also be familiar with narrative devices such as flashbacks (e.g. *Carrie's War*: Bawden, 1973) and traditional stories told from different points of view (e.g. *The True Story of the Three Little Pigs*: Scieszka and Smith, 1989) which make this kind of classification difficult.

The other thing to remember about this kind of structural analysis is that it is only one way of analysing texts. For example, we might choose to analyse the text by exploring the idea that *Little Red Riding Hood* is overtly about the dangers of child abuse. At first sight this might seem a bit extreme or that we are reading *too much* into the text (how can one read too much?). However, a useful website provides us with a translation of Perrault's original written version.

The wolfe seeing her come in, said to her, hiding himself under the clothes. Put the custard, and the little pot of butter upon the stool, and

come into bed with me. The little red Riding-Hood undressed her self, and went to bed, where she was very much astonished to see how her grandmother looked in her night-cloaths . . .
THE MORAL . . .
With luring tongues, and language wondrous sweet,
Follow young ladies as they walk the street,
Ev'n to their very houses and bedside,
And though their true designs they artful hide,
Yet ah! these simpring Wolves, who does not see
Most dang'rous of all Wolves in fact to be?

(Salda, 2000)

Our analysis here has been historical as we decided to locate one of the original versions – although like other traditional stories these started their lives as oral tales. The analysis also took a social dimension by hypothesising about the link with abuse. The 'moral' of the tale, written in rhyming couplets, once again leads us to question whether the narrative structure that we illustrated above can be universally applied.

In order to work effectively at text level, teachers and children need to become competent in evaluating texts and language critically. A range of fiction, poetry and non-fiction texts should be made available for these purposes, and children need to be encouraged to draw on all three sources to demonstrate their skills in textual analysis. There are a number of textual patterns and conventions that are discernible, and these can become focal points for classroom discussion. An important thing to remember is that the kind of analysis that you carry out should depend on your point of view and the context that you determine for the text. There is no agreed way of analysing texts. In fact students of English literature are subject to a wide range of analytic methods and university programmes differ in the kinds of analysis that they think is important.

INFERENCE

Some teachers find it difficult to teach children about inference. They see this as asking children to 'read between the lines', and interpret this as asking them to read what is *not* there'. This may be an unhelpful way to conceive of inference; the meaning *is* present in the text, there are just different clues to signal the meaning. Sometimes the author leaves deliberate clues to guide the child towards understanding that what has been *said* is not what is *meant*. For example:

'Termtimes are the worst, of course,' she went on. 'Coachload upon coachload of children. You'd wonder where they all came from.'
Her eye rested on Minty, now into her fourth scone.
'Not that I've anything against children,' she said. 'Dear little things . . 'she added vaguely and insincerely.
Minty choked.

(Cresswell, 1987: 9)

The clues here are open for children to read. The author leaves the trailing adverbs 'vaguely' and 'insincerely', then follows this with a description of the main character choking on her scone (because the child has picked up the inference that children are *not* welcome).

At other times, the clues are less deliberate. For example, any text which contains sarcasm is an example of inference, since the physical words contain one set of meanings, but in the context of the larger text, or the way in which the words are spoken, the same words have a very different meaning. For example:

> Michael picked up the loose ball and knocked it past one of the oncoming defenders. At last, here was his chance! Sprinting now, he headed towards the penalty area. He kept his concentration on the ball, not allowing the oncoming goalkeeper to intimidate him and, pulling back his right foot, he sent the ball scorching into the back of the net. Suddenly he was aware of the noise around him, his team-mates shouting and whistles blowing.
>
> 'What a brilliant goal!' exclaimed his captain, 'one of the most magnificent shots I've ever seen'.
>
> Michael finally felt the sense of pride he'd lacked in his performance, then noticed the opposing side celebrating.
>
> His captain went on: 'What a shame it was in your own net!'

If the above example of text were to be simplistically decoded (and the last sentence ignored), the suggestion would be that Michael's captain believed that Michael's goal was one of the best he had ever seen. By reading the whole text and relating the captain's statements to the last sentence, it is possible to use inference to deduce that the captain's earlier praise was an example of sarcasm.

USING POETRY

A good way to develop children's understanding of inference is to use poetry. Several poetic devices require the reader to look beyond the literal meaning of the word on the page in order to attain closer understanding. The temptation to move into 'what does the poet really mean?' should be resisted, however, as this is not the point of poetry. A better approach is 'what are the different ways that we all *read* this poem?'

Ted Hughes wrote many 'animal' poems, but his first, 'The Thought-Fox', is one which lends itself quite readily to extended investigation. Hughes says that the poem was composed in only a few minutes after a year of not writing. It clearly makes a connection between suddenly, unexpectedly getting a glimpse of a fox and suddenly, unexpectedly getting the idea for a piece of writing. He says 'It is about a fox, obviously enough, but a fox that is both a fox and not a fox' (Hughes, 1967: 20). He makes the distinction between the image created of the fox, the act of writing about it and the resulting animal which he has created. Throughout the poem though, it is possible to deduce these meanings through the range of poetic devices. As an extended metaphor, there are several opportunities for readers to make inferred connections. For example, the first sight of the fox is described in tentative terms, as if the animal does not know whether to make itself known or not, its nose 'touches twig, leaf' and we are unsure whether we will see the full beast or not. The idea for writing (or the thought-fox) comes at the same time, in the same way. The two ideas are developed together until the fox has disappeared back into the darkness and the page is written.

A poem such as 'The Thought-Fox' offers several opportunities for teachers to introduce analytical terms and concepts. It is not unreasonable to suggest (for example) that children would be able to establish a meaningful correlation between the white snow and the blank paper, or the 'neat prints' left by the fox and the gradually emerging writing on the page.

Children towards the top end of Key Stage 2 should also be offered opportunities to work with poetry which has themes appropriate to their experience and understanding. Adrian Mitchell, in his poem 'By the Waters of Liverpool' deals openly with the Hillsborough tragedy (Mitchell, 1996). Here is an opportunity for primary teachers to address boys who claim that they don't like poetry or that they don't understand the language. Mitchell establishes the colour red as a metaphor for the city's football, poverty, it's historical links with the slave trade, and, finally, the deaths at Hillsborough.

There are no simple equations by which text can be analysed; to reduce *Hamlet* to a sequence of textual devices leaves us none the wiser about the play's wider issues. For some teachers the analysis of text is a grey area which instantly becomes problematic because there is no set of answers to act as a safety net. For others it is the kind of activity which begins to genuinely engage children with the act of understanding the written and spoken word, and as such becomes the most dynamic and exciting part of literacy teaching. As ever, in primary classrooms, there is a balance to be achieved; structural analysis should not diminish the importance of personal engagement with texts and growing sensitivity towards language.

Practice points

- Encourage children to think about texts in a variety of ways: some structured by you, and others taken from their own ideas.
- Develop your critical appreciation of texts including a strong understanding of inference and bias.
- Keep a balance between analysis and straightforward enjoyment.

Glossary

Cohesion – the way that different parts of a text work together to convey meaning.
Inference – the knowledge of textual meanings beyond the literal or 'obvious'.
Narrative – a text which retells events often in chronological sequence.

References

Bawden, N. (1973) *Carrie's War*. London: Victor Gollancz.

Cresswell, H. (1987) *Moondial* London: Puffin.

Hughes, T. (1967) *Poetry in the Making*. London: Faber and Faber.

Martin, J. R., Christie, F. and Rothery, J. (1987) Social Processes in Education: A reply to Sawyer and Watson (and others), in I. Reid (ed.) *The Place of Genre in Learning*. Victoria: Deakin University.

Mitchell, A. (1996) *Blue Coffee*. Newcastle-Upon-Tyne: Bloodaxe.

Salda, M. N. *The Little Red Riding Hood Project*. University of Southern Mississippi. Version 1.0, December 1995. Drawn from the 'de Grummond Children's Literature Research Collection. [online – cited 23-1-00]
http://www.dept.usm.edu/~engdept/lrrh/lrrhhome.htm

Scieszka, J. (1989) *The True Story of the Three Little Pigs!* London: Penguin.

Wilson, A. (1999) *Language Knowledge for Primary Teachers*. London: David Fulton

Wray, D. and Medwell, J. (1997) *QTS English for Primary Teachers*. London: Letts.

Annotated bibliography

Hayhoe, M. and Parker, S. (1990) *Reading and Response*. Buckingham: Open University Press.
A useful link between education and studies of English literature. Tackles the idea that texts are never one-dimensional and that readers apply all kinds of different interpretations and analyses to the texts that they read.
L3 ***

Hughes, T. (1967) *Poetry in the Making* London: Faber and Faber.
As educators concerned with reading and writing it would be unforgivable not to take account of the views of people who write for a living. Ted Hughes shows how children respond with excitement to the most complex challenges that poetic meaning can offer.
L2 ***

Sarland, C. (1991) *Young People Reading: Culture and Response*. Milton Keynes: Open University Press.
Sarland raises the question of popular versus classical texts. He found that children's views about popular films such as *Rambo* were worthy of interest by teachers.
L3 ***

University of Teesside. School of Social Sciences: Student Network. [online – cited 26-6-00] Available from:
http://sss-studnet.tees.ac.uk/politics/studyskills2/textanal.htm
Succinct and well worked example which analyses two statements supporting different points of view and considers a variety of interpretations.
L2

Chapter 6

Listening to children read

The skills required to interact effectively when reading with children are vital. These skills are considered initially in the context of paired and shared reading. The chapter concludes by looking at reading conferences with individual children.

Listening to individual readers is a fairly recent phenomenon. Reading round the class or in unison was much more common in primary school classrooms up until the middle of the twentieth century. Following new thinking in psychology in the 1930s and 1940s, resulting in the development of graded reading schemes (☞), teachers began to listen to children reading individually. The strategy was deemed to be particularly useful for the teaching of struggling readers who benefit from individualised support.

The Bullock Report (DES, 1975) broke new ground by recommending that every child should be heard individually several times a week and have their comprehension of the text assessed. This seemed to reflect current practice in schools at that time. But only six years later, the Extending Beginning Reading Project (Southgate et al, 1981) found that the time given to hearing reading was minimal – often only 2–3 minutes per child – and that checking up on how much the child had read was given precedence over any actual *interaction*. One of the main findings of the project was that children should be heard reading less often but with a higher quality of interaction and for a longer period of time.

During the 1980s teachers continued to persevere with individualised reading aloud but took on board some of the criticisms of the 'Extending Beginning Reading Project'. Schools began to look more critically at their reading schemes, the amount of time they were giving to hearing readers and the quality of what went on in these sessions. A number of important developments resulted, such as 'paired reading', 'shared reading', 'reading apprenticeship' and the use of 'big books' (☞) (Campbell,1995).

WORKING WITH INDIVIDUAL CHILDREN: PAIRED AND SHARED READING

Paired reading began in the USA in the late 1970s and was aimed at struggling readers. It was used extensively by a number of Local Education

Authorities (LEAs) – including notably the West Yorkshire authority Kirklees – and involved many parents who found the technique relatively easy to handle. Paired reading lasts between 5 and 15 minutes and comprises the following procedures:

- Ideally, the child chooses the book or text to be read
- The book should be briefly discussed before reading aloud commences
- The adult and the child begin by reading the text aloud together
- The child may follow the text with a finger
- When the child wants to read alone they indicate this by tapping the table or arm of the adult
- The adult ceases reading immediately and praises the child for signalling.
- The child continues alone
- When a child makes a miscue the adult supplies the word
- The child then repeats the word
- Praise is given for the correct reading of difficult words and for self-corrections (☞)
- If a child is unable to read a word or correct an error in about 5 seconds, teacher and child return to reading in unison
- The child makes the signal when they feel confident enough to resume reading alone
- Further praise and encouragement is given at the end of the session.

An important feature of paired reading is that the adult provides a model of appropriate reading behaviour for the child alongside the child's own attempts at reading satisfactorily. It is a tightly structured way of reading a text with the set guidelines being strictly followed.

The notion of 'shared reading' emerged in the 1980s. You will notice when you read Chapter 8, 'Routines for Reading', that the idea of shared reading in the National Literacy Strategy is significantly different from the practice we are about to describe. Originally shared reading was a strategy for working with an individual child not with a large group.

Shared reading is different to paired reading in that the session is loosely structured to make it a collaborative and enjoyable experience between adult and child. The teacher determines at what point the child should read unaccompanied though the young reader is allowed to take over whenever they want without signalling. Some of the child's miscues (☞) are ignored where the general meaning is unaffected and more time and latitude is given for the child to make use of all reading cues (☞) and to self-correct.

Shared reading also involves extended interaction between teacher and child lasting 10 or even 15 minutes rather than five. The simplest form of shared reading consists of little more than hearing the child read. Where necessary the teacher will prompt the child and provide appropriate words. Often the child's attention is drawn to different features of the text or illustrations and the teacher generally encourages and supports the child. The teacher might read parts aloud while the child follows the text or they might read in unison every so often. The session is usually concluded with some discussion of the text as a whole and the teacher will often record evidence of the child's reading behaviour.

A type of shared reading that became known as reading apprenticeship was described by Waterland (1985: 29) as 'a relationship in which the adult demonstrates the craft [of reading] and supports the children in whatever contribution they are able to make'. The child starts by listening to the adult reading then reads alongside and finally begins to take over the greater part of the reading. Waterland went on to describe the role of teachers: 'we are not listening to the child perform, we are performing with the child.' She made the point of stressing the importance of high-quality texts in the process and recommended the use of so-called 'real books' (☞) in preference to reading scheme books (➡ Chapter 4, 'Texts for Children'). She also emphasised the importance of parental involvement. Waterland's short book was one of the most popular of its time.

A later version of shared reading put forward by Campbell (1990) is similar to that of Waterland though his approach is even more interactive than hers and the role of the teacher more complex and investigative. He offers the example of 5-year-old Kirsty sharing a new book with her teacher. Firstly the teacher reads the story while Kirsty looks at the pictures. Then they read through the story again with the teacher asking Kirsty questions that draw her into conversation about different incidents in the story. Then, when she feels Kirsty is ready, she asks her to read aloud:

Teacher:	Your turn to read it, All right, let's see.
Kirsty:	The dog sees a box.
Teacher:	Mmmh.
Kirsty:	He sniffs in the box.
Teacher:	He sniffs it, doesn't he?
Kirsty:	He kicks the box. He climbs in the box.
Teacher:	Oh, now what happens.?
Kirsty:	He falls down the stairs. The dog falls out the box. The (hesitates)
Teacher:	The (pauses)
Kirsty:	The dog falls over.
Teacher:	He does, doesn't he? Then what does he try to do?

Original text:

The dogs sees the box.
The dog sniffs the box.
The dog kicks the box.
The dog gets in the box.
The dog gets out of the box.
The dog falls over.

Campbell (1990: 29–30)

Although Kirsty makes a number of miscues, the full meaning of the text has been more or less retained, so the teacher decides not to comment although she does make several interjections to support and encourage Kirsty's reading. When the child hesitates, the teacher simply restarts the sentence with rising intonation and pauses thereby prompting Kirsty to respond appropriately. She then confirms the accuracy of this response with her next two remarks. This is an extract from a shared reading session that took place over a period of approximately five minutes and ended with the teacher and Kirsty discussing the story for a few more minutes and the child telling of her own pet's adventures. Such interactions can effectively take place with all levels and ages of children learning to read in the primary school. The level of text may change, but the principles of encouragement, support, discussion, instruction and enjoyment will not.

The Framework for Teaching clearly states that additional time outside of the literacy hour might be found for: 'continuing the practice of reading to the class; pupil's own independent reading for interest and pleasure; and extending writing for older pupils' (p. 14). There is no mention of the teacher listening to children on an individual basis, but at the time of writing many schools were still attempting to do this, particularly with struggling readers. The circular 4/98 (DfEE, 1998) sets out the criteria which all Initial Teacher Training courses must meet, and stresses that trainees should know how to teach reading through whole class shared reading, guided group and individual reading as well as 'focused reading sessions with individual pupils'.

THE READING CONFERENCE

The notion of a reading conference is partly based on the idea of the 'shared reading interview', which is a mixture of hearing reading and assessing reading (Arnold, 1982), and partly on writing conferences – used notably by Graves (1983) – in the context of children's writing. Both ideas involve extended interactions between teachers and children and reading conferences last for anything between 5 and 15 minutes.

The elements of a reading conference consist of:

- Discussing titles, authors and other features of the text
- Encouraging the child to use various cues to decode the text
- Helping the child with difficult words and sections
- Checking comprehension by engaging the child in discussion about the text
- Discussing the child's opinions about the text
- Finding out how the child's reading is going generally
- Offering advice on how to choose future texts if appropriate
- Making a written record of the conference.

It might not be possible to cover all of these items each time so the teacher decides which elements to focus on with each individual child from one occasion to the next.

A less ambitious type of reading conference involves a quick check on an individual child's progress. This is often done at the beginning of the year and enables the teacher to get a quick overview of reading standards. However, it is a good idea to mix short conferences and long conferences throughout the year as they can achieve different objectives. Often if can be beneficial to have a series of short conferences over say a two-week period in order to develop more understanding of a child with reading problems.

Practice points

- Make time for extended reading conferences with individual children at least once per term.
- Constantly work at refining your skills of interaction when supporting children's reading aloud.
- Beware of an inappropriate reliance on one cueing strategy at the expense of a balance of strategies.

Glossary

Big books – enlarged versions of children's books designed to aid group reading.

Miscues – reading mistakes that can reveal the readers' strategies.

Reading cues – mental strategies that people use to read texts. Most commonly described as semantic (using meaning), syntactic (using grammar) and graphophonic (using sounds and symbol correspondences).

Reading schemes – collections of reading books that are graded to match children's reading levels.

Real books – books that are written for children and published in the standard way. Designed primarily for enjoyment rather than as a teaching aid.

Self-correct – the ability to recognise miscues during reading and to correct them yourself. An important facet of reading skills.

References

Arnold, H. (1982) *Listening to Children Reading*. London: Hodder & Stoughton in association with The United Kingdom Reading Association (UKRA).

Campbell, R. (1990) *Reading Together*. Buckingham: Open University Press.

Campbell, R. (1995) *Reading in the Early Years Handbook*. Buckingham: Open University Press

Department of Education and Science (DES) (1975) *A Language For Life (The Bullock Report)* London: HMSO.

Department for Education and Employment (DfEE) (1998) *Teaching: High Status, High Standards: Requirements for Courses of Initial Teacher Training (Circular 4/98)*. London: DfEE.

Graves, D. H. (1983) *Writing: Teachers and Children at Work*. Portsmouth, NH: Heinemann Educational.

Southgate, V., Arnold, H. and Johnson, S. (1981) *Extending Beginning Reading*. London: Heinemann Educational Books for the Schools Council.

Waterland, L. (1985) *Read With Me: An Apprenticeship Approach to Reading*. Stroud: Thimble Press.

Annotated bibliography

Beard R.(1990) *Developing Reading 3-13* (Second Edition) London: Hodder & Stoughton.
This book covers a wide range of issues related to the reading process and contains an excellent source of useful references. Plenty of practical examples are included as well as possible teaching strategies.
L2 **

Campbell, R. (1995) *Reading in the Early Years Handbook*. Buckingham: Open University Press.
Sixty different topics relating to reading are presented alphabetically and succinctly. Each of these is followed by suggestions for further reading in the very useful form of annotated bibliographies. A number of interesting classroom examples are included to focus on specific concerns.
L1 *

Southgate, V., Arnold, H. and Johnson, S. (1981) *Extending Beginning Reading*. London: Heinemann Educational Books for the Schools Council.
The main findings of the Extending Beginning Reading Project that investigated the reading development of 7–9 year olds. The report received a lot of publicity for suggesting that teachers spent too long on hearing individual children reading aloud and that the sessions were too superficial and open to constant disruption.
L3 ***

Topping, Keith. *Read On Read O Read On (The Read on Project)* [online – cited 22-6-00] Available from:
http://www.dundee.ac.uk/psychology/ReadOn/#whatis
Keith Topping is an expert on paired reading. In this website he also gives excellent information about peer-tutoring.
L1 **

Chapter 7

Phonics

In the section on 'The teaching of reading' in Chapter 3 we illustrated how there has been much research, particularly from the discipline of psychology, that has shown that phonics teaching is important. In this chapter we look at the way that phonics is taught in the classroom.

'Phonics' is commonly known as a method of teaching children to read. Originally it was based on the idea of encouraging children to sound out letters. In recent years simple systems of teaching sounds have been replaced by a more sophisticated understanding called 'new phonics'. However, at the heart of all phonics teaching is the idea that you can and should teach children about 'phonemes' (☞). Many children develop some general knowledge of sounds – i.e. they develop some 'phonological awareness' (☞) – before they enter school.

One of the ideas that has emerged from the research on phonics is the significance of onsets (☞) and rimes (☞), the beginnings and ends of syllables. An understandable mistake is to confuse 'rime" and 'rhyme': the following poem helps us to illustrate this.

> **Spellbound**
> I have a spelling chequer
> It came with my PC
> It plainly marks four my revue
> Miss takes I cannot sea.
> I've run this poem threw it
> I'm shore your pleased too no;
> It's letter perfect in it's weigh
> My chequer tolled me sew.
> (Vandal, 1996: 14)

The *rhymes* in lines 2 and 4, and 6 and 8, are present because the 'rime" of the words 'C' and 'sea', and 'no' and 'sew' are the same. This poem nicely illustrates the problems that we can have when representing phonemes with letters.

Using the concept of onset and rime Goswami (1995: 139) emphasised the importance of reading by analogy: 'Analogies in reading involve using the spelling-sound pattern of one word, such as *beak*, as a basis for working out the spelling-sound correspondence of a new word, such as *peak*.' Young children find it easier to understand analogies between the ends of words than they do between the beginnings of words. This is because children's development of phonological understanding tends to proceed from the ability to identify syllables, then onsets and rimes, and finally the ability to segment phonemes. The use of analogies draws on children's early recognition of onsets and rimes.

THE IRREGULARITIES OF ENGLISH

In order to see further potential for analogies it is necessary to briefly look at the irregularity of English. It has often been pointed out that the links between sound and symbol in the English language are notoriously irregular and Frank Smith (1978: 50) raised this in his controversial chapter 'The fallacy of phonics'. For example, what is the sound of the vowel phoneme in the following word: 'read'? You may have assumed that it was /ee/. However, if we explained that the sentence context is 'Yesterday I read a good book' then it is clear that not just the meaning of the word but the meaning of the sentence as a whole has an impact on the particular vowel phoneme. This perhaps reaches the height of irregularity in the name of the university department 'The centre for reading in Reading'. Also, consider the way that the /sh/ phoneme is represented in the following words: Appreciate, ocean, machine, moustache, stanchion, fuchsia, schist, conscious, extension, pressure, admission, sure, initiate, attention and luxury.

A short anecdote helps us to explore further the irregularities of sounds and symbols. A child in one of the classes we were teaching was writing a book with the following joke:

Saima: Will you remember me tomorrow?
Dominic: Yes.
S: Will you remember me in a week?
D: Yes.
S: Will you remember me in a month?
D: Yes.
S: Will you remember me in a year?
D: Yes.
S: Knock, knock.
D: Who's there?
S: You've forgotten me already!

Saima was stuck on the spelling for 'remember' and I was about to suggest that she sound out the word, when it struck me that each time the letter 'e' is used in 'remember' it represents a different phoneme.

The examples that have been given illustrate an important point. Phonemes are constant and it is broadly agreed that there are 44. The irregularities occur when phonemes are represented by graphemes (☞) because there are various ways that a phoneme can be represented in writing. So, to return to

Goshwami's work on analogies, she argued that a focus on rime units as analogies can reduce the spelling/sound ambiguities of written English. Children are more likely to guess the correct spelling of words by using rime analogies than phoneme analogies

One of the important aspects of onset and rime is that when young children learn nursery rhymes and simple songs their awareness of sounds is raised and it is often their attention to the *rime* of the words that is strong. Because this is the case it has been argued that teaching which emphasises onset and rime can be beneficial particularly if it is linked with the different ways that onsets and rimes can be written down. Children's understanding of rime seems to be part of a normal developmental process whereas the ability to segment phonemes does not come so naturally.

TEACHING PHONEMES

The fact that children do not segment words into phonemes naturally has led to the idea that they need to be systematically taught. There is strong evidence that teaching methods that systematically teach phonic knowledge result in readers, particularly at Key Stage 1, who learn to decode quicker. The Framework for Teaching has a set of objectives for the teaching of phonics: there are 35 numbered objectives and 51 with bullet points giving 86 in total between reception and year 4. However, when we look in more detail at classroom practice things become more complex.

In order to support some of the recent ideas about 'good practice' OFSTED produced a video to help teachers in the classroom. This video put forward an unequivocal message about phonics teaching; Ruth Miskin was one of the headteachers who was featured in the video. Since then she has published her method of teaching phonics.

> I have taught children to read for 20 years in six different local authorities. During that time, I have tried every possible method and combination of methods: look and say, 'mix and muddle' reading schemes, real books – and what I now know to be very basic phonics. The one constant has been my drive to ensure that my pupils came to share my love of reading.
>
> (Miskin, 1999: 19)

Miskin's method includes some of the following features:

- In reception and year 1 children are taught the alphabetic code for 30 minutes per day
- This knowledge is then consolidated using a shared book projected on to a screen using a 'True Image Projector'
- The final ten minutes is used to select books for the children to take home
- The children are praised constantly
- Throughout, books are read and discussed that are above the children's decoding level in order to develop their vocabulary

- If children learn the whole alphabetic system quickly, they should not need a reading scheme past Year 1
- The approach uses both 'synthetic' (☞) and 'analytic' phonics approaches (☞).

Miskin illustrates the teaching of the letter 'c' and the sound /cuh/ in stage one of her first four stages. Each sound is learned by hearing it, writing it, reading it and saying it:

> (a) Hear it: collect objects, pictures and photographs of people beginning with 'c'; say the names quickly with the children; listen to the first sound /cuh/ in each word; split the /cuh/ from the rest of the word.
> (b) Read it: show a caterpillar and the things it likes eating; say the alliterative phrase; show how the caterpillar turns into the letter 'c'; look at the words in a picture dictionary that start with 'c'.
> (c) Write it: 'Tell the children that the caterpillar likes you to smooth the hairs on its body downwards, starting at its eyes. The caterpillar curls as you stroke it. It likes its face pointing to the sun so it always chews in the reading direction. (Draw a sun on the right hand side of the page.)
> (Miskin, 1999: 22)

Miskin has very forceful views about what constitutes good practice, she considers the teaching of reading to be full of 'obvious truths'. Some of her ideas represent important strategies, such as the multi-sensory (☞) approach; the use of characters to support the memory of letters; books that are read above the children's decoding level to extend their vocabulary; and reading schemes not used past year one. Another interesting aspect of her school's work is that they do not follow the letter of the Framework for Teaching. Miskin believes that her method works better than the framework (Miskin, 1998) and she has had some support from OFSTED for this view.

However, her ideas are not without critics. Davies (1997) pointed out that there were a number of problems with her school's work as shown in the OFSTED video. Davies suggested that the pronunciation that Miskin and her teachers used for some phonemes was inaccurate: 'the three sounds in mat as (mer) (a) (ter) as opposed to (m) (a) (t)' (1997: 13). The important point he made was that there are a number of phonemes that are 'unvoiced' and should only be illustrated by forming the shape with the mouth but not making a sound, for example the 'th' in thumb is unvoiced. Davies is also critical about the 'one-letter-makes-one-sound-method (OLMOSM)' because it gives misleading information to children yet it is a method that continues to be used widely.

Consideration of Miskin's published scheme raises the issue of whether to use published schemes of work or not; this issue is one that has caused controversy in primary education. Although we would argue that the use of such schemes is often very questionable, and the Framework for Teaching is built on the idea of using high quality 'real' texts, the reality is that many schools continue to use published schemes; phonics is no exception.

One of the most popular schemes is 'Jolly Phonics'. The example from this

th th

voiced and unvoiced th

ACTION
Child pretends to be a little rude by sticking out tongue a little and saying *th* (as in them), and very rude by sticking tongue further out and saying *th* (as in thumb).

that   thin

then   thumb

this   thick

feather thunder

with   moth

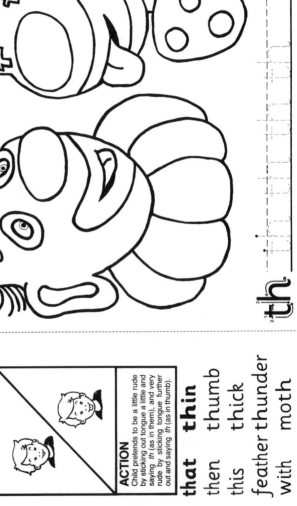

th i th

Figure 7.1 A page from the 'Jolly Phonics' Scheme

series shown in Figure 7.1 is from *The Phonics Handbook* which provides photocopiable worksheets with each sheet covering one phoneme. Like the Miskin work, multi-sensory approaches are used so that each sheet is accompanied by an action that the children have to carry out. The phonemes are linked to a storyline to help the children remember them.

There are a number of more questionable ideas. The sheets include a picture related to the suggested storyline which are left blank for children to colour in; something that is not good practice. Additionally, a handwriting exercise is offered which encourages the children to write two letters that represent the phoneme. The problem here is a confusion of learning objectives (handwriting and learning phonemes) and the fact that most phonemes can be represented by a range of letter combinations, not just the ones that are offered.

One of the most worrying aspects appears in the introduction to the handbook.

> During the first 8–9 weeks the aim is to prepare the children for reading books. Stories and poems are read to them, but the children are not expected to try and read books for themselves.
>
> (Lloyd, 1998: 20)

There is now a wealth of evidence pointing to the fact that pre-school children acquire a range of sophisticated understandings. Many two-year-old children enjoy choosing books from their book shelves in the home and flicking through the pages or sharing the books with siblings or parents. The idea that when children come to school this opportunity to read books should be denied for 8–9 weeks seems extraordinary. This also does not fit with the Framework for Teaching which emphasises the importance of using high quality texts to contextualise sentence and word level work.

Practice points

- Phonics teaching should be regular, brief and as enjoyable as possible.
- Make a clear distinction between sounds and letters names. Help children to understand that various letter combinations can produce the same sound.
- Look out for children who use phonic cueing too much resulting in nonsense words when reading aloud.

Glossary

Analytic phonics – involves breaking words down into their phonemes.
Grapheme – written representation of a sound: e.g. a letter of the alphabet.
Multi-sensory – approaches that use sight, sound and touch to reinforce language learning
Onset – any consonant sounds that come before the vowel, in a syllable.
Phonemes – the smallest unit of sound in a word.
Phonological awareness – understanding of the links between sounds and symbols.

Rime – the vowel and any consonants that follow the onset in a syllable.
Synthetic phonics – involves the teaching of sounds prior to word building.

References

Davies, A. (1997) 'Sounding out'. *Literacy and Learning*, Autumn, Issue 1: 13–14.
Goswami, U. (1995) 'Phonological development and reading: what is analogy, and what is not?' *Journal of Research in Reading*, 18 (2): 139–145.
Lloyd, S. (1998) *The Phonics Handbook*. Chigwell: Jolly Learning.
Miskin, R. (1998) 'R is for enjoying'. *Times Educational Supplement*, November 13.
Miskin, R. (1999) 'Fast Track to Reading'. *Times Educational Supplement Primary*, 22 January.
Smith, F. (1978) *Reading*. Cambridge: Cambridge University Press.
Vandal, N. (1996) Spellbound, in J. Foster (compiler) *Crack Another Yolk and Other Word Play Poems*. Oxford: Oxford University Press.

Annotated bibliography

BBC ONLINE. Education: Schools Online. [online – cited 26-6-00]. Available from:
    http://www.bbc.co.uk/education/schools/primary.shtml
    Includes various interactive areas that support the development of reading. Words and Pictures has activities for phonics.
    L1
Department for Education and Employment (DfEE) (1999) *Phonics: Progression in Phonics: Materials for Whole-class Teaching*. London: DfEE.
    Practical guide to the teaching of phonics in the classroom. Includes a range of useful classroom activities and photocopiable resources. Official view of how phonics should be taught.
    L1 *
Dombey, H., Moustafa, M. and the staff of the Centre for Language in Primary Education (CLPE) (1998) *Whole to Part Phonics: How Children Learn to Read and Spell*. London: CLPE.
    A practical alternative to standard phonics approaches. This book shows how phonological understanding can be successfully developed in the context of whole texts first and foremost.
    L1 **
Oakhill, J., Beard, R. and Vincent, D.(eds) (1995) 'The contribution of psychological research'. *Journal of Research in Reading*, 18 (2).
    An impressive and challenging collection of articles about phonics. The range of research evidence that is presented should lead to teachers questioning their assumptions about aspects of the reading process. Published later in book form by Basil Blackwell Publishers, Oxford.
    L3 ***

Chapter 8

Routines for reading

The aim of reading teaching is to develop enthusiastic and independent readers. This chapter illustrates some of the practical techniques that teachers need to adopt to support this aim. Thoughts on independent reading are followed by outlines of two significant strategies: shared and guided reading.

An initial consideration in any teacher's classroom is how space is utilised to the best possible effect. There are many advantages to a comfortable and attractive carpeted area which allows the class to sit together and share ideas. It has to be acknowledged, however, that the size of many classrooms makes this difficult to achieve. Whether there is a carpeted area or not, the space must allow for the delivery of whole class activities such as the class reader, shared reading, word- and sentence-level work, plenary sessions. In the past it was considered 'good practice' to have particular designated areas that would support language work. These included book 'corners' with comfortable seating or cushions; listening points with audio-cassettes and headphones; display areas such as 'author of the week'; message boards; role-play areas. Although we feel that these kinds of organisation are still very important we regret that the advent of the literacy strategy has meant that this kind of practice is more difficult to prioritise.

Resources within the classroom need to be carefully considered. There should be a wide range of fiction (☞) and non-fiction (☞) including: home-made books, a daily newspaper, magazines, brochures, pamphlets, catalogues, etc., for use in silent reading time and to support thematic work. These should all be well displayed and easily accessible. Materials for book-making, such as paper, card, scissors and glue, and resources for independent working, such as reference books, dictionaries and thesauri should also be clearly labelled and accessible. The Literacy Strategy has seen much wider use of big book holders, large pointers, flip charts, overhead projectors, text masking devices, letter fans, etc.

The management of time is problematic. How much time *beyond* the literacy hour should be spent on language and literacy activities such as reading? The Framework for Teaching acknowledges that time needs to be found for pupils' own independent reading and for the traditional practice of reading stories, poems and non-fiction to the class. Many schools still include part of the week or even part of the day for children to engage in their own personal 'silent reading' to allow young readers to develop their skills in a supportive environment and to emphasise the importance of reading for interest and pleasure. Everyone in the class reads at this time and noise and movement in the classroom is minimised. Sometimes the teacher models the process by also reading silently. The time spent on this can vary from about five minutes with the youngest primary school pupils to 20–25 minutes with the oldest. Story readings should also form an important part of the timetable. Texts, authorship and concepts about print can be examined and analysed profitably in the literacy hour but an important benefit to be had from story reading is pure enjoyment. The sight of a class of children all engrossed in a story reading is a very powerful one.

INDEPENDENT READING

The aim of any approach to reading is that children learn to read independently: they make informed *choices* about their reading material and they become critical and sensitive readers. If children are to achieve this, it is important that they are given the opportunity to make choices. In recent years this opportunity has steadily declined, so much so that even as late as years 5 and 6 some children are still restricted to graded reading schemes (☞) for their reading at school. An anecdote serves to illustrate this. The daughter of a parent who was a teacher had been able to read before she started school. In spite of this, by year 5 she was still restricted to reading scheme texts at school. This contrasted with the unrestricted reading she was able to do at home including some of the best literature written for children. On one occasion the daughter said to her parents that she found that most of the reading schemes lacked suitably interesting plots and that the characters were rather limited. At a parents' evening the child's views were explained to the class teacher who realised that the reading scheme books were not sufficiently challenging so she agreed to allow the girl to choose her own texts in future.

As far as the National Literacy Strategy is concerned, at Key Stage 1 independent reading forms part of guided reading (see below), but it also takes place in independent working time during the literacy hour and at other times of the school day. The reading material is matched to the attainment of the children (which is significantly different from encouraging children to choose their own books) and allows independent reading with adult support where necessary.

At Key Stage 2 the pupils are more likely to concentrate on analysing texts. The texts need to be demanding and interesting but sufficiently understandable for the pupils to be able to work independently of the teacher. Examples of independent tasks include children taking on character roles in playscripts; identifying settings of familiar stories and comparing them with settings within their own experience; discussing what makes a good story; and so on.

With information texts, children are expected to interrogate the texts in various ways (➡ Chapter 9, 'Reading for information') including exploring the range of presentation devices such as bullet points, dropped capitals, sub-headings and other visual devises.

SHARED READING

As we mentioned in Chapter 6, 'Listening to children read', shared reading in the literacy hour is considerably different from its original practice. One of the hallmarks of shared reading in the literacy hour is the use of enlarged texts. Don Holdaway (1979) pioneered this idea and it is important to realise that his aim was to extend the benefits that he saw for individualised reading by giving access to larger groups to the intimacy of shared reading. The motivation of the literacy strategy stems more from a dissatisfaction with individualised reading and a corresponding belief in whole class teaching. When Holdaway started there were no professionally published large texts so he involved the children in their design, including the artwork. With the recent emphasis on enlarged texts including 'big books' in the literacy hour publishers have realised the marketing opportunities that are available and have produced a number of such texts or 'big books'. However, it should be remembered that Holdaway's work with his children *creating* their own texts had many learning outcomes beyond the production of enlarged texts which were in themselves practically useful; this part of Holdaway's work seems to have been neglected recently. In addition to the pleasure of sharing whole texts, Holdaway also emphasised the teacher's role in modelling reading strategies for the children, including helping them to understand the conventions of print and examining sentences and words in detail.

Shared reading helps to form a bridge between the teacher reading to the pupils and independent reading by children. Its main feature is that the whole class (teacher and pupils) read a text together. Sometimes the teacher reads aloud with the children following and sometimes teacher and pupils read aloud together. The texts chosen for shared reading can be beyond pupils' independent reading levels because the exercise is co-operative and the teacher is there to demonstrate and support, allowing all children to access challenging texts. The key features of shared reading are as follows:

- Uses high quality enlarged texts
- Demonstrates a range of reading strategies
- Develops word recognition skills
- Encourages understanding of sentence structure
- Differentiates (☞) through appropriate interaction
- Discusses the children's response, ideas and understanding of textual features.

GUIDED READING

Guided reading in the literacy hour is one of its most important organisational strategies, yet as Beard (1999) points out it is a fairly recent development with limited related research. In the past, the majority of educators believed that effective teaching of reading needed a mix of work with individual children, small groups of children and the whole class. However, the Inspectorate became concerned that too much individualised reading was taking place and not enough group 'instruction'. The OFSTED report 'The Teaching of Reading in 45 Inner London Schools' (OFSTED, 1996) is a controversial but important document as you can clearly see the way that it strongly suggests the importance of small group and whole class work in the teaching of reading. The Framework for Teaching clearly points out that guided reading replaces the individualised teaching of reading. The books that are used should be of a high quality (➡ Chapter 4, 'Texts for children') and may be graded reading scheme books at times.

The main features of guided reading are as follows:

- Multiple copies of books in sets of about six are used
- Books are matched to the achievement levels of the group
- It sometimes involves introduction to new texts, at other times could involve reflections on a chapter read earlier in the week
- It can develop ideas from shared reading and will often lead to an independent group activity
- Teachers are to support the children as they read independently
- The other groups are engaged in independent group work
- At Key Stage 1 the emphasis is on helping children learn to read (➡ Chapter 6, 'Listening to children read' for examples of interaction strategies)
- At Key Stage 2 the objectives are to analyse and discuss the text although some children will still require help in learning to read.

Although the outlines of shared and guided work in this chapter have been related to reading, it is important to remember that there should be an equal amount of time spent on shared and guided *writing*. Some teachers have ensured that this happens by alternating on a weekly basis between reading and writing. Many of the principles are the same for both although clearly the objectives differ.

Practice points

- Selection of texts of the highest quality is a vital first step in your reading teaching.
- Constantly work to improve your skills interacting with individual children and use these during guided reading in particular.

- Give plenty of opportunities for independent reading including choice over reading materials.

Glossary

Differentiation – methods for ensuring that the range of achievement levels in a class are supported.

Fiction – text which is invented and in the main is not factual; most novels are fictional.

Non-fiction – texts which are factual. Information books are non-fiction.

Reading schemes – collections of reading books that are graded to match children's reading levels.

References

Beard, R. (1999) *National Literacy Strategy Review of Research and Other Related Evidence*. London: DfEE.

Holdaway, D. (1979) *The Foundations of Literacy*. London: Ashton Scholastic.

Office for Standards in Education (OFSTED) (1996) *The Teaching of Reading in 45 Inner London Primary Schools. A Report by Her Majesty's Inspectors in Collaboration with the LEAs of Islington, Southwark and Tower Hamlets*. London: OFSTED Publications.

Annotated bibliography

Centre for Language in Primary Education (CLPE) Barrs, M. and Thomas, A. (Eds) (1991) *The Reading Book*. London: CLPE.
An important practical guide based on close work with London teachers. Introduces the idea of a 'core' selection of high-quality books to support reading. Equal opportunities is a strong strand to the work.
L1 *

Department for Education and Employment (DfEE) (1998) *The National Literacy Strategy: Literacy Training Pack. Module 5: Shared and Guided Reading and Writing at Key Stage 2 (Fiction and Poetry)*. London: DfEE.
The official position on shared and guided reading and writing; these packs are used for professional development and in-service training. Thorough and clear description of the national requirements. Pack includes teacher's notes, trainer's notes, overhead projector transparencies, and activity sheets. There is a similar pack for Key Stage 1.
L2 *

Graham, J. and Kelly, A. (1997) *Reading Under Control: Teaching Reading in the Primary School*. London: David Fulton.
A very useful account with a particularly strong section on 'Reading Routines' which develops a number of the points about reading that we touch on in this book.
L1 **

Holdaway, D. (1979) *The Foundations of Literacy*. London: Ashton Scholastic. A very important book that has had a strong influence on language education. The approach to shared reading in the National Literacy Strategy is heavily influenced by Holdaway's work.
L2 **

Chapter 9

Reading for information

As children progress they move from learning to read to an emphasis on reading to learn. The acquisition of knowledge is a central part of learning and much of this takes place through the reading of texts. We look at a range of strategies that encourage reading for information.

In the past, information texts were used much less than other texts, particularly stories. As we explain in Chapter 14, 'Genre and the process of writing', the genre theorists (☞) have been influential in reminding us about the importance of a range of genres including information texts. Since the advent of the Framework for Teaching the specific strand 'Non-Fiction: Reading Comprehension' has been established. This means that all children will receive teaching about the use of information texts.

Although there was less teaching involving information texts in the past this does not mean that there was not any effective practice taking place. Traditionally primary teachers had encouraged children to research topics of their choosing and use the resources of the classroom and schools libraries for this purpose. At its best this resulted in children being highly motivated to explore areas that were of genuine interest to them. When these projects were presented to the class in the form of live presentations and/or books, this gave all the children the opportunity to learn from their peers. Some education authorities also established impressive collections of books and artefacts which could be linked with cross-curricular topic work that the teacher had planned.

Littlefair identified 'expository' writing as one of the genres of information texts. She defines the purposes of expository writing as to 'explain, describe, argue' (Littlefair, 1991: 27). She points out that writers of expository writing often select a style which distances them from their reader by using the passive (☞) voice in the third person (☞). One of the examples she offers is from newspapers:

Four police forces have been alerted. . . . (*Cambridge Evening News*, 13 October 1989)

Initial inquiries by Avon and Somerset police were made last year. (*Guardian*, 18 October 1989)

Here we can illustrate use of the passive voice as the grammar which the journalists have chosen to report news. We can show that by making this choice, they have achieved a sense of objectivity.

(Littlefair, 1991: 29)

Although it is true that the passive voice is used we should question the idea that this automatically results in 'objectivity'. Most people would argue that newspapers are notoriously subjective if not downright misleading and that the particular use of this kind of language can give them a *false* objectivity.

DIRECTED ACTIVITIES RELATED TO TEXTS (DARTs)

During the late 1970s and early 1980s the Schools Council classified reading for learning into three key areas: locating information, organising information and reconstructing information. The DARTs were further classified into those that used *unmodified* texts and those that used *modified* texts. Cloze (☞) procedure is a classic example of a modified text activity. This involves presenting children with a text where some of the words are missing which they have to replace. Various levels of difficulty can be achieved by offering the solutions or not, and including words that are wrong, as a distraction.

The approach to the teaching of reading for information in the Framework for Teaching is informed by the research of David Wray and Maureen Lewis. They carried out a research project which examined this area and they established the Extending Interactions with Texts (EXIT) model. The training materials developed to help teachers with the implementation of the Framework for Teaching use the EXIT model (DfEE, 1998) (see Box 9.1).

The idea of 'activation of prior knowledge' (1) is an important one. This is a recognition that children have a vast amount of knowledge already and the task of finding new information can be made easier if they are reminded of their prior knowledge. Another significant aspect of the EXIT model is the planning that is required before the information is retrieved. KWL grids are simply tables with three columns or rows which ask: What do I Know? What do I Want to know? What have I Learnt? Children are expected to initiate such tables before they actually start to search for the information.

'Metacognitive discussion' (☞) (4) can involve discussing the best ways of retrieving the particular information that is required. For example as students you might be wanting to find research papers related to a particular area. The most basic search would involve manually flicking through the books and journals in the library to try and find something useful. A more sophisticated way of retrieving the information would involve using the British Educational Index online. This might be carried out at the same time as checking the reference lists of key books in the area which might suggest particularly significant papers, and so on.

As we saw at the beginning of this section 'interacting with the text' (5) is not a new idea. However, it is a current idea that has changed the meaning of

EXTENDING INTERACTIONS WITH TEXTS: THE EXIT MODEL	
Process stages	**Teaching strategies**
1 Activation of prior knowledge	Brainstorming, concept mapping, KWL grids
2 Establishing purposes	Question-setting, KWL (Know, Want, Learnt) and QUADS (Questions, Answers, Details, Source) grids
3 Locating information	Situating the learning in meaningful contexts, teacher modelling
4 Adopting an appropriate strategy	Metacognitive discussion, teacher modelling
5 Interacting with the text	Text marking and restructuring, genre exchange, cloze activities, sequencing, etc.
6 Monitoring understanding	Teacher modelling, strategy charts
7 Making a record	Writing frames (☞), grids, teacher modelling
8 Evaluating information	Discussion of biased texts
9 Assisting memory	Review, revisit, restructuring
10 Communicating information	Different types of writing frames, drama, alternative outcomes

Box 9.1

the word 'interacting' and that has added new strategies to this way of working with texts. It should be remembered that an individual child engaging with a book of their own choice is often a powerful example of 'interacting' with a text. However, the meaning in the case of the Framework for Teaching implies acting on the text in particular ways that have been defined by the training materials.

If we take *Making Tracks* (a 'Walker: Bright Sparks' information book by Steve Parker) it is possible to illustrate 'interacting with the text'. One of the sections is about bicycles and features this kind of information:

PEDAL PUSHING

1   Believe it or not, the air slows us down! It pushes against us – and the faster we move, the harder it pushes.
2   That's why the wheels and frame of these track bikes are streamlined – with a sleek shape to help them to slip smoothly through the air.

(Parker, 1998: 6)

A text marking activity could involve the children highlighting key words and phrases which explain why these bikes are particularly fast. The information could then be restructured into a series of bullet points. A 'genre exchange' could be carried out by suggesting that the children design a poster for a local bicycle shop which aims to sell their particular brand. The poster should include some of the points which show why the bike is particularly fast. A 'sequencing' activity might involve the children thinking about ways to order the six paragraphs featured in the 'pedal pushing' section.

REFERENCE SKILLS

Although EXIT activities are an important way to increase children's knowledge of information texts there is one area of the primary school that is vital – the library. A well-resourced and well-organised school library can fulfil many functions including providing the teacher with sets of books related to a particular topic or theme. The library also provides children with the resources to pursue their own areas of interest. Although many children will work out the organisational structures of libraries and information books if they are offered helpful guides, there can be benefit in setting up focused library and book activities.

The Dewey decimal system is used to categorise non-fiction (☞) books in a library. A simplified version has been established to make the task of searching for texts easier for children. The simplified Dewey system includes colours and broad categories to help young children start to understand how libraries are structured. An introductory activity could encourage children to locate various pieces of information based on knowledge of the categorisation system: Find a book about science and write down the title; What kind of books are shelved between 550 and 579?; What colour is the label on geography books?

Children need to understand the difference between fiction and non-fiction. This knowledge enables them to disregard fiction texts if they are searching for particular information. The knowledge of the terms fiction and non-fiction is an objective in the literacy hour which can be consolidated and made more meaningful through library work. A hands-on approach to these terms can involve sorting a range of books into the two categories and suggesting why the books fit into particular categories.

The understanding of what constitutes a fact as opposed to an opinion can be a lifelong learning process. In the early stages children need to distinguish between simple statements such as 'two add two equals four' or 'I think it will rain tomorrow'. For older children this progresses towards an appreciation of bias, perhaps in the media.

Skimming and scanning are important skills when searching for information. Scanning can be improved by using timed reading of text extracts. The answers to key questions have to be found and noted (not necessarily in complete sentences) within a given timescale. The timed element ensures that the children cannot read every word of the text if they are to complete all the answers.

The most purposeful way to learn about contents pages and indices occurs when children search for the answers to specific questions that they have set themselves. When they have such a goal in mind they are often motivated to use the contents and/or index to help them find the answer to their question quickly. However, it can be useful to raise their awareness of the nature of these things through structured activities. A full knowledge of alphabetic order is required for using both indices and dictionaries.

One of the classic dilemmas with dictionaries is that you need to know how to spell most of a word if you are to check its spelling in a dictionary. For children whose spelling is at a very early stage of development this can create difficulties as their limited knowledge of standard spelling is accompanied by lack of knowledge about alphabetic order. The better picture dictionaries are useful in order to introduce the idea of what dictionaries contain, but their problem is that they rarely include some of the most common and difficult words that are not nouns or verbs, such as their, she why. For older children we recommend the use of high-quality adult dictionaries rather than those that are specially prepared for children. Invariably the ones that are prepared specially for children lack the kinds of words that they might want to look up, and they also often lack more than one meaning. This is a serious limitation when so many English words have multiple meanings. CD ROMS are offering other opportunities for finding information (➡ Chapter 4, 'Texts for children' for an example of internet information), but most rely on knowledge of alphabetic order. For example *My First Incredible Amazing Dictionary* published by Dorling Kindersley allows access to a wide range of words through an alphabet at the top of the screen. It also features animated pictures, spoken definitions, hypertext links to other words in the dictionary and a number of other lively features.

Practice points

- Encourage children to *interact* with texts not just copy information uncritically.
- Organise opportunities for children to create their own research projects.
- Use the internet as an important source of information.

Glossary

Cloze – activities that involve filling in missing sections of text, usually words.

Fiction – text which is invented and in the main is not factual; most novels are fictional.

Genre theorists – group of mainly Australian academics who suggested that English teaching in primary schools should focus more on the larger text structures.

Metacognitive discussion – talking about the kinds of mental strategies that we use. In this case with regard to locating information.

Passive voice – description of particular clause grammar: 'The cat was seen by the dog.' (passive); 'The dog saw the cat.' (active).

Third person – a grammatical form shown by the use of verbs and pronouns: 'she said; they are'.

Writing frames – a structured prompt to support writing. May include useful phrases and/or layout ideas.

References

Department for Education and Employment (DfEE) (1998) *The National Literacy Strategy: Literacy Training Pack. Module 6: Reading and Writing for Information*. London: DfEE.

Littlefair, A. (1991) *Reading All Types of Writing*. Buckingham: Open University Press.

Parker, S. (1998) *Making Tracks*. London: Walker.

Annotated bibliography

Department for Education and Employment (DfEE) (1998) *The National Literacy Strategy: Literacy Training Pack. Module 6: Reading and Writing for Information*. London: DfEE.
One of the six in-service training packs which teachers used in preparation for the National Literacy Strategy. Includes teacher's notes, trainer's notes, overhead projector transparencies and activity sheets.
L2 *

Moon, C. and Bourne, J. for The Open University (1994) *Learning to Teach Reading*. Milton Keynes: The Open University.
A thorough and thoughtful overview of the issues related to the teaching of reading. Prepared as a pack for postgraduate teaching students. Interesting section on 'Directed Activities Related to Texts'.
L2 **

Wray, D. and Lewis, M. (1997) *Extending Literacy: Children Reading and Writing Non-fiction*. London: Routledge.
This book is based on the Exeter University Extending Literacy project which has been influential. Practical examples are given that show how children can be encouraged to engage with non-fiction texts.
L2 **

Chapter 10

Reading recovery

The work of Marie Clay in the field of struggling readers has been outstanding. Her work is central to this chapter because she mixes down-to-earth practice with rigorous research. Descriptions of the practice she recommends are given, following some general considerations. Research on reading recovery is reviewed.

One of the main concerns for many primary school teachers is what to do with children who struggle with their reading. The ability to read gives access to so many areas of learning. For some children their difficulties may not be recognised early enough and this can make the job of catching up even more difficult. Some children start school already being able to read (Clark, 1976), many children become confident with their reading around age 6 or 7, but what is usually a small minority of children do struggle. There is growing evidence to suggest that nationally this minority of children are a problematic feature of education in England; this has been called a 'long tail' of under-achievement (Brooks et al, 1996:19). There is also evidence that the numbers of functionally illiterate adults in Western societies such as Britain is alarmingly high.

This chapter is dominated by the work of Marie Clay whose work is internationally famous in relation to the early detection of children with reading difficulties. An overview of her techniques is followed by reflections on some of the evaluations that have been carried out that show that improvements in children's reading can be achieved by using Clay's ideas.

GENERAL CONSIDERATIONS

First and foremost it is important to remember that the reasons for struggling with reading are many and complex. Some people would suggest that the quality of teaching is the main reason why children struggle. However, factors such as confidence, self-esteem, motivation can all be part of the picture. Whatever the nature of the child's needs it should be remembered that collaboration with parents is a vital aspect of supporting children with reading difficulties. It is also important to remember that for a small number of children there may be problems with eyesight and/or hearing that contribute. Such children will be supported through the code of practice for special educational needs. In the course of assessing children's needs it may be decided that they are dyslexic. The nature of dyslexia (☞) is a complex and hotly debated area to which we could not do justice in this chapter.

Multi-sensory approaches have had considerable success in supporting children with reading difficulties. The basic underlying idea is that the combination of touch, sight, hearing, and speaking can enhance the development of language. Specific examples of multi-sensory techniques include: the way that handwriting movement can support spelling memory; the forming of letter shapes in a range of media such as sand and paint; using actions to reinforce memory of letter sounds and shapes; hearing and seeing onsets and rimes; and so on.

To illustrate aspects such as the importance of building relationships with children, their confidence, their motivation, and collaboration with parents, consider this comment offered by an experienced teacher who is also the special needs coordinator:

> Darren had struggled with his reading throughout the school. I asked if I could read with him one day. It was an uncomfortable experience. His intonation and expression was very low. He stopped and stared when he didn't know a word. If he was stuck on a word he would sound out every letter. The result of this often didn't give him enough of a clue to the word because he wasn't using the other cueing strategies to support his reading. When I asked him about sections that he had read he would only offer minimal information. The class teacher felt that I should give him more phonics practice and that perhaps we should try earlier books in the reading scheme. My heart sank because I knew that the boy had had phonics and reading schemes throughout the school. It was clear to me that he already had enough phonic knowledge. Knowing that my daughter had learnt to read by the time she was three simply by sharing and discussing books and other texts I wondered whether a variation on this would work with Darren.
>
> The following academic year he joined my own class having progressed very little. I decided that the first thing I had to tackle was his motivation. I collected ten picture books that I thought he might be interested in which I labelled with green stickers. These books were kept for him alone. The next thing I knew I had to do was to start talking to him about why he didn't like reading. At the time I was in contact with his mum who was quite sceptical that this would work after so many years. I followed these two main ideas of talking to the child and trying to find texts that would motivate him for the best part of the year. When it came to his next assessment the educational psychologist gave Darren a standardised reading test and was astonished.
>
> I wondered if some extra tuition that he had at home had contributed

but his father said that until his motivation changed Darren wasn't prepared to work with a tutor. That child had gone through repeated systematic phonics programmes in the past and they had simply not worked.

THE WORK OF MARIE CLAY

The reading recovery (☞) initiative was introduced throughout the UK in 1992 and funding was withdrawn in 1995. According to the Literacy Task Force report, their evidence suggested that reading recovery had been shown to be effective by national and international evaluations and the report recommended that it be 'kept under review' (Literacy Task Force, 1997: 31). It was also argued that it was expensive: certainly the training and employment of specialist reading recovery teachers, who worked on a one-to-one basis with children, did cost a significant amount of money. In spite of the recent lower national profile and the lack of finances to support reading recovery, some of the ideas are still being usefully employed by schools and classroom teachers in a modified form.

'Reading recovery' is a term that was coined by Marie Clay and it sums up a necessarily complex view of the strategies that are necessary to support struggling readers. Clay maintains that selected teachers should undergo a training programme in order to become experts in reading recovery techniques. This happened in the UK during the time when money was available, and schools had individual teachers who supported children with reading difficulties on a one-to-one basis outside their ordinary lessons. However, many of Clay's ideas can be used to underpin class teachers' thinking about how to help children who are struggling.

One of the most important features of reading recovery is the idea that children who are struggling should be identified by the time they have been at school for one year. In order to do this, systematic observation is required. Clay outlines a diagnostic survey that includes a range of assessments. One of these is the 'running record': it is important to remember that running record is a specific strategy for recording children's ability to decode (➡ Chapter 11, 'Assessing reading').

Reading recovery is an early intervention programme for children with reading difficulties and it is important to point out that:

> Most children (80–90%) do not require these detailed, meticulous and special reading recovery procedures or any modification of them. They will learn to read more pleasurably without them.
>
> (Clay, 1979: 47)

The teaching procedures for reading recovery include a range of ideas for enhancing children's reading. As far as the use of text is concerned, although Clay is critical of the controlled vocabulary of reading schemes (she emphasises the importance of natural language) she does not particularly emphasise the significance of the particular texts that children read. The teacher's comment above showed the importance that he placed on the choice of text; the significance of the texts themselves is something that Meek (1988) has strongly advocated (➡ Chapter 4, 'Texts for children').

Clay's procedures include: learning about direction of text and pages; 'locating responses' that support one-to-one correspondence (☞) (e.g. locating words and spaces by pointing or indicating); spatial layout; writing stories; hearing the sounds in words; cut-up stories (i.e. cutting up texts and reassembling them); reading books; learning to look at print; linking sound sequences with letter sequences; word analysis; phrasing and fluency; sequencing; avoiding overuse of one strategy; memory; children who are hard to accelerate.

Another procedure that Clay emphasised is the importance of 'teaching for operations or strategies' (1979: 71). Within this, is the idea that readers need to be able to monitor their own reading and solve their own problems. It is suggested that teachers should encourage children to explain how they monitor their own reading. The process of explanation helps to consolidate the skills. Clay offers useful examples of language that teachers might use.

Teacher: What was the new word you read?
Child: Bicycle.
Teacher: How did you know it was bicycle?
Child: It was a bike (semantics)
Teacher: What did you expect to see?
Child: A 'b'.
Teacher: What else?
Child: A little word, but it wasn't.
Teacher: So what did you do?
Child: I thought of bicycle.

Teacher: (reinforcing the checking) Good, I liked the way you worked at that all by yourself.
Teacher: You almost got that page right. There was something wrong with this line. See if you can find what was wrong.
Child: (child silently rereads, checking) I said Lizard but it's Lizard's.
Teacher: How did you know?
Child: 'Cause it's got an 's'
Teacher: Is there any other way we could know? (search further)
Child: (child reruns in a whisper) It's funny to say 'Lizard dinner'! It has to be Lizard's dinner like Peter's dinner doesn't it?
Teacher: (reinforcing the searching) Yes that was good. You found two ways to check on that tricky new word.

(Clay, 1979: 73–74)

EVALUATIONS OF READING RECOVERY

As we said at the beginning of this chapter, reading recovery is an internationally recognised approach for supporting children with reading difficulties. It was pioneered in New Zealand and because of this questions have been asked about whether it is possible to adopt such a programme in the UK.

This is a matter that is a serious consideration when thinking about any initiatives that have been developed in another country because the varying cultural and historical backgrounds of countries do make a difference. A number of research projects have tried to discover how effective reading recovery is.

Surrey Education Authority was the first authority in the country to introduce reading recovery in 1990. Wright (1992) carried out an evaluation to compare the success of reading recovery in the UK with the New Zealand experience. She found that on average, children took about two weeks longer before they could finish the reading recovery tuition. She also found that 'only three of the 82 children taken into the programme in the two years did not achieve average levels for their classes after 20 weeks of teaching' (Wright, 1992). Achievements in the SATs were also improved and overall Wright concluded that reading recovery could be successfully implemented in the UK. Her positive views about reading recovery are supported by Clay's own research carried out over a number of years where she found that 'as a result of accelerated progress the children typically leave the programme with average levels of performance in three to six months' (1979: 105).

There have also been studies that are more critical of reading recovery. *The Times Educational Supplement* screamed '**Poor recovery** An expensive programme of individual literacy lessons has failed to raise standards amongst struggling pupils' (Bald, 1998). But a proper reading of the actual research report itself reveals a different picture. The research compared reading recovery with a particular phonological training (☞) intervention, and control groups. Immediately after the interventions were completed the research found that the effects of the reading recovery were large: 'approximately an 8 month reading age advantage over the control children' compared with the phonological training where there was 'no measurable effect on reading' (QCA, 1998:20). An advantage for reading recovery was maintained in the second follow-up. The third follow-up had a more complex picture. Reading recovery had been particularly successful for those children who 'started as complete non-readers' but the phonological intervention was more successful for those children 'who had a slightly better grasp of reading before they were given the intervention' (QCA, 1998: 26). Which all goes to show that you shouldn't believe everything you read in the papers!

Practice points

- Identify children who are struggling as early as possible.
- Decisions should be made in terms of time and resources for extra support including the use of classroom assistants.
- Improve the relationship with the child and try to understand and empathise with their particular problems.

Glossary

Dyslexia – a formally recognised condition which results in specific difficulties with reading and writing.

One-to-one correspondence – the understanding that one word on the page corresponds with one spoken word. Evidence comes from finger pointing at words and numbers.

Phonological training – teaching children to understand sound/symbol links.

Reading recovery – a set of techniques developed by Marie Clay designed to eradicate children's reading problems.

References

Bald, J. (1998) 'Poor Recovery'. *Times Educational Supplement*, October 13.

Brooks, G., Pugh, A. K. and Schagen, I. (1996) *Reading Performance at Nine*. Slough: NFER.

Clark, M. M. (1976) *Young Fluent Readers: What Can They Teach Us?* London: Heinemann Educational Books.

Clay, M. M. (1979) *The Early Detection of Reading Difficulties* (third edition). Auckland: Heinemann.

Literacy Task Force (1997) *The Implementation of the National Literacy Strategy*. London: DfEE.

Qualifications and Curriculum Authority (QCA) (1998) *The Long-term Effects of Two Interventions for Children with Reading Difficulties*. London: QCA.

Wright, A. *Evaluation of the First British Reading Recovery Programme*. NISS EBSCO MasterFILE Service. *British Educational Research Journal*, 18(4): 351–368. July 1992 [online – cited 24-3-99]. Available from: http:www.niss.ac.uk/EBSCO-MF/cgi-bin/n

Annotated bibliography

Clay, M. M. (1979) *The Early Detection of Reading Difficulties*, third edition. Auckland: Heinemann.
This gives a full account of how to implement the reading recovery approach. One of the many useful aspects includes information on what a typical tutoring session looks like.
L2 **

Institute of Education University of London. Reading Recovery National Network. [online – cited 16-6-00] . Available from:
http://www.ioe.ac.uk/cdl/readrec.html
Some useful basic information about the Reading Recovery project in the UK.
L1 **

Qualifications and Curriculum Authority (QCA) (1998) *The Long-term Effects of Two Interventions for Children with Reading Difficulties*. London: QCA
A detailed research report which is useful because it does not hide the complexities of helping children with reading. Like many reports of its kind it

does not deal with qualitative issues.

L3 ***

Stainthorp, R. and Hughes, D. (1999) *Learning from Children who Read at an Early Age*. London: Routledge.

The most interesting part of this study is the kinds of experiences that the children had at home before they started school. An important reminder that children who are particularly advanced or 'gifted' need special support as well.

L3 ***

Chapter 11

Assessing reading

In this chapter you will read about assessing and recording children's reading progress through a range of strategies and procedures including the running record, miscue analysis and reading observations. The chapter should be read in conjunction with Chapter 19, 'Assessing writing' and Chapter 25, 'Assessing talk', as some strategies – such as diaries of observations – are applicable to all three modes and other strategies are specific to one mode.

Monitoring and assessing the reading progress of young children has invariably been a day-to-day part of classroom life. Listening to children read aloud has traditionally been the means by which teachers have done this. With the advent of the National Literacy Strategy, checking up on reading is now most likely to occur during guided reading within the literacy hour and reading conferences outside the literacy hour. It is also probable that children will be heard individually less and less, but with each session taking an increased importance. These sessions will sometimes need to focus specifically on assessing individual children's competence. Miscue analysis, and the simpler running record, are two practical procedures which support reading assessment in the classroom.

THE RUNNING RECORD

The running record represents a relatively easy way of recording and assessing the oral reading of the child. As the child reads aloud from a book or other text, the teacher encodes the reading onto a sheet of paper using a specified coding system such as the following one:

/ word read accurately
T word told by teacher
'is' substituted word written down
O omission of word
SC self-correction of word by child

For example, Helen, age 7, read the following text 'There was soup for dinner. Chicken soup for all the children' as:

'There is soup for dinner. Children . . . Chicken soup for all the children.'

The teacher duly coded this as / 'is' / / / SC / / / / / indicating that the child read the piece accurately apart from substituting the word 'is' for 'was'. Also, when she substituted 'children' for 'chicken' she immediately corrected herself when she realised that 'children soup' was very unlikely.

After the child finishes reading, the teacher might discuss with them some of the miscues (☞) made, particularly the substitutions (☞), to determine which cueing strategies the child is currently employing and how they might be taken forward in their reading development

The great advantage with a running record is that it is immediate, in the sense that special materials are unnecessary – just a pen and a sheet of paper. Provided you have memorised the codings, you can complete one or more records during reading conferences, or at any other suitable times of the day. There are limitations, however. Instant coding by the teacher is likely to be inaccurate from time to time, because some utterances by children need greater reflection or, at least, need to be listened to more than once or twice. The running record is one of the main techniques used in the SATs at Key Stage 1 for determining children's National Curriculum reading levels.

MISCUE ANALYSIS

All teachers find that children, when reading aloud, inevitably deviate from the written text in front of them from time to time. (They also do so when reading silently though this is, of course, not accessible to the teacher.) Goodman (1969) termed such departures from what is written on the page as 'miscues' rather than errors because they involve a child's interaction with the text which can be seen as positive or negative; the term 'errors' usually implies something purely negative. A child's miscues do, in fact, denote reading strengths as well as reading weaknesses and the fluent reader produces miscues as well as the struggling reader. The most common types of miscue include:

- The *substitution* of one word for another
- *Self-correction*
- *Non-response*, where the child is unable – or refuses – to supply a word or part of a word
- *Omission*, where the child leaves out a word in the general course of reading rather than non-response
- The *insertion* of a word or words, sometimes reflecting a particular dialect or personal pattern of language
- *Hesitation* involving a pause of more than three seconds
- *Repetition*, sometimes this can give the child the chance to think more about a difficult word coming next

Although there are others, these points constitute the most common children's miscues.

The following procedure is typical of the process of carrying out a miscue analysis:

- Choose a suitable text for the child to read aloud. Avoid anything that will be too easy. It should be something that the child will find challenging
- Allow the child to read the text silently beforehand and alert the child to the fact that you will be asking a few simple questions about the text after they have read aloud
- Tape-record the actual reading for future listening including your questions and the reader's responses to them
- Provide yourself with a photocopy of the text and mark it accordingly using the coding system
- Analyse the marked-up text and try to ascertain if the child is using positive or negative strategies and to what extent they are making full use of all reading cues
- Analyse the pupil's responses to your questions. According to Arnold (1982) this comprehension element is a very important aspect of miscue analysis. Can the reader recall what has just been read? Do they understand it? Are the finer points of the passage recognised and appreciated, and so on?

Once the miscues have been carefully interpreted and scored, the substitutions can be further categorised as falling into one or more of syntactic (☞), semantic (☞) and graphophonic (☞) strategy headings. A detailed analysis might then follow to furnish the teacher with a detailed picture of the child's reading strengths and weaknesses. A full description and explanation of such an analysis can be found in Arnold (1982) or Beard (1990).

A sample of marked-up text might be:

> Tom   over ✓   little
> When T̶i̶m̶ fell d̶o̶w̶n̶ the hole, he got extremely wet(and)his / sister began
> to sob.

The miscues in this example are made up of:

1   substitution ('Tom' instead of 'Tim')
2   self-correction ('down' read as 'over' then self-corrected to 'down')
3   non-response to 'extremely'
4   omission of 'and'
5   insertion of 'little'
6   hesitation before 'began'
7   repetition of 'to'

Self-correction is regarded as a positive strategy; the omission of 'and' is also positive because it retains the full meaning of the sentence. The hesitation and the repetition of 'to' could also, in this case, be regarded as positive rather than negative as the child appeared to be buying time to interact successfully with the text and use appropriate strategies. The insertion of 'little' was positive because the child had noticed from an adjacent illustration that the sister was indeed very small. The non-response to the word 'extremely' was, however, definitely negative since the child did not attempt to sound out the word or offer a substitution.

Substitutions, in fact, are the most common of all miscues and the most helpful to teachers. They give the most insight into the cueing strategies that the young reader is inclined to use. In our example, the substitution of 'Tom' for 'Tim' is positive since it suggests that the child might be operating all three cueing systems here. 'Tom' is syntactically acceptable in that it is a proper noun and hence fits grammatically into the sentence. 'Tom' is semantically appropriate as it is meaningful and does not affect the sense of the story (unless there is another character in the story named Tom who does not fall down the hole). Finally, 'Tom' is graphophonically similar to 'Tim' with both initial letter and word ending similarity. Substitutions like this one strongly suggest that the reader is making full use of all cueing systems. Other, less positive substitutions can indicate that one strategy is being overused at the expense of others.

Perhaps the most important aspect of carrying out a miscue analysis is the effect the process has on the teacher. As Bielby observes,

> [The] experience of doing miscue analysis changes the teacher's attitude and approach forever to listening to children read. Instead of seeing it as a chore that you devote half your mind to while marking on the side, it becomes an enthralling diagnostic exploration.
>
> (1994:147)

Although a miscue analysis might be administered formally to determine the child's reading ability, once a teacher is familiar with it, every reading conference (➡ Chapter 6, 'Listening to children read') or guided reading period will involve at least some analysis of the child's potential. These perceptions might be formally or informally recorded on a reading observation sheet.

READING OBSERVATIONS

It is very important that teachers keep reading records on each child in their care. These records should be informative, to enable teachers to reflect on suitable literacy activities for the pupils concerned and to discuss pupils' reading development with parents and other teachers. However, they should not be too demanding on teachers' time and energy. Data on individuals – gathered in reading conferences and Guided Reading sessions

READING OBSERVATIONS

Child's name:	Year group:	Child/teacher choice (underline)
Title, author: 1.	2.	
Genre/form: 1.	2.	
Date: 1.	2.	

Reading with accuracy, fluency and sense of meaning

Strategies used: • playing at reading • using book language • using pictures as cue • memory • focusing on print self correcting **Cueing:** • semantic (meaning) • syntactic (word order/ grammar) • graphophonic (phonic and visual) **Overview:** • independence • accuracy • fluency		

Understanding and response

• motivation and involvement • prediction • knowledge about text structure • known/unknown text • issues discussed • personal view • critical view **Child's own view of their reading**		
Future action		

Figure 11.1 Reading Observations Form

and, more specifically during running record or miscue analysis exchanges – can be recorded on reading observation sheets. We have used observation sheets with students for use in primary schools during student school experience and the example (see figure 11.1) is based on the 'Reading Sample Form' in the Primary Language Record (PLR) (CLPE: 1988). The PLR final document contains four A4 pages consisting of summaries of interactions between children and teachers and between parents and teachers. The Record also obliges teachers to identify different stages of reading fluency attained by young readers.

Reading diaries

The reading diary is one of the most flexible and open-ended forms of recording individual reading development. Some teachers include a series of brief observational jottings, appropriately dated, noting significant features of the child's reading as they occur, e.g. 'Leanne is trying very hard. She knows several words by sight and uses both phonics and picture clues to help her' or 'James appreciates nuances of text with lots of support – seems to understand 'puns' when they are explained to him'. Over time, patterns of development become evident and milestones and competences can be readily perceived and recorded.

Reading diaries can also provide a record of the child's reading at home. In this way, parents can become fully involved in their child's development in reading and useful dialogues can take place between the parent and the teacher about the child's reading:

18.11.98 'The Carnival'
In my opinion Cassie is reading very well. I only had to help her with a few words.

23.11.98 'The Carnival'
Cassie does know many of the key words now. Cue her into new words by using the pictures where it helps.

25.11.98 'The Carnival'
Cassie would not read to me. She says she won't read at home.

27.11.98 'The Carnival'
Cassie read very well and with a great deal of enthusiasm. Don't try to force her to read at home. Just encourage her as much as possible.

30.11.98 'The Carnival'
Cassie read wonderfully to me tonight. Can she have new book tomorrow?

Children too can keep reading diaries (sometimes called 'reading journals' or 'logs') and participate in a dialogue with the teacher about their reading, the books they like to read in and out of school and even problems they are having with their reading. Some of the comments taken from actual diaries read like this: 'I enjoyed this book because it was in English as well as Gujerati'; 'I found the story quite difficult because there were some very long words and lots of names that were a bit hard'; and 'I wish I could read like you, Miss. I enjoy it when you read to us because it makes the stories even better'.

There are, of course, other ways of assessing children's reading ability. Beard (1990) usefully examines other informal ways of accumulating information such as checklists, reading interviews and informal reading inventories together with formal measures such as tests. Vincent (1994) also has some interesting points to make about the usefulness of standardised reading tests. Chapter 19, 'Assessing writing' looks in more detail at the influence of the National Standard Assessment Tasks (SATs) which are another way of assessing literacy.

Practice points

- Carry out reading observations of all the children in your class very early in the year in order to identify those who need help. Talk to the previous class teacher to confirm your judgements.
- Decide the kinds of assessment strategies you will use throughout the year and plan for when they will happen.
- Adjust your planning regularly based on frequent analysis of the results of your assessments.

Glossary

Miscues – reading mistakes.

Semantic, syntactic and graphophonic reading cues – mental strategies that people use to read texts. Most commonly described as semantic (using meaning), syntactic (using grammar) and graphophonic (using sound and symbol correspondences).

Substitutions – words guessed in place of unknown printed words.

References

Arnold, H. (1982) *Listening to Children Reading*. London: Hodder & Stoughton in association with The United Kingdom Reading Association (UKRA).

Beard R. (1990) *Developing Reading 3–13* (second edition). London: Hodder & Stoughton.

Bielby N. (1994) *Making Sense of Reading: The New Phonics and Its Practical Implications*. Leamington Spa: Scholastic.

Centre for Language in Primary Education (CLPE) (1988) *The Primary Language Record: Handbook for Teachers*. London: CLPE.

Goodman, K. (1969) 'Analysis of oral reading miscues: applied psycholinguistics'. *Reading Research Quarterly*, 1 (3): 9–30.

Vincent, D. (1994) 'The assessment of reading', in D. Wray and J. Medwell (eds) *Teaching Primary English: The State of the Art*. London: Routledge.

Annotated bibliography

Centre for Language in Primary Education (CLPE) (1988) *The Primary Language Record: Handbook for Teachers*. London: CLPE.
One of the most thorough record-keeping systems that has been developed in recent years. One of its important features was the recognition of the needs of ethnic minority children.
L1 *

Clay, M. M. (1979) *The Early Detection of Reading Difficulties* (third edition). Auckland: Heinemann.
Marie Clay created the running record and she shows how its use can feed directly into teaching decisions.
L2 **

Coles, M. and Jenkins, R. (eds) (1998) *Assessing Reading 2: Changing Practice in Classrooms: International Perspectives on Reading Assessment*. London: Routledge.
One of two substantial books that look at the theory and practice of assessment. This book uses case studies to focus on practice and serves as a reminder that assessment is a complex process.
L3 **

Qualifications and Curriculum Authority (QCA) (1999) *Target setting and assessment in the National Literacy Strategy*. London: QCA.
Like many other QCA publications on assessment this manages to put forward realistic guidance on assessment. Particularly welcome is the reminder that not all assessment has to be written down.
L1 *

Teacher Training Agency (TTA). Assessing Your Needs in Literacy. [online] University of Derby. Scope Productions. [cited – 26-6-00]. Available from:
    http://www.derby.ac.uk/schools/ess/education/tta/needs/literacy/index.html
These materials were developed by the TTA to enable teachers to assess their subject knowledge. The literacy questions include knowledge that is necessary when making assessments of children's reading.
L2 *

Part III

Writing

Chapter 12

The development of writing

Historically, the teaching of writing has been much less of a focus than the teaching of reading. However, just as we illustrated for reading, in order to teach writing effectively it is necessary to be aware of how children learn. We return to the detailed picture of Paul Bissex (➡ Chapter 3, 'The Development of reading') in order to look at writing development. Spelling and composition development are summarised. This picture of development is followed by a large section on the teaching of writing and the different views that have been expressed in relation to the importance of creativity and expression.

It is important to understand the typical stages of development that children pass through in their writing. This knowledge helps you to pitch your planning and interaction at an appropriate level for the children you are teaching. People who have already experienced such development as teachers and parents are in an advantageous position. However, teachers who are inexperienced need to grasp the fundamental aspects of such development. One of the reasons for this is that it heightens their awareness of what to look for when they do have the opportunity to interact with young writers.

As you will have seen in Chapter 3 there are a number of in-depth case studies of individual children that can help in acquiring knowledge about children's development. Studies of individual children do not act as a blueprint for all children: one of the important things that such case studies show us is that children's experiences vary greatly. However, if we focus on certain key concepts and significant milestones these can be applied to larger groups of children. These milestones are likely to happen at roughly the same age for many children but there will be significant numbers of children whose development is different. Once again the seminal work (☞) by Bissex (1980) is used, on this occasion to examine the developmental characteristics of Paul's writing from age 5 to age 10.

PAUL BISSEX'S WRITING DEVELOPMENT

Age 5 to 10

Invented spelling

• *Age 5*

Paul started to experiment with spellings. On one occasion his mother was reading; in order to grab her attention he wrote a sign: RUDF (are you deaf?). At this stage he was still very much dependent on support from his mother so he would often ask questions about how to write particular sounds.

At age 5 years and 6 months Paul's confidence to invent spellings increased dramatically. He used a combination of letter name strategies (using the letter because its name sounds like the appropriate phoneme (☞)) and phonemic strategies (☞): A PAN A TIM (once upon a time). His interest in signs and notices was a consistent part of his development throughout his childhood and one sign in particular became the title to Bissex's book: DO NAT DSTRB GNYS AT WRK (do not disturb genius at work). Paul was interested in labels and captions and these were always accompanied by a picture: HAU. TO. DO. TH. ENDEN. WOR. DANS FRST. U. TAK. WAN. AV. UOR. FET (how to do the Indian war dance. First you take one of your feet).

Paul's main problem, which made his writing difficult to read at 5 years 8 months, was his lack of understanding of unconventional short vowel sounds. At this time he was occasionally including standard English spellings alongside his invented ones. His writing was mainly in the present tense and he made a second attempt at a newspaper which was modelled on the local paper. His second attempt at book writing resulted in four short books. During this stage for the first time he strongly expressed concerns about correctness and this may have been linked to his school experiences in year 1. His enthusiasm for writing was replaced by another burst of reading.

Towards conventional spelling

• *Age 6*

From 5 years 10 months to 6 years 3 months Paul wrote very little. One of the few texts he did compose was a game with letter cards and word cards. At this time he became aware of some words that he could read but not spell. At school the emphasis was on visual whole word learning which contributed to his visual spelling strategies. However, this resulted in the temporary mis-spelling of some words that previously he had spelled correctly using phonological knowledge (☞). At 6 years and 3 months there was evidence of logical over-generalisation: CACE (cake) and later CACK (cake) – in these cases he used his visual knowledge when he tried a final 'e' and the 'ck'. He was beginning to show greater awareness of affixes (☞): 'locked'; 'laughing'.

Up to 6 years and 7 months Paul started doing more writing again but reverted to some of his favourite earlier forms such as signs and labels, a list, a cookbook and notes. He also created four newspapers which included sections such as 'funnies, weather, news, advertisements'; these were constructed on large sheets of paper with lines and boxes drawn on them. Sometime later when he looked back over them he commented: 'It's got funnies and advertising and news and weather! How did I get all this? Did I have some interpretation of what was in a newspaper?' At this stage there was some evidence that he was moving towards conventional punctuation.

His new writing forms included rhymes, riddles and a personal notebook which later became a diary. He only chose to write one story: ONECS UPON A TIME THERE WAS A CAT. THE END. In contrast to the varied forms of Paul's spontaneous writing, his school writing was structurally monotonous. He would mainly write about a picture at school and frequently his stories started 'This is . . . '. It has been suggested by some people that offering choice results in children's writing becoming limited to a restricted number of forms. In this study there was evidence that the lack of choice at school resulted in narrowly focused and weaker writing.

- ● Age 7

One striking characteristic of this period was the way that Paul used writing in order to remember and keep track of things: PAULS COLECSHINS SPOONS 37, PETS 2, COMICS 4, MARBLES 4, MONY 2$, MAGIC ECT 3 (the ECT matched his pronunciation of etcetera). Between 7 years 4 months and 7 years 7 months Paul had another writing spurt possibly encouraged by his mother's analysis of his writing for her research.

Paul was now using multiple spelling strategies including phonemic, visual and possibly some rule guided strategies. One example shows Paul learning the 'oi' combination relatively early: NOIS (6:6), TOILET (7.5) but he struggled with the -tion ending: COLECSHINS (7.2), COLECTOIN (7.5), EXAM-ANATOIN (7.9), DIRECTIONS (8.1 but he was unsure until 8.5). His continuing interest in his favourite forms was not mere repetition as there was evidence of increasing sophistication. He continued to experiment with: signs, labels, notes, charts and organisers, newspaper, fun book, directions, school-type exercises.

Sustained and more mature writing

- ● Age 8

A change in teacher resulted in much more writing done at school. Paul's story (his third) written at this age showed evidence of greater awareness of audience. This was a very significant change in his development and resulted in the inclusion of dialogue and description: 'I suppose you want to know how you steer a magic carpet . . . ' Informational writing was introduced at school. On one occasion he chose to work with a friend on the subject of 'prisms' and was given a notebook for findings: 'a prism is a thick (mostly) piece of glass that puts the colors of sunlight visible to the human eye'. His awareness of the organisation of non-fiction was growing and he would include an index in his own books. His knowledge of impersonal forms of writing was also developing. Paul started a diary which was a new form for him.

- **Age 9**

At age 9 Paul was beginning to develop greater sophistication in his style of writing. For example, another attempt at a newspaper resulted in:

> 'PISTOL PAUL GONE GUNWACKY Pistol Paul just baught a new pistol and is using up ammo like a lawn mower uses of gasoline Scientists say that he must have a terrible earwax problem because anyone else in his position would be deaf by now.'
>
> (Bissex, 1980: 83)

The composition of a poster for 'Paul's Flea Market' resulted in close imitation of commercial advertising. At this stage Paul's peer group and culture were a strong influence and they enjoyed sharing quizzes, membership cards, booklets, etc. An example of a quiz book was 'THE STAR WARS MINI QUIZ BOOK' with many questions about Star Wars: '0 Who is the writer? 1. Who is the director?' etc. By 9 years 8 months Paul's spelling had become mainly standard and he had acquired most of the necessary strategies and knowledge such as: knowledge of affixes; the ability to distinguish homonyms (☞); awareness of consonant doubling, and awareness of uncommon spelling patterns.

Bissex's reflections on the development of Paul's spelling prompted Gentry(1982) to suggest five stages of spelling development (➡Chapter 15, 'Spelling') These are a very useful and quick way to locate a child's level of spelling development. However, there is the danger that the development of composition can be overlooked. Spelling and composition often develop at different rates so it would be simplistic to describe children's writing levels on the basis of spelling alone. The National Curriculum makes the distinction between spelling and 'writing' (composition) and the level descriptions give limited information from that perspective. Using case-study data such as Bissex's we can identify other common developmental features of composition.

1 Beginning writing

- Interested in environmental print
- Makes distinctions between text and pictures
- Enjoys playing at writing
- Attempts to communicate messages with writing
- Uses personal experience as influence for writing.

2   Learning to encode

- Has the confidence to invent spellings
- Will use various written forms as models
- Attempts story writing
- Revisits favourite forms with greater sophistication
- Increasing amount of writing
- Growing awareness of need for standard conventions.

3   Extending written forms

- Expresses preference for particular forms
- Exploration and increasing knowledge of wider range of forms
- Uses writing to organise and categorise
- Aware of multiple meanings for words
- Uses standard conventions of written English most of the time
- Experiments with presentational features and special effects.

4   Writing to learn

- Greater sophistication in narrative (e.g. awareness of audience) and/or other forms
- Will collaborate effectively on appropriate stages of writing process
- Uses impersonal language when appropriate
- Develops particular writing styles: personal and imitative
- Sustained concentration on writing projects
- Growing use of drafting and editing.

We have suggested that knowledge about the development of language and literacy can influence your teaching. At one level this can mean that your interaction is targeted more effectively. However, as in the section on reading development, having a knowledge about development also causes us to ask questions about pedagogy (☞). Bissex clearly signalled this when she referred to Paul's motivation and the range and amount of writing he chose to do at various stages. Once again it was a concern that some of the narrowly focused writing that was done at school seemed to be a factor in his periodic lack of motivation.

THE TEACHING OF WRITING

In Chapter 3 on the development of reading we described how the pedagogy of reading teaching had been dominated by the 'great debate'. As far as writing is concerned it is much more difficult to identify a central theme to the discussions about teaching. In part this reflects the fact that writing continues to attract less attention than reading: less research is devoted to writing and there are fewer publications on the subject. Writing also seems to attract less attention in the media although standards of spelling and grammar recurrently hit the news. However, overall the disagreements in relation to the teaching of writing have tended to centre on the amount of creativity and self-expression that is desirable and how these should be balanced with acquiring the necessary writing skills. As we work through a number of key moments in the history of writing pedagogy you will see that this central point about creativity and skills will recur.

In the past the teaching of writing was dominated by 'copywriting' (☞), this was accompanied by formal – usually grammar – exercises that were decontextualised from any meaningful purpose. One of the early National Curricula illustrates the kinds of teaching that was expected in 1900.

> *Standard I* (7 years)
> *Reading*   To read a short passage from a book not confined to words of one syllable.
> *Writing*   Copy in manuscript characters a line of print, commencing with a capital letter. Copy books to be shown.
> *'English'*   Pointing out nouns.
>
> *Standard 2* (8 years)
> *Reading*   To read a short passage from an elementary reading book.
> *Writing*   A passage of not more than six lines, from the same book, slowly read once and then dictated.
> *'English'*   Pointing out nouns and verbs.
>
> *Standard 4* (10 years)
> *Reading*   To read a passage from a reading book or history of England.
> *Writing*   Eight lines of poetry or prose, slowly read once, then dictated.
> *'English'*   Parsing easy sentences, and showing by examples the use of each of the parts of speech.
>
> *Standard 5* (11 years)
> *Reading*   To read a passage from some standard author, or reading book, or history of England.
> *Writing*   Writing from memory the substance of a short story read out twice; spelling, handwriting and correct expression to be considered.
> *'English'*   Parsing and analysis of simple sentences. The method of forming English nouns, adjectives, and verbs from each other.
>
> (Shayer, 1972: 4)

Shayer points out that

> 'Imitation' was not simply an isolated classroom exercise, but a whole way of thinking that was taken for granted by a great many teachers, if not by the vast majority, certainly until 1920 and even beyond. Briefly, the pupil (elementary or secondary) is always expected to imitate, copy, or reproduce.
>
> (1972: 10)

He goes on to give some examples from Nelson's *Picture Essays,* 1907 of typical activities of the time:

> 'Describe a cow; general appearance. Horns . . . teeth . . . hoofs . . . tail. Food. Breeds. Uses.'
> 'Write on "Our Town" as follows: 1. *Introduction* – Name; Meaning; Situation; Population. 2. *Appearance* – General appearance, chief streets, buildings, parks, etc. 3. *General Remarks.* Principle trades and industries. Any historical facts, etc.'
>
> (1972: 10)

> *The Story of a Shilling*
> Hints
> Where and when was it born?
> What did it look like?
> Who was its first owner?
> What did he do with it?
> Invent some adventures for it, and tell what became of it in the end.
> (J. H. Fowler, *A First Course in Essay-Writing,* 1902)

It is interesting to reflect on the specific ways that these kind of activities differ from those suggested in the Framework for Teaching.

Creative writing

As a reaction to rather formal approaches, 'creative writing' flourished in the 1960s. One of the most famous texts from this time is Alex Clegg's book *The Excitement of Writing.* Clegg also recognised the extensive use – and potentially damaging effect – of published English schemes and wanted to show examples of children's writing 'taken from schools which are deliberately encouraging each child to draw sensitively on his own store of words and to delight in setting down his own ideas in a way which is personal to him and stimulating to those who read what he has written'. (1964: 4)

Protherough (1978) provided a very useful summary of the impact of creative writing and his paper also signalled some of the criticisms that were emerging. Overall he felt that the creative writing movement was an important one and that 'the emphasis on personal, imaginative writing [needed] to be maintained and extended' (1978: 18). But he felt the model had some weaknesses. One of these weaknesses was the restriction on the forms of writing that were used. The teacher provided a stimulus (such as a piece of music or visual art) which was followed by an immediate response, and this implied brief personal forms of writing such as a short descriptive sketch or a brief poem. The model did not encourage the writing of other forms such as argument, plays, or even short stories. Protheroe recommended that 'the stimulated writing is to be seen *not* as the end-product, but as a stage in a process. Pupils need to be helped to develop their work, and to learn form each other as well as from the teacher'. (1978: 18) As you will see later, the process approach took these ideas forward.

By the end of the 1970s, concerns were growing about the emphasis on 'feeling' in writing teaching and the fact that much of the creative stimuli required an immediate response which did not allow for suitable reworking or redrafting. Allen (1980) pointed out that too much focus on expressive writing could lead to a lack of emphasis on more 'abstract modes'. At this time it was suggested that the teaching of writing required tighter structures that were deemed to be missing from the creative writing ideas.

One of the influential thinkers of the period, James Britton, proposed that writing could be categorised into several key forms (figure 12.1). Britton offers a scientific report as one example of transactional writing (☞). He argued that this kind of writing 'may elicit the statement of other views, of counter-arguments or corroborations or modifications, and is thus part of a chain of interactions between people' (Britton, 1970: 175). He contrasts this with poetic writing where the reader is invited to share a particular verbal construct (☞). The sharing of the writer's thoughts in poetic writing does not 'elicit interaction' in the same way that transactional writing does.

Britton did not see the forms of writing as clear boundaries, he recognised that the reality of language in use meant that they would often be blurred. By looking at his diagram as a continuum Britton argued that expressive writing might become more explicit if the audience for the writing did not share the interests and experiences of the writer. In this case the piece would be described as moving towards the transactional end of the continuum. However, if expressive writing moves towards the poetic then Britton argued that writers deliberately emphasise implicit meanings in order to create 'sounds, words, images, ideas, events, feelings' (1979: 177). At this time there was a growing feeling that expressive writing could and should be a foundation for other more abstract forms. However, overall, Allen maintains that the mid- to late 1970s were characterised by uncertainty and lack of consensus on approaches to the teaching of writing.

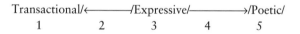

Transactional/⟵————/Expressive/————⟶/Poetic/
　　　1　　　　　2　　　　3　　　　4　　　　5

Figure 12.1 Britton's categorisation of forms of writing. (Reproduced from *Language and Learning.* Harmondsworth: Allen Lane The Penguin Press, 1970, second edition 1972. Copyright © James Britton, 1970, 1972).

Developmental writing

The creative writing movement had in part been based on the philosophies of Rousseau (➡Chapter 2, 'Theories of learning'), but there was a lack of research evidence to support claims about children's 'natural' development. One of the reasons that research like Bissex's was so important was that it documented children's development as language users in natural ways. This kind of data has also been collected from larger groups of children. Harste et al (1984) were able to extend our knowledge of children's writing by look-ing at 3- and 4-year-olds. Their conclusions signalled concern about the lack of 'uninterrupted' writing in most early years settings. One of the striking features of their work was the researchers' ability to focus on the positive features of early writing rather than the deficits: an extract from 'Lessons from Latrice' – a chapter from their book – is shown in Figure 12.2.

Uninterrupted Writing

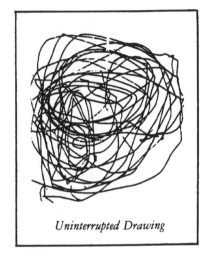

Uninterrupted Drawing

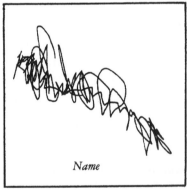

Name

Figure 12.2 Samples of Latrice's writing. (Reproduced from Harste et al (1984) *Language Stories and Literary Lessons,* Oxford: Heinemann. Used with permission).

The researchers initially confessed to being more unsure about Latrice's writing than any of the other children they studied: she was developmentally the least experienced child that they encountered. The researchers asked Latrice to write her name and anything else that she could write; she was then asked to draw a picture of herself. By positively and actively searching for evidence of Latrice's achievements they were able to understand her writing in great depth. The following is a list of some of the knowledge that Latrice had already acquired:

- Latrice was aware of how to use writing implements and paper
- She understood and demonstrated the difference between writing and pictures
- She switched between writing and drawing as a strategy to maintain the flow of her writing
- Each new mark represented a new or different concept
- She had developed some knowledge of the importance of space in relation to text
- She was aware of the permanance of meaning in relation to written language.

Another important point that Harste et al made is that judgements about children's writing based on the final product do not give us enough information about their writing achievements. It is only by analysing the process of writing, in addition to the product, that valid information can be gathered.

The research evidence on children's natural literacy development supported philosophies like those of Rousseau and led to new theories on writing pedagogy. It was argued that as children seemed to develop to a large extent by using their own natural curiosity and ability, perhaps formal teaching should take account of this reality. The theories of 'emergent literacy' developed alongside approaches such as 'developmental writing'. The term 'emergent literacy' was popularised by Hall (1987) in his book *The Emergence of Literacy*. The basis of the philosophy is the notion of the child as an active and motivated learner who experiments with a wide range of written forms out of a sense of curiosity and a desire to learn. Hall described emergent literacy as follows:

> It implies that development takes place from within the child . . . 'emergence' is a gradual process. For something to emerge there has to be something there in the first place. Where emergent literacy is concerned this means the fundamental abilities children have, and use, to make sense of the world . . . things usually only emerge if the conditions are right. Where emergent literacy is concerned that means in contexts which support, facilitate enquiry, respect performance and provide opportunities for engagement in real literacy acts.
>
> (1987: 9)

The theory of emergent literacy was very closely linked with the practice of developmental writing. The following list identifies some of the key features of developmental writing and was influenced by Browne's (1993: 21) points that characterise such writing:

1 Builds on children's literacy experience prior to coming to school.
2 Encourages independent writing from day one of the nursery.
3 Modelling is provided by physical resources and the actions of the teacher.

4   Transcription errors are dealt with after the meaning has been established. A smaller number of errors are corrected but each one in more detail.
5   Learning to write developmentally can be slow but the benefits in future motivation for writing are the result.
6   Writing tasks emphasise purpose and real reasons.
7   Children have time to develop pieces of writing in depth.
8   The confidence to take risks is encouraged.

Developmental writing differs from the creative writing of the 1960s and 1970s in two main ways. Both approaches share the recognition that children must be given opportunities to carry out uninterrupted writing which uses their previous knowledge and experience. However, with developmental writing there is a stronger expectation that the teacher will interact, particularly with individual children, in order to take learning forward. The second difference relates to the first in that the teacher's interaction during developmental writing is based on a high level of knowledge about common developmental patterns in the children's writing and this informs the focus of their interaction. With these clearer pictures of development came different and more realistic expectations of children's learning.

The freedom of developmental writing was replaced in the early 1980s by a continuing recognition of the importance of children's self-expression, but with the realisation that routines to support the process of writing were helpful.

The process approach to writing

The uncertainty of the 1970s was finally transformed by the process writing of the 1980s. The work of the New Zealander Donald Graves became very influential culminating in international recognition for his work and great demand for him as a keynote speaker. Czerniewska (1992: 85) described Graves as 'one of the most seductive writers in the history of writing pedagogy'. Graves's approach to writing became known as the 'process approach' and had a significant influence on the teaching of writing in the UK. It is difficult to assess exactly how many schools and teachers took up the approach in the UK but, for example, the National Writing Project and the Language in the National Curriculum Project both involved many schools in the UK, and it is clear from their reports of practice that the process approach was influential. Frank Smith was also very popular at the time and although his theories on reading have taken some severe criticism, his theories on writing have remained better intact. Nevertheless some of these theories are still regarded as controversial.

> It has been argued that writing is learned by writing, by reading, and by perceiving oneself as a writer. The practice of writing develops interest and with the help of a more able collaborator provides opportunity for discovering conventions relevant to what is being written . . . None of

this can be taught. But also none of this implies that there is no role for a teacher. Teachers must play a central part if children are to become writers, ensuring that they are exposed to informative and stimulating demonstrations and helping and encouraging them to read and to write. Teachers are influential, as models as well as guides, as children explore and discover the worlds of writing – or decide that writing is something they will never voluntarily do inside school or out.

(Smith, 1982: 201)

Smith expresses some of the key ideas of the process approach and particularly the notion of children being regarded as writers from the start. However, the idea of the teacher as primarily a demonstrator, as role model, and as an 'encourager' has recently received repeated criticism because of the perception that this does not involve direct instruction. Graves's work was in sympathy with these ideas and he developed classroom routines which turned the theories into a practical reality for many teachers.

One of the fundamental principles of Graves's process approach has been downplayed in the UK. He was quite clear that children needed to be offered choices in their writing.

Children who are fed topics, story starters, lead sentences, even opening paragraphs as a steady diet for three or four years, rightfully panic when topics have to come from them . . . Writers who do not learn to choose topics wisely lose out on the strong link between voice and subject . . . The data show that writers who learn to choose topics well make the most significant growth in both information and skills at the point of best topic. With best topic the child exercises strongest control, establishes ownership, and with ownership, pride in the piece.

(Graves, 1983: 21)

It has been argued that the National Curriculum and more recently the Framework for Teaching do recognise the influence of the process approach. However, this influence is mainly restricted to the important notion that writing often needs to pass through a series of drafts. The central and fundamental point about child choice and children as authors is not part of national curricula.

The previous point illustrates one of the many ways that ideas from educators in other countries are usually modified in order to fit the UK system. In spite of this fact Graves's most popular work *Writing: Teachers and Children at Work* is still usually cited as an account of the process approach. It is perhaps time to reappraise Graves's specific influence on the UK. Wyse (1998) does this in *Primary Writing* where he shows that one of the striking differences with, for example, the USA is the way that British teachers have used the process approach to enhance other writing approaches. In a more recent article he also suggests that a renaissance of a more child-centred approach to writing might be achieved by using the recent statutory strengthening of children's rights (Wyse, 1999).

The genre theorists

In the late 1980s the popularity and optimism of the process approach began to be attacked by a group of Australian academics called the 'genre theorists' (➡ Chapter 14, 'Genre and the process of writing'). Once again the tide began to turn away from the importance of self expression towards greater emphasis on skills and direct instruction. The three authors who perhaps have been referred to most in relation to genre theory are J. R. Martin, Frances Christie and Joan Rothery. One of the key texts from 1987 was 'The Place of Genre in Learning' where these three authors put forward some of their ideas as a response to other authors in the book. They also offered some criticisms of the process approach.

In a section of Martin et al's chapter they examine the notion of 'freedom' during the process approach. They ask a series of important questions:

> What is freedom? Is a progressive process writing classroom really free? Does allowing children to choose their own topics, biting one's tongue in conferences and encouraging ownership, actually encourage the development of children's writing abilities?
>
> (Martin et al, 1987: 77)

To answer these questions the authors report on a school in the Australian Northern Territory with a large population of Aboriginal children. They claimed that over the course of the year the children had only written about one of four topics: '(a) visiting friends and relatives; (b) going hunting for bush tucker; (c) sporting events; (d) movies or TV shows they have seen' (Martin et al, 1987: 77). This example is used to cast doubts on the effectiveness of the process approach claiming that the range of forms that children choose is limited.

Martin et al's answer to the perceived problems of the process approach was didactic teaching on the structure and range of various genres that are available. For example, if the teacher were reading *Little Red Riding Hood* she might refer to the stages of a genre. In the narrative genre they suggest that these stages are 'Orientation, Complication and Resolution'. Later in the chapter they suggest that these could be added to: 'Abstract/Orientation/Complication/Evaluation/Resolution/Coda' (➡ Chapter 5, 'Analysing texts').

Their strong views on direct instruction are illustrated by a specific criticism the genre theorists make of Graves's (1983) work. They examine an extract from Graves' seminal book.

Mr Sitka: What is this paper about, Anton?
Anton: Well, I'm not sure. At first I thought it was going to be about when we won the game in overtime with the penalty kick. But then I got going on how our team had won because we were in such good shape for overtime. You see, the other team hardly move at the end. Took me way back to our earlier practises when I hated the coach so much. Gosh, I don't know what it's about.

Mr Sitka: Where are you now in the draft?

Anton: Oh, I've just got the part down about when we won in over-time.

Mr Sitka: So, you've just got started then. Well, its probably too early to tell what it's about. What did you figure to do with the next draft then?

Anton: I don't know. I don't want to just write and wander around. I've written about when we've won but it just sort of has me stuck at that point.

Mr Sitka: Tell me about that coach of yours.

Anton: God, how I hated him! I almost quit three or four times maybe. I thought he couldn't stand me. He'd yell, catch every little thing I did wrong. We'd run and run until we couldn't stand up. Have some passing drills. Then he'd run us some more. He'd just stand there yellin' and puffin' on his cigar. Course he was right. When we won the championship, I think it went write back to those early practices.

Mr Sitka: The way you tell it sounds as though you have quite a live beginning to your story. Try writing about early practises, then see what your piece is about.

(Graves, 1983: 114)

Martin et al cite this extract as an example of 'unfocused conferencing'. They criticise the teacher for not directly helping the young writer to 'shape the structure of his narrative'. They go on to suggest that this kind of indirect guidance will only benefit bright middle-class children who are 'sure to read between the lines and learn to write, apparently effortlessly, without being taught'.

In addition to these crude views about class and ability, their criticisms reflect a distorted view of effective teaching and learning. In the extract the pupil does the bulk of the talking. It seems that the teacher has developed a good working relationship as the pupil is confident to express a range of ideas and issues. The teacher is clearly encouraging the pupil to think independently and resists telling him what to do. Instead he encourages the pupil to reflect on, and begin to solve, some of his own problems. The charge that the teacher does nothing to directly help the writer shape the narrative is plainly mistaken. Each of the teacher's questions directs the writer's attention to important aspects of the written structure such as: the theme of the writing; the direction of the piece; where the pupil is in the process; a potentially interesting addition to the plot; how the piece might begin. The teacher's final piece of dialogue does just what Martin et al say the teacher does *not* do, i.e. directly help the writer with the structure: 'The way you tell it sounds as though you have quite a live beginning to your story. Try writing about early practices, then see what your piece is about.' The teacher offers some focused positive feedback designed to support the pupil's self-esteem and to signal a potentially effective opening to the narrative. The teacher is quite clear in the suggestion that Anton should use the 'early practices' as the beginning of the story. Following this suggestion the teacher presumably feels that Anton is capable of taking that opening further so he does not offer other specific recommendations. However, the teacher would, of course, be aware that later on he might return if Anton struggles with the subsequent section, but he has at least given him the opportunity to solve the next problem himself.

The Framework for Teaching

In spite of a number of serious criticisms (Barrs, 1991; Cairney, 1992) the views of the genre theorists have proved to be influential, and the Framework for Teaching reflects a number of their views. There is an equal emphasis on fiction and non-fiction that has been informed by the view that there was too much 'story' writing happening in primary schools, although the genre theorists were not the only people to suggest this. The objectives for written composition are no longer about writing to interest and excite readers, finding a vehicle for expression, writing to explore cross-curricular themes, writing as art, but are much more about the analysis of texts. The importance of writing for real purposes and reasons in order to communicate meaning has been replaced by an emphasis on textual analysis as this selection from the Framework for Teachers indicates (DfEE, 1998: 38–39).

Year 4 Term 1

Text-level work

4   to explore narrative order: identify and map out the main stages of the story: introductions → build-ups → climaxes or conflicts → resolutions;

10 to plan a story identifying the stages of its telling;

16 to identify different types of text, e.g. their content, structure, vocabulary, style, lay-out and purpose;

26 to improve the cohesion of written instructions and directions through the use of link phrases and organisational devices such as sub-headings and numbering.

Here we see the emphasis on the larger text structures that the genre theorists thought were so important (➡ Chapter 14, 'Genre and the process of writing' for further information). The phrase 'pupils should be taught' that is a subheading to all sections of the Framework ensure that these text structures will receive direct teaching.

There can be little doubt that the Framework for Teaching has moved English education much closer to the nineteenth century models than to those of the 1960s and 1970s. At the beginning of this chapter we described how Shayer (1972) argued that at the beginning of the twentieth century the primary child was expected to imitate, copy, or reproduce in order to learn English.

'Imitation' has been respun: 'to study in depth one genre and produce an extended piece of similar writing; parody a literary text; to use different genres as models to write', but the objectives in the Framework are certainly concerned with imitation rather than authorship. As we currently write, creativity and self-expression are temporarily seen as less important than the acquisition of skills but, undoubtedly, serious questions will continue to be asked about the status of writing in the Framework for Teaching, and changes will be made. This is not to cynically suggest that history simply repeats itself; the evidence in this chapter has shown that this is not the case. However, as our understanding of how children learn to write is still incomplete it is inevitable that aspects of teaching will continue to be modified while others will continue unchanged.

Practice points

- Improve your observation and interaction skills by increasing your knowledge of writing development.
- Use time outside of the literacy hour to develop extended writing including classroom publishing.
- Use your observations to adjust your planning for writing so that children's actual needs are met.

Glossary

Affixes – letters that are added to the roots of words to produce suffixes and prefixes.

Construct – in this context the word is a noun – as opposed to a verb – and means a specific way of thinking about something.

Copywriting – A method for teaching writing that encourages children to copy before they write for meaning.

Homonyms – a word with the same spelling or pronunciation as another, but with different meaning or origin.

Pedagogy – approaches to teaching.

Phoneme – the smallest unit of sound in a spoken word

Phonemic strategies – the use of sounds to help reading or writing

Phonological knowledge – understanding of the links between sounds and symbols

Seminal work – classic (often old) academic work that continues to be referenced by large numbers of writers.

Transactional writing – concerned with getting things done: e.g. information, instructions, persuasion, etc.

References

Allen, D. (1980) *English Teaching Since 1965: How Much Growth?* London: Heinemann Educational Books.

Barrs, M. (1991) 'Genre Theory: What's it all about?' *Language Matters*, 1991/92 (1): 9–16.

Bissex, G.L. (1980) *GNYS AT WRK: A Child Learns to Write and Read.* Cambridge, MA: Harvard University Press.

Britton, J. (1970) *Language and Learning.* Harmondsworth: Penguin.

Browne, A. (1996) *Developing Language and Literacy 3–8.* London: Paul Chapman.

Cairney, T. (1992) Mountain or Mole Hill: The Genre Debate Viewed from 'Down Under'. *Reading,* 26 (1): 23–29.

Clegg, A. B. (1964) *The Excitement of Writing.* London: Chatto and Windus.

Czerniewska, P. (1992) *Learning about Writing.* Oxford: Blackwell.

Department for Education and Employment (DfEE) (1998) *National Literacy Strategy Framework for Teaching.* London: DfEE.

Gentry, J. (1982) 'An analysis of developmental spelling in GNYS AT WRK'. *Reading Teacher,* 36: 192–200.

Graves, D.H. (1983) *Writing: Teachers and Children at Work.* Portsmouth, NH: Heinemann Educational Books.

Hall, N. (1987) *The Emergence of Literacy.* Sevenoaks: Hodder & Stoughton.

Harste, J.C., Woodward, V.A. and Burke, C.L. (1984) *Language Stories and Literacy Lessons.* Portsmouth, NH, Heinemann Educational Books.

Martin, J.R., Christie, F. and Rothery, J. (1987) Social Processes in Education: A reply to Sawyer and Watson (and others), in I. Reid (ed.) *The Place of Genre in Learning.* Victoria: Deakin University.

Protheroe, R. (1978) 'When in doubt, write a poem'. *English in Education,* 12 (1): 9–21.

Shayer, D. (1972) *The Teaching of English in Schools 1900–1970.* London: Routledge and Kegan Paul.

Smith, F. (1982) *Writing and the Writer.* Portsmouth, NH: Heinemann Educational Books.

Wyse, D. (1998) *Primary Writing.* Buckingham: Open University Press.

Wyse, D. (1999) 'Turning Children on to Writing'. *Literacy and Learning* October/November, (4): 37–39.

Annotated bibliography

Bissex, G.L. (1980) *GNYS AT WRK: A Child Learns to Write and Read.* Cambridge, MA: Harvard University Press.
An extremely thorough and insightful account of one child's development. A rich picture is combined with knowledgeable academic analysis: an important book.
L2 ***

Campbell, R. (1999) *Literacy from Home to School: Reading with Alice.*
Another single case study of a child's development. Fewer links with academic literature than Bissex's, but a rich picture of the kinds of experiences that Alice had with reading at home.
L1 **

Czerniewska, P. (1992) *Learning about writing.* Oxford: Blackwell.
Summarises many of the experiences of the National Writing Project which was so influential during the 1980s.
L2 *

Chapter 13

Composition

The composition side of writing is one that has at times been neglected. This chapter starts by making the distinction between composition and transcription. The important ideas of audience and purpose are followed by examples of writing activities both within and outside the literacy hour.

During the 1980s many teachers were realising that all was not well in the teaching of writing. One of the key problems was that many children were being turned off by writing, and this was supported by some evidence from the Assessment of Performance Unit (APU) (☞). The APU found that as many as four in ten children did not find writing an enjoyable experience and 'not less than one in ten pupils [had] an active dislike of writing and endeavour[ed] to write as little as possible' (DES, 1988: 170). Somewhat later the National Writing Project gathered evidence that many children, particularly young children, tended to equate writing with presentation skills rather than content. Wray (1993) also acknowledged that previous research evidence confirmed this but his own research suggested that there may be a developmental influence. He argued that perhaps children are concerned about the aspects that are 'bothering them at the time' (Wray, 1993: 7), suggesting that children in the early stages might naturally be concerned with particular skills as they try to master them.

One of the problems in the teaching of writing is to ensure that the balance between content and the presentational aspects of writing is correct. Throughout the history of the teaching of writing, presentational aspects have frequently dominated the curriculum. The following quote from a research study that looked at the teaching of initial literacy summed this up very well:

In commenting on the teaching of writing, it is important to note what appeared to be a concentration on 'secretarial' aspects of written work: the focus in some cases on surface features of writing as opposed to matters relating to content, form, and style; the simplistic notions of 'redrafting' that prevailed in some classes; and the relative lack of exploitation of the word-processing facilities that were available to pupils in some cases, particularly with regard to redrafting.

(Cato et al 1992: 36)

Frank Smith (1982: 20) made the distinction shown in Box 13.1 between composition and transcription.

Composition (author)	Transcription (secretary)
Getting ideas Selecting words Grammar	Physical effort of writing Spelling Capitalisation Punctuation Paragraphs Legibility

Box 13.1 (Reproduced from F. Smith (1982) *Writing and the Writer,* Oxford: Heineman Educational, p. 20. Used with permission)

The NLS Framework for Teaching makes the distinction by having 'writing composition' as text level work. Transcriptional aspects are covered in word and sentence level work though: sentence construction and punctuation, spelling conventions and rules, and handwriting.

The Framework for Teaching is built on the idea that the explicit teaching of the various genres (➡Chapter 14, 'Genre and the process of writing') will help children to be able to compose them. Although there is evidence from research that this does indeed help children's writing, it should be remembered that all writers approach composition in different ways. Carter (1999) collected together the thoughts of a number of writers including the routines that they used for writing. Helen Cresswell, a prolific and talented author for both children and adults, describes her way of composing:

> With most of my books I simply write a title and a sentence, and I set off and the road leads to where it finishes. All my books are like journeys or explorations. Behind my desk I used to have this saying by Leo Rosten pinned up on the wall that went 'When you don't know where a road leads, it sure as hell will take you there.' When I first read that, I thought, that's exactly it! That's what happens when I start on my books – I really don't know what's going to happen; It's quite dangerous, in a way. I often put off starting because it seems a bit scary. Yet at the end of the day, I feel that a story has gone where it's meant to have gone.
>
> (Carter, 1999: 118)

There are other writers who plan in detail before they write a word. Children as writers should be given the same opportunities to find ways to compose that suit their style.

AUDIENCE AND PURPOSE

In order to compose meaningfully writers need to have clear audiences and purposes. Genuine audiences are sometimes difficult to find, but one example that has been well used in primary schools is the publication of books by older children for their younger peers. The purpose of this task can be made more meaningful if the children interview the readers to try to find out the kind of book they might like. The internet is also offering the chance of audiences around the globe who can be contacted with ease. Political activity is another fruitful area for generating real audiences and purposes. For example, the environment is something that children are often interested in to the extent that they can be committed to writing to organisations with a view to limiting environmental damage. It is not practical to organise real audiences all the time so teachers have successfully created imaginary audiences and have used the available audiences of the school community to good effect.

Czerniewska (1992) illustrated the work of a reception teacher who was involved in the National Writing Project. A traditional early years activity – baking cakes – was used as the basis for generating audiences and purposes. At the local supermarket the children had to match their shopping lists with items on the shelves; spare cakes were sent to the nursery with a greeting card; the nursery children replied with a large thank you letter and asked for the recipe; the resulting recipe took the form of pictograms, packaging and some phrases 'scribed' (☞) by the teacher. More recently the internet has also been presenting many opportunities for communicating with real audiences, for example the Tesco Schoolnet 2000 gives young authors the chance to publish their work on the world wide web (http://www.tesco.schoolnet2000.com/welcome/1.html).

Collins highlights the importance of different purposes for writing:

> The purpose of the writing also affects composition, whether it be to entertain, persuade or explain. Purpose influences the linguistic structure of the piece and helps the child consider the language choices to be made. The purpose of the writing also links with the form that the writing will take; maybe a letter, diary or pamphlet. It should not be forgotten that one form of writing can be used for different purposes and different audiences; just think of all the different pamphlets that you see in a week.
>
> (Collins, 1998: 44)

STIMULI FOR WRITING

One of the key questions when planning the teaching of writing is 'what kind of stimulus should I offer?' In other words the teacher has to decide what kind of encouragement, activities and experiences children need in order to help them to write. These decisions should be affected by consideration of children's motivation. Most teachers make the sensible assumption that when children are not motivated they do not learn as well as they could.

When planning the kind of activities to stimulate children's writing it is helpful to think of a continuum between open and closed activities (see Figure 13.1). The Framework for Teaching rarely emphasises the open end of our continuum. If we take Year 6 Term 3 as an example, we can see that some of the objectives are closed: '4 to revise and consolidate work from previous five terms with particular emphasis on: unstressed vowel spellings in polysyllabic words'. These kinds of objectives test the skills of the teacher who is trying to achieve a meaningful purpose for writing, particularly with the strict timings and organisation that are recommended by the literacy hour. However, the more open objectives are no less testing within the timings of the hour: '8 to use a reading journal effectively to raise and refine personal responses to a text and prepare for discussion'.

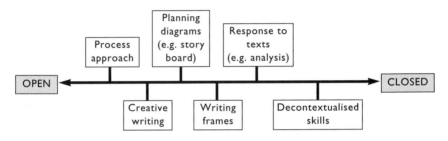

Figure 13.1 Writing tasks continuum

The most successful open activities are based on creativity, personal expression and the process of writing. As an example of open activities the 'process approach' has an enviable track record in motivating children to write and is based on establishing authorship in the classroom supported by a publishing process (➡ Chapter 14, 'Genre and the process of writing'). The more structured use of artefacts and first-hand experiences are also a well-established means of encouraging writing which the three following examples illustrate.

1   Kirklees Local Education Authority had an extensive range of boxed artefacts and books available from the library service that supported cross-curricular work. One of the highlights was 'granny's attic' which contained a treasure trove of historical artefacts and documents that could be used as the basis for children's stories about the origins of the objects and a wide range of historical work.

2   A maths lesson was postponed for an hour when it began to hail and the children's collective attention was focused on the sudden change in light, the noise, the heightened sense of unease and danger. Standing outside, underneath a canopy, they began to write what they saw. Rebecca (8) wrote:

Hail

Suddenly, the light changed
Crisp, bright, yellow
I rushed outside and stood
Waiting impatiently
Just as the hail fell
Heavy ricochets
The air smelt, strangely
And the breath was sucked
From my lips
The wind changed the weather vane
And made the bushes dance
In a moment it was gone
The air hung grey empty
The clanging flagpole signalled
All clear

3   Many children are not able to sustain observational writing in this way, but they should still feel their work has worth and potential. A class of children on a field trip to the Northumbrian coast sat beside the harbour watching the day developing. One girl wrote a series of unrelated observations which neither inspired nor interested her. She was asked to select two or three elements of her writing which might 'feel right' together, and to express them in the smallest space which achieved what she wanted to say. Charlotte wrote:

Soon the tide
And the birds will follow

It took Charlotte some considerable time to arrive at these two lines, and it brings to mind an anecdote from Oscar Wilde. He once said that he had spent the morning working on a piece of writing and by lunch had added a comma. In the afternoon he took it out again.

In the past there have been criticisms that too much writing in primary schools has been dominated by story and expressive forms. One influential group of academics dubbed the 'genre theorists' (☞) had particularly strong views about this (➡ Chapter 12, 'The development of writing'). They offered two main ideas: (1) Children need explicit teaching about the characteristics of different genres (➡ Chapter 5, 'Analysing texts' for example of narrative structure); (2) Children should be exposed to a much wider range of genres than mainly narrative ones. The genre theorists are not without their critics, but they did highlight the fact that non-fiction genres were being neglected.

NON-FICTION TEXTS

One of the things that teachers are currently required to know is the way that instructional texts (one example of a non-fiction text) use imperative (☞)

language. The Framework requires that children should be taught:

> **Year 2 Term 1**
>
> **Text-level work:**
>
> **Non-Fiction**
>
> **Writing composition**
>
> **18** to use appropriate register in writing instructions, i.e. direct, impersonal, building on texts read.

An example of a typical instruction text is a *recipe*, but we should be careful before we assume that all recipes are 'direct and impersonal'. First of all one of the important aspects of many cookery books is the introductory material for the recipes that is designed to whet your appetite:

> This simple chicken dish is a great favourite with our children. I generally serve it with plain long-grain rice and 'Whole green lentils with garlic and onion'.
>
> (Jaffrey, 1982: 75)

Even in the instructions for the recipes the texts are made more interesting by personalising the commentary:

> Add the eggs and blitz for a further 1 minute. Add the cream, brandy and jus if using. (The jus is optional for this recipe, but I find it gives a little depth and flavour to the parfait.)
>
> (Rhodes, 1994: 62)

In spite of the use of different written voices for effect it is undoubtedly true that recipes do use imperative language, and this is clearly signalled by the regular placing of the verb at the beginning of the sentence: e.g. 'Add the eggs . . .'. It is important that you ask yourself when is the best time to analyse imperative forms in recipes. Perhaps after doing some real cooking, eating the food, painting the ingredients, talking about the tastes, inventing recipes, blind tasting, etc. It is important that you continue to do these things which contextualise the abstract analytical work that is expected in the Framework for Teaching.

The research from the 'Exeter Extended Literacy Project' (EXEL) developed the idea of 'frames' as a way of supporting children's non-fiction writing. Lewis and Wray explain the notion of writing frames:

> Writing frames are outline structures, enabling children to produce non-fiction writing in the different generic forms. Given these structures or skeleton outlines of starters, connectives and sentence modifiers, children can concentrate on communicating what they want to say. As they prac-

tise building their writing around the frames, they become increasingly familiar with the generic forms.

(Lewis and Wray, 1995: 53)

One of the important ideas behind writing frames is that they are intended to support writing done in meaningful contexts; the sort of contexts where appropriate audiences and purposes have been facilitated. Lewis and Wray are quite clear that 'using the frames for the direct teaching of generic structures in skills-centred lessons' is inappropriate.

There are six writing frames: recount, report, procedure, explanation, persuasive argument, discussion. Of these it is perhaps the writing of argument that has proved the most demanding for teachers and children alike. The following example shows how a child used the writing frame: the child's text is in italic and the frame text is normal.

Although not everybody would agree, I want to argue that
Children should not wear school uniform.

I have several reason for arguing for this point of view. My first reason is
That they feel more comfortable in clothes which they choose to wear. They would feel more relaxed and be able to work better and concentrate more on their work.

Another reason is

There wouldn't be the problem of parents not wanting to buy uniforms because they think they are too expensive.

Furthermore

Sometimes you might wake up and find your two lots of uniform in the wash.

Therefore, although some people argue that

Children might take it past the limits.

I think I have shown that

Children should be able to choose their clothing just as adults do, as long as they wear sensible clothes.

(Lewis and Wray, 1995: 85)

It is pointed out that prior to using this kind of structure, teacher modelling and shared construction of texts is important. We would also point out that children need to experience the extensive reading of any genre that they are trying to write themselves. In terms of written argument and persuasion, adverts offer a rich resource: significantly they combine text and image to communicate their message, sometimes requiring a higher level of thought to read the underlying meanings.

The writing frames are designed to be flexibly applied, and it is intended that children should move towards independence. This means that the form of the frame can be modified to offer a different level of support. If we return to written argument, Box 13.2 gives an example that includes a list of connectives:

I would like to persuade you that	These words and phrases might
	help you
	because
There are several points I want to make	*therefore*
to support my point of view. Firstly	*you can see*
	a supporting argument
	this shows that
	another piece of evidence is

Box 13.2 (Source: M. Lewis and D. Wray (1995) *Developing Children's Non-Fiction Writing*. Leamington Spa: Scholastic, p. 85)

OTHER RESEARCH

One of the features of writing in the Framework for Teaching is that it tends to focus on products: write a balanced report; parody a literary text; summarise a passage; write own poems experimenting with active verbs and personification, and so on. This contrasts with some of the most important research in the field which has identified the writing process as an area of particular importance. At the beginning of this section we outlined Frank Smith's distinction between composition and transcription. In the composition column of his diagram the first line says 'getting ideas'. As you probably realised after reading Helen Cresswell's thoughts on her professional writing, the job of getting ideas is fundamental to the task of composition. Although many of the objectives do require young writers to generate ideas they are not ideas such as 'what shall I write?', 'What form shall I write it in?', 'Who shall I write with?', 'Who do I want to read my writing?'.

Donald Graves's research and writing has been very influential on the teaching of writing in English-speaking countries. His research led him to believe that the process of writing should be the main focus of teacher's work not particular products. He was convinced that children should be encouraged where possible to decide on their own ideas for writing and that this would motivate them and help them develop a voice as a writer. Although Graves' ideas have been very popular Dahl and Farnan point out: 'Our review of writing workshop references reveals that there are far more books about how to conduct these programs than systematic studies about their effectiveness'. (1998: 49)

Wyse's (1998) research generated two models of composition: one through the analysis of the process of children's writing and the other through the analysis of teacher's reflections on their teaching of writing. He concluded that children need to control five key areas if they are engaged in purposeful writing:

1   They must be clear about the meaning they are intending to convey.
2   They must organise their time and resources.
3   They need to generate ideas.
4   They have to learn how to structure text.
5   They need a strong awareness of the connections between readers and writers.

The analysis of teacher's reflections revealed the importance of: (1) the ways that language is chosen and constructed; (2) the control of written forms; (3) the generation of ideas. Like the Framework for Teaching the importance of genre or written forms is once again apparent and this relates to the importance that Bereiter and Scardamalia (1993) attach to 'discourse schema'. Where Wyse differs from the Framework is in the belief that the command of particular genres should come through choice and can only be developed through extended opportunities over considerable periods of time not through 20 minute bursts.

The teaching and learning of language and literacy has to focus on activities that motivate learners and encourage them to engage in a higher order of thinking while learning essential skills. As teachers these are ideas that we need to apply critically to the approach to the teaching of writing evident in the National Literacy Strategy. As Fox (1999) has found, teachers are already modifying the prescriptions of the strategy. For example, ways are being found to enhance extended writing, to offer more one-to-one support, to encourage children to make choices and to find more imaginative ways to stimulate writing.

Practice Points

- Be clear about the distinction between composition and transcription.
- In the early stages of writing, composition is most important. Without composition there is no transcription.
- Remember that different drafts of writing can emphasise different aspects of either composition or transcription.

Glossary

Assessment of Performance Unit – a government initiated unit that monitored standards during the 1980s.

Genre theorists – group of mainly Australian academics who suggested that English teaching in primary schools should focus more on the larger text structures.

Imperative – a sentence which is a request for action.

Scribe – the teacher or other experienced writer who writes down what the child says.

References

Bereiter, C. and Scardamalia, M. (1987) *The Psychology of Written Composition*. Hillsdale, NJ: Lawrence Erlbaum Associates. Quoted in R. Beard (ed), *Teaching Literacy Balancing Perspectives*. London: Hodder & Stoughton, 1993, pp. 159,162.

Carter, J. (1999) *Talking Books: Children's Authors Talk about the Craft, Creativity and Process of Writing*. London: Routledge.

Collins, F. M. (1998) 'Composition', in J. Graham and A. Kelly (eds) *Writing Under Control: Teaching Writing in the Primary School*. London: David Fulton.

Czerniewska, P. (1992) *Learning about Writing*. Oxford: Blackwell.

Dahl, K. L. and Farnan, N. (1998) *Children's Writing: Perspectives From Research*. Chicago, IL: National Reading Conference.

Department of Education and Science Assessment of Performance Unit (APU) (1988) *Language Performance in Schools. Review of APU Language Monitoring 1979–1983*. London: HMSO.

Fox, R. (1999) 'Effective Teachers of Writing at Key Stage 1: A Summary of Impressions'. Personal correspondence: Draft paper for UKRA conference.

Jaffrey, M. (1982) *Madhur Jaffrey's Indian Cookery*. London: BBC Publications

Lewis, M. and Wray, D. (1995) *Developing Children's Non-Fiction Writing: Working with Writing Frames*. Leamington Spa: Scholastic.

Martin, J.R., Christie, F. and Rothery, J. (1987) 'Social processes in education: A reply to Sawyer and Watson (and others)', in I. Reid (ed.) *The Place of Genre in Learning*. Victoria: Deakin University.

Rhodes, G. (1994) *Rhodes Around Britain*. London: BBC Publications.

Wray, David. *What Do Children Think About Writing?* [online] NISS EBSCO MasterFILE service. *Educational Review*, 45: 67–78. Carfax. 1993 [cited 14-11-97]. Available from:
   http://www.niss.ac.uk/cgi-bin/ebbrowse.p

Wyse, D. (1998) *Primary Writing*. Buckingham: Open University Press.

Annotated bibliography

Click software. [online – cited 26-6-00]. Available from:
   http://www.cricksoft.com/index.htm
   'Clicker 4' is award winning software that can support the writing process. It allows children to click onscreen cells to insert text into documents. This site includes clicker screens (called grids) that can be downloaded and used to support teaching.
   L1 *

Collins, F. M. (1998) Composition. In J. Graham and A. Kelly (eds) *Writing Under Control: Teaching Writing in the Primary School*. London: David Fulton.
   This chapter looks in more depth at a number of the issues that we discuss. Includes useful reminders about bilingual children and the use of drama to stimulate writing.

Lewis, M. and Wray, D. (1995) *Developing Children's Non-Fiction Writing: Working with Writing Frames*. Leamington Spa: Scholastic.
A thorough account that includes the rationale for the use of writing frames and examples of practice.
L2 *

Ramsden, S. and Ahmed, R. (1997) *NATE Shared Reading: Journey to Jo'Burg*. Sheffield: NATE.
Examples of useful writing activities related to key texts. At the time a rare example of such a resource aimed at KS2.
L1 *

Riley, J. and Reedy, D. (2000) *Developing Writing for Different Purposes: Teaching about Genre in the Early Years*. London: Paul Chapman.
Useful reminder of many of the main issues in the teaching of writing. Includes interesting six-point theory on the teaching of writing developed in New Zealand.
L2 **

Chapter 14

Genre and the process of writing

Our understanding of the process of writing has grown over the last 20 years. The 'process approach' has been very successful in motivating children and teachers and the first part of this chapter outlines the approach. In recent years genre theory has come to exert considerable influence on literacy teaching and the second half of the chapter looks at this. We conclude with thoughts on critical literacy.

In the past, writing in primary classrooms was synonymous with copying and handwriting practice in addition to the use of decontextualised (☞) grammar exercises (➡ Chapter 12, 'The development of writing'). The idea that children needed to experience the writing and composing of their own texts was alien to these earlier methods. There was also a lack of understanding of the ways that all writing is created as part of a process. Since that time we now understand much more about the differences between the process of writing and the end products.

THE PROCESS APPROACH

One of the movements that has contributed to our understanding of the process of writing is the approach called the 'process approach'. It is important to make a distinction between the process of writing, which occurs whenever someone does some writing, and the process approach which is a distinct method for the teaching of writing. The process approach is typified by several key features within the classroom: the teacher establishes a developing community of young writers; most of those writers are offered high levels of control over the process of writing; children's earliest attempts at mark-making are seen as writing, and the writing develops within a publishing cycle that mirrors aspects of the publication processes in the world outside the classroom.

The idea of children making choices over what they should write, who they should write with, how they should publish, when they should finish, etc., seems somewhat radical in the present climate. However, in the experience of one of the writers of this book – as a primary teacher and language coordinator – one of the great successes of the process approach was the motivation for writing that it generated: two anecdotes illustrate the flavour of this motivation.

My first job was for the Inner London Education Authority (ILEA) in a school situated between King's Cross and Euston stations. I had chosen to focus on writing for my college dissertation so I was very keen to get some writing going with the children in my first class. Each weekend I prepared what I hoped would be interesting tasks for the children, looking forward to working on them during the week. But as the year reached the half way point I became aware that the children were not particularly motivated by the writing tasks. When one of the boys called David said 'Oh no not writing again' I hit a bit of a low point. At this time I took part in one of the excellent INSET courses that were organised by the ILEA. One of the advisory teachers recommended one of Graves' books which I read. From that point I decided to initiate a regular writing workshop in the classroom. The transformation in the children's motivation was remarkable. Now David said 'When are we doing writing workshop again?'.

Some years later I was once again struck by the particular motivation that the process approach could generate. Following some very heavy snow in West Yorkshire only a handful of the children had been able to attend school for a few days. Once the majority of the class returned the regular writing workshop sessions continued.

Teacher:	As you know this morning is writing workshop
Various children:	Yesss!
	Yes! I've got this idea . . .
	What are you gonna do? (*Excited whispering*)
Teacher:	I'm sure you all missed school when it was closed because of the snow!
Children:	Yeah, yeah . . . (*Sarcastically*).
Saiba:	(*Aside*) I did, I wanted to do writing workshop.

Motivation is essential if children are to achieve the highest possible standards in their work. This motivation can only be achieved if children are offered regular opportunities to make decisions about their learning. In terms of writing this means sometimes being encouraged to generate their own ideas and carry them out. It also requires the recognition that in order to learn, people need to make mistakes and to have those mistakes viewed by their teachers as positive moments in the learning process.

The main teaching vehicle for the process approach is the regular writing workshop. The classroom is organised so that children have independent access to all the resources they need when progressing from initial idea through to published final product. The writing workshop begins with a 15 minute 'mini lesson' which tackles a variety of issues and objectives. At the beginning of the year strategies for generating ideas and the organisational details of the workshop are covered. As the year progresses the mini lessons are designed to link with the children's needs as demonstrated in the workshops. The whole class discussions at the beginning and end of the workshop contrast with 'writing conferences'. These are the periods when the teacher sits with children as they are writing and offers advice on how to progress (➡ example of dialogue in Chapter 12, 'The development of writing'). Writing folders are used by the children to keep the various drafts of writing in progress, and these folders can also be used to facilitate record-keeping. The reading area of the classroom contains books that children have published in the classroom and these become extra reading resources for all.

If all literacy lessons were to consist of mechanistically timed activities supporting government prescribed objectives, children would not necessarily learn the skills and knowledge that are necessary to make productive and meaningful decisions about writing. So although there are those who will argue that the National Literacy Strategy does not preclude initiatives such as the process approach, and informed teachers will make sure that the hour is subverted in the best interests of their children, there can be no doubt that the growing recognition of children as authors that was developed in the National Writing Project and extended in the Language in the National Curriculum Project will face a stern challenge. The notion of children as authors and child choice are not concepts that are readily found in the Framework for Teaching. As we have indicated in the last chapter, teachers are concerned about the place of extended writing in the literacy hour, and in the light of this many are using approaches like the process approach outside of the hour.

GENRE THEORY

The influence of the process approach on the Framework for Teaching has been minimal in spite of the importance that is attached to 'drafting' and revising in the National Curriculum; genre theory has had a more profound influence. Some of the objectives from the Framework for Teaching illustrate this:

> **Year 6 Term 2**
> **Text-level work:**
> 1   to understand aspects of narrative structure.
> 10   to use different genres as models to write.
> 12   to study in depth one genre and produce an extended piece of
>   similar writing.

Genre is usually regarded as a structural form. *Chambers English Dictionary* defines genre as 'a literary or artistic type or style'. For example, in music genres include the symphony, the quartet and the concerto. In writing genres include narrative, poetry, article, diary etc. However, the genre theorists' definition was radical: any 'staged, goal oriented social process'

(Martin, Christie and Rothery, 1987: 59). This wider definition allows the inclusion of genres that emphasise the spoken form as well as written forms, and includes consideration of the links between the two modes. So 'jokes, sermons, appointment making, anecdotes, weather reports' etc. are all included as examples of genres.

The genre theorists are a group of mainly Australian academics who put forward strong opinions on the teaching of writing in primary schools. One of their key ideas was that the larger structures of texts should be explicitly taught and not left to develop through experience alone. This idea was contradictory to the philosophies of the process approach.

Littlefair (1991) carried out an analysis of a range of books used in upper primary and lower secondary contexts. She concluded that they could be categorised into four genres.

Books in the literary genre

Authors who have a purpose of narrating, of describing personal or vicarious experience, or of experimenting with the use of language itself.

Books in the expository genre

Authors who plan to describe or explain objectively, to inform, or discuss, or argue.

Books in the procedural genre

Authors who wish to give instruction, or to initiate activities, will write books which fall within the procedural genre. These authors tell us how to undertake various learning strategies or how to complete tasks.

Books in the reference genre

Authors whose purpose is to write sequential information about particular topics, will write books which fall into the reference genre. These authors intend to provide information which can be reasonably referenced.

(Littlefair, 1991: 4)

Other writers have added to these. As far as non-fiction genres are concerned Lewis and Wray (1995) suggest six categories: recount, report, procedure, explanation, persuasion or exposition, discussion and, as we saw in the last chapter these have been used to develop 'writing frames'.

The recent work of Christie and Misson, describes an analysis of some children's texts. One of the texts is by a year 6 child and it is about 'gold mining'. Christie and Misson comment on a number of linguistic features (☞) of the text which they say are characteristic of such a genre. The child uses technical language efficiently and in particular the way it is introduced.

The process starts
when the ore is blasted from the mine
and brought up to the surface.
The ore is very big
when taken from the mine
so before it can be processed
it has to be crushed.
The first stage is 'primary crushing',
when the ore passes through the jaw crusher, the cone crusher
and finally the screen
which only lets particles smaller than 10 mm pass.

(Christie and Misson, 1998: 59)

Christie and Misson point out that the series of conjunctive (☞) relations (in bold) are more varied than the texts they analyse from the younger pupils. The child also uses an authoritative voice towards the reader using the third person (☞) throughout the text.

The introduction to Christie and Misson's book raises some intriguing possibilities for the future direction of literacy frameworks. Two theoretical frameworks are proposed: the first, based on 'systemic functional linguistics', is a familiar one and this formed the basis for genre theory. The crucial aspect of this framework is to think about language not as rules, but 'as offering systems of choices for making meaning '(Christie and Misson, 1998: 10). However, the second framework, although again familiar, is not one that has traditionally been associated with the genre theorists: *'critical theory . . .* does provide a serious, attractive and challenging vision of what literacy teaching might achieve' (1998: 13).

Critical theory is attributed to the brilliant Brazilian educator Paulo Freire. Freire believed that the learning of literacy could not be separated from the political context in which it took place. Much of his work was with the poor people of the world, and he argued that literacy learning had to be closely tied to their political struggles against oppression and poverty.

In the UK, Chris Searle's career in teaching was founded on the importance he placed on the notion of critical literacy. His work with secondary pupils in deprived areas used Freire's ideas as the basis for encouraging his students to make a stance against injustice using literacy as a weapon against those in power. He was sacked on at least two occasions as his fascinating book reveals. We conclude this chapter with an example from Searle's (1998) book that describes the outcome of him being made redundant at one school.

Their own 'cultural action' was confirmed on the green outside the school, next to the churchyard where many of them had composed their poems. Eight-hundred students – virtually the entire school, came out on strike and rallied against the sacking of a teacher who had published their poems. Even as they boycotted class they sang and proclaimed poems. They held aloft a banner with their own poem in support of their sacked teacher and sang an old music-hall song, 'Roll out the Barrel' punning on the name of the headteacher, Geoffrey Barrell.

(Searle, 1998: 23)

We do not anticipate that this latest development in the thoughts of the genre theorists will become national educational policy in the foreseeable future.

Practice points

- Think about using the process approach to encourage extended writing.
- Encourage your children to investigate the different genres and to notice the ways that texts often do not conform.
- Engage the children in creation and analysis of whole texts as a vital part of literacy learning.

Glossary

Conjunctive relations – the use of conjunctions to links parts of text.

Decontextualised – removed from normal context. In the case of writing this means where letters, words and/or sentences are analysed without reference to original text.

Linguistic features – describe the ways that texts are structured including the choice of particular words.

Third person – indicated by the particular use of verbs and pronouns: e.g. 'she said'; 'they are'.

References

Christie, F. and Misson, R. (1998) *Literacy and Schooling*. London: Routledge.

Graves, D. H. (1983) *Writing: Teachers and Children at Work*. Portsmouth, NH: Heinemann Educational Books.

Lewis, M. and Wray, D. (1995) *Developing Children's Non-Fiction Writing: Working with Writing Frames*. Leamington Spa: Scholastic.

Littlefair, A. (1991) *Reading all Types of Writing*. Buckingham: Open University Press.

Martin, J. R., Christie, F. and Rothery, J. (1987) Social Processes in Education: A reply to Sawyer and Watson (and others), in I. Reid (ed.) *The Place of Genre in Learning*. Victoria: Deakin University.

Searle, C. (1998) *None But Our Words: Critical Literacy in Classroom and Community*. Buckingham: Open University Press.

Annotated bibliography

Graves, D. H. (1983) *Writing: Teachers and Children at Work*. Portsmouth, NH: Heinemann Educational Books.
   The classic and seminal text that encouraged people to think again about the process of writing.
   L1 **

Littlefair, A. (1991) *Reading all Types of Writing.* Buckingham: Open University Press.
Relates the ideas of genre and register to both primary and secondary classrooms.
L3 **

Searle, C. (1998) *None But Our Words: Critical Literacy in Classroom and Community.* Buckingham: Open University Press.
Radical and fascinating account of critical literacy in practice.
L3 **

Tesco, Ultralab, Exemplar, Intuitive Media. (1998) Tesco Schoolnet 2000. [online – cited 26-6-00]. Available from:
   http://www.tesco.schoolnet2000.com/welcome/1.html
Schools who register for this project can publish children's writing on the site. The writing is based on a series of projects that children carry out. Includes work in progress and finished work.
L1

Wyse, D. (1998) *Primary Writing.* Buckingham: Open University Press.
The first book length analysis of the process approach in the UK. Practical advice on motivating children to write. In-depth analysis of the composing process. Recognised by DfEE 'National Literacy Strategy Review of Research and other Related Evidence'.
L2 **

Chapter 15

Spelling

In this chapter you will read about some of the changes that have taken place in attitudes towards the teaching of spelling. It also covers the emphasis now given to the use of visual strategies (☞), in particular, and a range of other strategies. Assessing spelling is considered, including the pros and cons of spelling tests.

Do you know what 'ghoti' means? The answer is 'fish'. The idea behind the word is attributed to Bernard Shaw, one of the great thinkers of the twentieth century. It has been used to illustrate the way that English contains many words that seem to have irregular spellings. If you take the sound of 'gh' in enough, the 'o' in women, and the 'ti' in station, you get 'fish'! It is the irregularities of English that make it demanding for children to learn and teachers to teach.

In her seminal book *Spelling: Caught or Taught?* Peters (1985) argued that in the past spelling had not been taught effectively. She suggested that spelling is a particular skill, or set of skills, that requires direct instruction for the majority of school pupils. Children who are not taught to spell properley, often develop a poor self-image as far as spelling is concerned and lack self-confidence in their writing as a whole. Crucially, she emphasised the significance of children acquiring visual rather than auditory (☞) strategies in learning to spell, though she also acknowledged the usefulness of kinaesthetic strategies (☞). She strongly recommended the 'Look-Cover-Write-Check' approach which is advocated by the National Curriculum:

- Look carefully at the word noting particular features such as familiar letter strings, suffixes, etc. and memorise it by saying the word silently, thinking of the meaning of the word and trying to picture it in the mind's eye
- Cover the word
- Write the word from memory
- Check that the word written is correct by matching it with the original
  NB If the spelling is incorrect, the whole process should be repeated.

Having to inspect letters and letter strings closely to reproduce them, initially by copying and later from memory, helps children to develop their general visual strategies. Peters' research also led her to believe that there is a direct correlation between confident, clear and carefully formed handwriting and the development of competent spelling (➡ Chapter 16, 'Handwriting').

Todd (1982) also advised teachers to stress the visual aspects of words to be learned and to explain to their pupils why dependence on auditory aspects can be unreliable. For example writing down what they hear is not helpful to children with a group of words such as *but, mother, book, could, does*. However, Mudd (1994) points out that some children, often poor spellers, can have a visual memory deficit which requires remediation through multi-sensory techniques (☞) or mental linking by remembering sets of objects placed within their sight.

One of the important issues addressed by Mudd concerns the teaching of spelling rules. Her view is that generalisations, not rules, should form the basis for instruction in school. Rules suggest immutability and correctness whereas generalisations suggest something less precise. A generalisation in spelling will be helpful, but it has exceptions. The so-called 'Magic E' rule, for instance, is better taught as a generalisation because there are so many exceptions to it such as *one, have, give, where*. Children can be taught to perceive this as a generalisation rather than a rule and be urged to discover words which confirm or disprove it. Another example is the adding of one consonant or two when adding '*-ing*' to verbs that end in a consonant preceded by a short or long vowel, such as *run* and *shop* or *sleep* and *eat*. This necessitates children being able to distinguish between long and short vowels and, ideally, being able to hear whether the preceding syllable is stressed or not. Mudd clearly has doubts about this and suggests that most novice spellers will need very specific, clearly worded teaching on this to avoid confusion.

SPELLING DEVELOPMENT

A number of writers cite the importance of the work of Gentry (1982) in relation to stages of development for spelling.

> The first stage is the *pre-communicative* stage, when young children are making their first attempts at communicating through writing. The writing may contain a mixture of actual letters, numerals and invented symbols and, as such, it will be unreadable though the writer might be able to explain what they intended to write.
>
> When children are at the second stage, that is *semi-phonetic* stage, they are beginning to understand that letters have sounds and show some knowledge of the alphabet and of letter formation. Words and pictures might be mixed, some words abbreviated or the initial letter might be used to indicate the whole word.
>
> At the *phonetic* stage, children concentrate on a sound–symbol correspondence, their words become more complete and they gain an understanding of word division. They can cope with simple letter strings such as *-nd, -ing* and *-ed'* but have trouble with less obviously phonetic strings such as *-er, -ll* and *-gh*.

During the *transitional* stage children become less dependent on sound–symbol strategies. With the experience of reading and direct spelling instruction they become more aware of the visual aspects of words. They indicate an awareness of the accepted letter strings and basic writing conventions of the English writing system and have an increasing number of correctly spelt words to draw upon.

Finally, the fully competent speller emerges at the *correct* stage. Correct spellings are being produced competently and confidently almost all the time and there is evidence of the effective use of visual strategies and knowledge of word structure. Children at this stage have an understanding of basic rules and patterns of English and a wide spelling vocabulary. They can distinguish homographs (☞), such as tear and tear and homophones (☞), such as pear and pair and they are increasingly able to cope with uncommon and irregular spelling patterns.

Teachers will be able to use the model to identify what stage individual pupils are at, what sort of expectations they might have of these individuals, what targets they might set for these children and what teaching strategies they might usefully employ at any one time. But as with all models, particularly those relating to language, the stages should not be interpreted in a narrow way.

Beard (1999) refers to Gentry's model as being very influential, but he does strike several notes of caution. He maintains that the different stages represent 'complex patterns of thinking and behaviour' and aspects of several stages might be evident in one piece of writing. The teacher therefore needs to evaluate the individual's progress through the stages on the basis of a wide sample of writing each time. He also points to the importance of parental support (making reference to the case-study of Paul Bissex: ➡ Chapter 12, 'The development of writing') and the significance of effective teaching of spelling in school. The rate of children's progression through the stages will vary greatly depending on these factors and, of course, individual differences. Beard also makes the point that 'spelling development should be related to reading development' and that

> Many children seem intuitively to use their phonological knowledge (☞) much more in their early writing than they do in their early reading. However, children clearly need to draw on their learning from the one in order to develop their learning in the other.

> (1999: 44)

SPELLING STRATEGIES AND THE NATIONAL LITERACY STRATEGY

The way in which teachers might use the relationship between spelling and reading is still open to question. The approach taken by the Framework for Teaching is to combine phonics and spelling (along with vocabulary) under 'word-level work' and prescribe spelling strategies that enable visual and aural modes of learning to support and enhance each other.

Visual strategies include recognising common letter strings such as '-*ing*' and grouping words according to spelling patterns: e.g. *could, should, would*. Aural strategies, on the other hand, imply a concentration on sounds. The Framework for Teaching stresses the importance, for very young learners, of a phonemic strategy which involves sounding out words phoneme (☞) by phoneme. The National Literacy Strategy Training Pack (DfEE, 1998) suggests that children in the reception year use the phonemic strategy almost exclusively but as they progress through Key Stage 1 and then Key Stage 2, the frequency of this strategy declines for most children and a range of strategies take over. These include visual strategies, but also morphemic strategies, graphic knowledge, mnemonics and principles of spelling:

- Visual strategies include checking critical features of the word such as shape and length (asking 'Does it look right?'), looking for words within words, e.g. *for* in *before*, *the* in *they*, recognising tricky bits in different words, e.g. *oo* in *book*, *ai* in *said* and using the 'Look, Cover, Write, Check' procedure
- A morphemic approach will involve using known spellings as a basis for correctly spelling other words with similar patterns or related meanings, and building words from awareness of the meaning or derivation of known words
- Using graphic knowledge entails knowing about the serial order of letters in the language, that is the order in which letters in a word are likely to occur
- Mnemonic approaches involve inventing and using personal mnemonic devices for remembering difficult words, such as 'there's an "e" for envelope in the middle of stationery' or 'an "i" (eye) in the middle of "nose" makes a noise', etc.
- Principles of spelling incorporate applying knowledge of spelling rules and learned exceptions to these rules.

By the end of year 6, children should be using all of these strategies. The phonemic strategy has all but disappeared for most children at this stage, though some individuals might still use it as a starting point for unfamiliar words, though with only limited success. Despite this useful range of strategies it seems particularly unfortunate that the use of games is not suggested. Games such as Scrabble, hangman, crosswords, word searches, Boggle, words-within-words, Countdown, etc. can all be useful in stimulating children's interest in words and spelling.

ASSESSING SPELLING

Weekly spelling tests are one of the most common ways that children's spelling is assessed, but all teachers must ask themselves what the pros and cons are. One of the most positive features of spelling tests is that lists of words are sent home to be learned. If this is carefully thought through, word lists can provide an activity that many parents feel confident to support their children with, although every week is a little excessive. However, there are also a number of problems with spelling tests. Teachers must ask themselves about the purpose of spelling tests. It is often suggested that they are used to enhance standards of spelling, but as you have seen there are many other strategies that can achieve this more effectively. Daw et al (1997) used their experiences as advisory teachers to argue that there were 11 key strategies that effective schools used to enhance standards of spelling including:

- Teaching methods and resources are deployed in ways that encourage pupils to experiment and become quite independent as spellers from an early age.

(Daw et al, 1997: 44)

The claim that spelling tests are used as an assessment tool is also questionable. Every piece of writing that a child carries out gives teachers an opportunity to assess their spelling, and it should be remembered that the kind of writing that the child is doing will affect the nature of their spelling mistakes. A diary, for example, will create different challenges from a piece of scientific writing. In addition, however sensitively tests are handled there will always be children who are poor spellers whose self-esteem will be damaged each time they have to carry out a spelling test.

The most useful assessment of children's spellings will, arguably, take place at the time that the children are actually engaged in the writing process in the classroom. This might be during the literacy hour, during an extended writing session beyond the literacy hour or, more specifically, within the kind of writing workshop described by Wyse (1998) where children are encouraged to 'have a go' at words they are not sure of. This results in children producing 'invented spellings' based on words they already know or on the use of other strategies. These spellings are analysed and discussed by the teacher and the child during conferencing. As Wyse points out, the different developmental stages children pass through provide a systematic framework by which children's progress can be monitored and individual conferences can be informed.

Practice points

- In the early stages phonic strategies are important, but in time children need to understand the importance of visual and semantic strategies (☞) for standard spelling.
- Every piece of writing provides an opportunity for the assessment of a child's spelling.
- There needs to be a careful balance between encouraging invented spelling which can aid composition and standard spelling which is the final goal.

Glossary

Auditory strategies – the use of sounds to help spelling of unknown words.

Homophones – words which sound the same, but have different meanings or different spellings: 'read/reed'; 'right/write/rite'.

Homographs – words with the same spelling as another but different meaning: 'a lead pencil/the dog's lead'.

Kinaesthetic strategies – the use of the memory of physical actions to form words.

Multi-sensory techniques – the use of as many senses as possible through movement, vision, touch, and hearing in order to remember words.

Phonological knowledge – knowledge of the links between sounds and symbols.

Phoneme – the smallest unit of sound in a word.

Semantic strategies – strategies which rely on the use of meaning, e.g. working out homophones.

Visual strategies – the use of visual memory of words including common sequences of letters.

References

Beard, R. (1999) *National Literacy Strategy: Review of Research and Other Related Evidence.* London: DfEE.

Bissex, G. (1980) *GNYS AT WORK: A Child Learns to Read and Write.* Cambridge, MA: Harvard University Press.

Daw, P. with Smith, J. and Wilkinson, S. (1997) 'Factors associated with high standards of spelling in years R-4'. *English in Education,* 31 (1): 36-47.

Department for Education and Employment (DfEE) (1998) *The National Literacy Strategy: Literacy Training Pack. Module 2 Word Level Work.* London: DfEE

Gentry, J. (1982) 'An analysis of developmental spelling in GNYS AT WRK'. *Reading Teacher,* 36: 192–200.

Mudd, N. (1994) *Effective Spelling: A Practical Guide for Teachers.* London: Hodder & Stoughton.

Peters, M. (1985) *Spelling: Caught or Taught: A New Look.* London: Routledge and Kegan Paul.

Todd, J. (1982) *Learning to Spell.* Hemel Hempsted: Simon & Schuster.

Wyse, D. (1998) *Primary Writing.* Buckingham: Open University Press.

Annotated Bibliography

Brooks, P. and Weeks, S. (The Helen Arkell Dyslexia Centre) (1999). *Individual Styles in Learning to Spell: Improving Spelling in Children with Literacy Difficulties and All Children in Mainstream Schools.* London: DfEE.
A very significant piece of research. In common with other research demonstrates that important aspects of literacy learning need to be individualised. Includes fascinating ideas on 'neurolinguistic programming'.
L3 ***'

Mudd, N. (1994) *Effective Spelling: A Practical Guide for Teachers*. London: Hodder & Stoughton.

As the title suggests, this book gives sensible, systematic, practical guidance to the effective teaching of spelling at Key Stages 1 and 2, as well as providing some interesting insights into the history of the English language and past and present approaches to spelling in school.

L1 *

Peters M. (1985) *Spelling: Caught or Taught: A New Look*. London: Routledge and Kegan Paul.

First published in 1967 *Spelling: Caught or Taught* was a seminal work based on doctoral research in the 1960s arguing for teacher intervention in the field of spelling and young children and setting out certain strategies, particularly visual strategies, for teaching spelling in school. In this later work she covers similar ground and brings to bear additional research carried out with various colleagues.

L2 **

Temple, C., Nathan, R., Burris, N.A. and Temple, F. (1988) *The Beginnings of Writing* (second edition). Newton: Allyn & Bacon.

This realistic account of children's development includes three significant sections on the beginnings of spelling. It includes some analysis of the links between spoken pronunciation and spelling strategies.

L2 **

Chapter 16

Handwriting

Handwriting is an important transcriptional skill. The development of a fluent, comfortable and legible style helps children throughout their schooling, not least in exams. The basic concepts of handwriting are described and these are followed by a discussion of handwriting in the National Curriculum and a section on handwriting problems.

Venerable Will played jazz sax 'til 3 o'clock in the morning before he quit.

The five boxing wizzards jump quickly.

(Jarman, 1989: 101)

These examples of sentences that contain all the letters of the alphabet serve to remind us that quick brown foxes are not the only subjects for such sentences. Learning to form the individual letters of the alphabet and produce legible handwriting at a reasonable speed, involves a complex perceptuo-motor (☞) skill that many children find difficult to pick up. As Sassoon (1990a) points out, individual people are often judged by their handwriting: in writing letters of application for example. Children in school can experience criticism of their handwriting early on that can lead to a poor self-image and can contribute to underachievement in all written work.

BASIC HANDWRITING CONCEPTS

Sassoon (1990a) puts forward the concepts behind our writing system. Direction, movement and height are all crucial: left to right and top to bottom; the fact that letters have prescribed flowing movements with specific starting and exit points; the necessity to ensure that letters have particular height differences. In addition, the variance between upper and lower case must be recognised and correct spacing consistently applied. She also stresses the importance of taking particular care when teaching certain letters that have mirror images of each other, such as *b-d*, *m-w*, *n-u* and *p-q* to avoid confusion among young learners. She suggests that speed – but not too much speed – is also important as this can lead to fluency and greater efficiency.

Modern classroom situations do require pupils to think, work and write reasonably quickly.

Sassoon also points out that children cannot be expected to produce their best handwriting all the time, so she advocates different levels of handwriting for children. A calligraphic (☞) standard for special occasions might require a careful, deliberate approach which will be more time-consuming than a legible day-to-day hand. There might, however, be times when pupils are drafting text or making notes that they alone will read where a lower standard of legibility will be appropriate. A keen sense of the audience for the writing is particularly important here.

For teachers there are a small number of technical terms that are useful when talking about handwriting. *Ascenders* are the vertical lines that rise above the mid-line (or *x*-line) on letters like 'd'; *descenders* are the vertical lines that hang below the baseline on letters like 'g'. Most letters have an *entry stroke* where you start the letter and an *exit stroke*. Some letters such as 'i' may not have entry or exit strokes and are called 'sanserif', meaning without the stroke (the origin of 'serif' is obscure but possibly came from a Dutch word). The letter 't' is interesting in that its horizontal line is called a *crossbar* and the height of the letter should only be three-quarters. This means that the top of the letter finishes between the mid-line and the ascender line. You will have worked out that there are four important horizontal lines: the *descender line*, the *baseline*, the *mid-line* and the *ascender line*. For adults only the baseline is visible; for children other lines have to be used carefully because there is a danger that they can measure the length of a stroke by the distance to the line not by understanding the differences in letter size. Children need to understand these concepts if they are to have legible and fluent handwriting.

Jarman (1989) like Sassoon suggests that letters can be taught in families that are related by their patterns of movement. There are slight differences between their approaches, but both underline the importance of the idea of letter families. Jarman links specific patterns – which he regards as beneficial – with the families of letters. He also suggests that there are two kinds of join or 'ligature': horizontal joins and vertical joins. He points out that it is sensible to leave some letters unjoined, such as b g j p q and y when joined to most vowels. Sassoon links together the following letters: (1) i l t u y j; (2) r n m h b p k; (3) c a d g q o e; (4) s f; (5) v w x z.

Posture and working space are important elements of handwriting. For right-handed pupils the paper is tilted to about 45° anticlockwise. It is important that the writing implement is not gripped too hard as this can lead to muscle tension in the shoulder and pain in the wrist and hand. It is important that you are aware of all the left-handed children in your class from the beginning of the year. As far as handwriting is concerned left-handed children have particular needs. Their writing moves inwardly, that is, in towards their bodies thus tending to make it difficult for them to read what they have just written. Left-handers should be encouraged to turn their paper clockwise (to about 45°), not to hold their pen or pencil too near to the actual point and to sit on a higher chair if possible – all this can increase visibility. A rather obvious way in which left-handers can be helped is by ensuring that they sit to the left of a right-hander so that their elbows are not competing for space.

HANDWRITING, SPELLING AND CURSIVE WRITING

According to Bearne (1998), the connection between handwriting and spelling relates to kinaesthetic (☞) memory, that is the way we internalise things through repeated movements. Writing out a spelling to be learnt by writing it in the air with a finger or on the desk or table or even writing out misspellings several times is attempting to make use of kinaesthetic techniques to remember the particular shapes of words.

Peters (1985) similarly discusses perceptuo-motor ability and argues that carefulness in handwriting goes hand in hand with swift handwriting, which in turn influences spelling ability. Children who can quickly write letter strings such as *ing*, *able*, *est*, *tion*, *ous* and so on in a connected form, are more likely to remember how to spell words containing these strings:

> Quality of handwriting is highly correlated with spelling attainment, so also is the speed of handwriting, for it is a myth that the slow writer is the careful writer and vice versa. The slow writer is often one who is uncertain of letter formation . . . and . . . often . . . makes a random attempt at the letter he is writing. The swift writer is one who is certain . . . [and] can make a reasonable attempt at a word he may never have written before.
>
> (Peters, 1985: 55)

It is also Peters's view that the teaching of 'joined up' or cursive writing, should begin long before the junior school, that is to say at Key Stage 1 rather than 2. The main advantages of this are that (1) the concept of 'a word' (and the spaces between words) is acquired from the outset as distinct from 'a letter' (and the spaces between letters); (2) correct letter formation with appropriate exit strokes is learned from the beginning; (3) the movement of joined-up writing assists successful spelling and is quicker than printing; (4) children do not have to cope with changing from one to the other at seven or eight years of age.

Sassoon (1990a) suggests that with sufficient preparation in the 'movement' of letters and the different exit strokes required, pupils can begin to join up the simple letters by the end of the reception year or year 1 at least. She advocates the teaching of the letters and the joins in family groups and puts forward a clear analysis as to how this might be achieved in school.

The National Curriculum treats handwriting as a 'key skill'. At Key Stage 2 the emphasis is not just on legibility, fluency and confidence, but also on adaptability. Handwriting should be adaptable to a range of tasks such as presenting clear, neat final copy, taking notes, printing headings and subheadings, labelling diagrams, lettering for posters, presenting information in tabular form, map making and so on. In the National Curriculum 2000, there is also an emphasis on presenting work in a variety of ways. This includes different kinds of handwriting for different purposes and the use of other devices such as a range of computer-generated fonts, bullet points, borders, shading etc. and even pictures and moving images.

Arguably the NLS Framework for Teaching does incorporate these sorts of ideas into word-level work. For example, in year 1, it prescribes correct letter orientation, formation and proportion in a style that can be easily joined later on and in year 2 the use of basic handwriting joins. In year 3 consistency of letter size and spacing between words and the building up handwriting speed, fluency and legibility is required. Finally in year 4 the Framework concentrates on knowing when to use different kinds of handwriting: a neat hand for finished work and an informal hand for everyday work such as drafting. It also refers to the use of a range of presentational skills such as printscript for captions etc., capitals for headings etc. and a range of computer-generated fonts for different types of writing and different purposes.

DIAGNOSIS OF PROBLEMS

Pupils entering the Key Stage 2 phase of schooling often arrive with handwriting problems. These might have been caused by indifferent teaching or they might, according to Sassoon (1990a), be symptomatic of pupils' particular condition or set of circumstances. They may have been described as 'clumsy' or they might be considered 'dyspraxic', that is prone to particular motor coordination problems. For example, they might not be able to catch a large ball, or cope easily with gymnastics or play games using the simplest of equipment. For these children neat, regulation handwriting might be impossible. Teachers need to acknowledge this, not continually chastise them but help them to develop handwriting that is reasonably swift and legible.

Sassoon argues that handwriting can be regarded as a diagnostic tool in itself, indicating certain problems that pupils have and teachers need to address. Hesitancy and a lack of confidence in spelling will interrupt the flow of handwriting. If this is accompanied by frequent attempts at correcting mistakes, the result is 'messy' handwriting that many teachers find unacceptable. This may well bring to their attention that these children need help in spelling as well as handwriting. Occasionally, children have psychological problems to cope with, too, such as bullying, bereavement, divorce and so on. which, in addition to a range of behavioural changes, can be evident in their handwriting. Often the writing becomes very variable and sometimes illegible, when previously it was conventional.

Poor handwriting might also indicate to the teacher that some pupils have poor understanding of directionality, as pointed out by Alston and Taylor (1987). Similar letters are often confused, e.g. *b* and *d*, *p* and *q*, *d* and *p*, *m* and *w*. Many young children experience such difficulties, which can be overcome to an extent by letters being taught and learned in families.

Some children with poor handwriting skills are found to have weak auditory, perceptual and memory skills and are not able to remember sequences of movements or sequences of verbal instructions. Difficulties with handwriting might indicate poor eyesight or a squint and perhaps the need for spectacles for an individual child. Children suffering from fatigue due to the after-effects of an illness, a physical disability or just insufficient sleep at night might also reflect this in their handwriting. Finally, a poor hand might bring the teacher's attention to the poor posture of some children when writing or even generally. Thus alerted and made aware of any of these cognitive, psychological or physical problems, teachers will be able to take steps, possibly with support from other professionals, to remedy them and aim to improve, not just children's handwriting, but other important features of their pupils' learning and development in school.

Practice points

- The individual support for handwriting during the writing process should be supplemented by whole group handwriting sessions on a weekly basis.
- A balance needs to be found between emphasis on standard letter formation and encouraging legibility and fluency.
- Joined-up writing should be encouraged as early as possible.

Glossary

Calligraphic – description of a particualarly skilled way of writing. Handwritten italic script is often seen as calligraphy.

Kinaesthetic – our sense and memory of movement/muscular control.

Perceptuo-motor skill – skills that rely on use of the senses, the brain and learned physical movement.

References

Alston, J. and Taylor, J. (1987) *Handwriting: Theory, Research and Practice.* London: Croom Helm.

Bearne, E. (1998) *Making Progress in English.* London: Routledge.

Jarman, C. (1989) *The Development of Handwriting Skills: A Resource Book for Teachers.* Oxford: Basil Blackwell.

Sassoon, R. (1990a) *Handwriting: A New Perspective.* Leckhampton: Stanley Thornes.

Sassoon, R. (1990b) *Handwriting: The Way To Teach It.* Leckhampton: Stanley Thornes.

Peters, M. L. (1985) *Spelling: Caught or Taught: A New Look.* London: Routledge and Kegan Paul.

Annotated bibliography

British Institute of Graphologists. Last revision 1 June 2000. [online – cited 26-6-00]. Available from:
  http://www.britishgraphology.org/
Includes a monthly analysis of someone's handwriting. An interesting view of how some people believe that it is possible to make judegements about character based on handwriting.
  L1

Fidge, L. and Smith, P. (1997) *Nelson Handwriting Teacher's Book*. Walton-on-Thames: Thomas Nelson.
This is the teacher's book from one of the most popular handwriting schemes. Graded progression of pupil activities which are attractively presented.
  L1 *

Jarman, C. (1989) *The Development of Handwriting Skills: A Resource Book for Teachers*. Oxford: Basil Blackwell.
Jarman makes a strong case for the teaching of eight specific patterns which he suggests account for all lower case letters. The book includes fascinating information about a range of handwriting related topics. The main part of the book consists of photocopiable handwriting sheets.
  L1 *

Sassoon, R. (1999) *Handwriting of the Twentieth Century*. London: Routledge.
Rosmary Sassoon has contributed a huge amount to our understanding of handwriting. This book, her most recent, gives a recent historical perspective on the teaching of handwriting. Her book *Handwriting: The Way To Teach It* (Sassoon, 1990b) focuses more on classroom practice.
  L1 *

Chapter 17

Punctuation

A brief reminder about some of the historical aspects of punctuation is followed by reflections on the current position including the use of colons, semi-colons and apostrophes. Children's development of punctuation is shown as more complex than previously thought. The chapter conludes with some examples of punctuation activities.

In the past punctuation has tended not to receive much attention in the primary classroom. There were more pressing concerns with spelling, handwriting and the development of fluent writing in general. Nor has it received much attention in the research literature. However, in recent years Hall's (1998) work has been some of the first to look closely at punctuation and this has included historical perspectives. For example, Richard Browne in 1700 said this about punctuation:

> What is the use of stops or points in reading and writing? To distinguish sense; by resting so long as the stop you meet with doth permit.
>
> (Hall, 1998: 2)

In Roman times it was the readers who inserted the punctuation into texts not the writers: this was related to the need to declaim texts orally. Since that time the function of punctuation has changed. However, the idea that punctuation is primarily designed to support oral reading – through pauses – still persists.

Since the introduction of the National Curriculum the expectations for punctuation have become increasingly demanding. The Framework for Teaching first introduces the various punctuation marks at the following stages:

Year 1
Recognise full stops and capitals. Begin to use full stops.
Use question marks.

Year 2
Recognise and take account of commas and exclamation marks in reading.
Identify speech marks. Use commas for lists.

Year 3
Speech punctuation.
Use of comma as grammatical boundary.

Year 4
Use of comma as grammatical boundary.
Use the apostrophe accurately.
Identify common marks including: commas, semi-colons, colons, dashes, hyphens, speech marks.

Year 5 and 6
Secure knowledge and understanding of colon; semi-colon; parenthetic commas, dashes, brackets.

The earlier requirements in this list are not too much of a problem, however, some of the punctuation required from year 4 onwards can sometimes stretch the knowledge of adults as well as children. The troublesome apostrophe is something that continues to catch out many adults. The following profession-ally printed banner appeared on a pub wall:

Qs monster meals won't scare you but the portion's might

Well, one out of three for the apostrophes in that one! It is worth reminding ourselves of the common types of apostrophe: (1) contraction: didn't = did not; (2) possession singular: the cat's tail, the child's book; (3) possession plural: the cats' tails, the children's books (as 'children' is an irregular plural form the apostrophe comes before the 's'); (4) possession with name ending in 's': Donald Graves's book. Common errors include: this first happened in the 60's. – 60s is plural not a contraction; was that it's name? – because of the confusion with *it's* (as in: It's (it is) my party and I'll cry if I want to) this pos-sessive form is irregular and does *not* have an apostrophe (was that its name?).

The colon and the semi-colon are particularly problematic and an exami-nation of some definitions gives us a clue to this:

Longman Concise English Dictionary
colon *n*, *pl* **colons, cola 1** a punctuation mark : used chiefly to direct attention to matter that follows . . .
semicolon *n* a punctuation mark ; used chiefly to coordinate major sen-tence elements where there is no conjunction (☞).

Framework for Teaching – Glossary
Colon a punctuation mark used to introduce: a list, a quotation or a sec-ond clause which expands or illustrates the first: *he was very cold: the temperature was below zero.*
Semi-colon a punctuation mark used to separate phrases or clauses in a sentence. It is stronger than a comma, but not as strong as a full

stop. Semi-colons may be used more flexibly than colons. The semi-colon can be used to separate two clauses, when they are of equal weight; in these cases it acts as a connective: *I love Indian food; John prefers Chinese.*

The Chicago Manual of Style

5.97 The colon is used to mark a break in grammatical construction equivalent to that marked by a semicolon, but the colon emphasizes the content relation between the separated elements. The colon is used, for example, to indicate a sequence in thought between two clauses that form a single sentence or to separate one clause from a second clause that contains an illustration or amplification or the first:

> The officials had been in conference most of the night: this may account for their surly treatment of the reporters the next morning.

In contemporary usage, however, such clauses are frequently separated by a semicolon or are treated as separate sentences:

> The officials had been in conference most of the night; this may account for their surly treatment of the reporters the next morning.

5.89 Though the semicolon is less frequently employed today than in the past, it is still occasionally useful to mark a more important break in sentence flow than that marked by a comma. It should always be used between the two parts of a compound sentence (independent, or coordinate, clauses) when they are not connected by a conjunction:

> The controversial portrait had been removed from the entrance hall; in its place had been hung a realistic landscape.

The New Fowler's Modern English Usage makes the important point that the 'rules' for the use of the colon have changed since its adoption in English in the sixteenth century. It then offers the following on the colon and semi-colon:

Whereas the semicolon links equal or balanced clauses, the colon generally marks a step forward, from introduction to main theme, from cause to effect, premiss [sic] to conclusion . . .

The semicolon separates two or more clauses which are of more or less equal importance and are linked as a pair or series: *Economy is no disgrace; for it is better to live on a little than to outlive a great deal. . . .*

As can be seen from these four authoritative sources it is a difficult matter establishing clear differences between the two punctuation marks. With all such discussions we also have to be aware that punctuation conventions continue to change as the *Chicago Manual of Style* points out. As far as colons and semi-colons are concerned the most difficult idea is perhaps that of the balance between the clauses: how do we decide if the clauses are of 'equal weight'? As we were writing the previous sentence we applied the Framework for Teaching definition. In the end we decided on a colon because the second part of the sentence expands the first, also the punctuation mark does not seem to naturally replace a conjunction. However, this is a debatable point! Our own feeling is that overall the colon is being used much less in the middle of a sentence unless it is introducing a list which is a better understood use. This means that the semi-colon can be used mid-sentence to replace conjunctions or to separate items in a list when a comma is inappropriate.

CHILDREN LEARNING TO PUNCTUATE

Until Hall's work an important area of omission in the research was knowledge about the way children developed their understanding of punctuation. One of the few early projects was carried out by Hutchinson (1987) who worked closely with a child on a piece of writing that was a re-enactment of 'Come away from the water Shirley' by John Burningham (1977). One of the points to emerge was the way that the child used his speech to support his structure of the writing:

> shirley and her mum and dad were going to the seaside and her dad told her to go and play with the other children and her dad didn no she went saling with a dog and a pirate ship was folling and the pirates corght her.

An important aspect of teachers' knowledge is recognising the significant differences between speech and writing. As far as the punctuation in this piece is concerned Hutchinson makes the point that Danny's reliance on speech results in the use of conjunctions where full stops would be more appropriate in writing. However, he also points out that an analysis based on one text is not sufficient for assessing understanding. The following day when they reloaded the writing Danny decided to put a full stop after the title. When asked if he could put some more in he demonstrated a better knowledge than he had the day before. The importance of redrafting is clearly indicated in this example.

As a result of his research Hall (1998) produced a very useful overview of the subject, offering some important principles and ideas to support the teaching of punctuation. Hall reiterates that punctuation is no different to writing in general in that the generation of *meaning* is the primary function of written language: one of the main points that he makes is that punctuation is learned most successfully in the context of 'rich and meaningful writing experiences' (1998: 9).

He usefully differentiates between 'non-linguistic punctuation' and 'linguistic punctuation'. An example of non-linguistic punctuation is where a child puts full stops at the end of every line of a piece of writing rather than at the end of the sentences. This illustrates the child's belief that punctuation is to do with position and space rather than to indicate meaning and structure. With regard to non-linguistic punctuation the idea of 'resistance to punctuation' is discussed. One of the reasons that children can remain resistant to using punctuation appropriately is exacerbated by teachers whose comments are often directed to naming and procedures rather than explanation:

> As already indicated, teacher comments which are simply directed to the placing of punctuation rather than to explaining its function can leave the child with no sense of purpose. Yet research suggests that teacher practices are, probably quite unconsciously, dominated by procedure rather than explanation.
>
> (Hall, 1998: 5)

Standard punctuation is linked with grammar and sentence structure. The necessary understanding of these complex concepts does not happen suddenly. Children gradually begin to realise that spatial concepts either do not work or do not match what they see in their reading material. Hall illustrates this with an example from his research:

> This dissonance is illustrated in a conversation between three children who were jointly composing a piece of text which was being scribed for them (see figure 11). After two lines, one child insisted on having a full stop at the end of each line. The rest of the piece was written with no more punctuation. Then there was a scramble for the pen and one child wanted to put a full stop after 'lot' on line three.
>
> Derek   You're not supposed to put full stops in the middle.
> Rachel You are!
> Derek   No, they're supposed to be at the end, Ooh!
> Rachel You are, Derek.
> Fatima Yeah. So that's how you know that (meaning the 'and' at the end of line 3) goes with that (meaning line 4).
>
> (Hall, 1998: 12)

PUNCTUATION ACTIVITIES

We conclude this chapter with some further brief reflections on practice. Waugh (1998) looks at some practical approaches to teaching punctuation in the primary school and he makes an important point about 'response partners'. One of the most effective ways of improving punctuation is to work with someone who is proficient at proof-reading. All professionally published materials pass through a proofreading stage: this book will be passed to a proofreader and a copy-editor; newspaper articles go to sub-editors who work on style and presentation, etc. This is in part a recognition that proof-reading is often more efficient if it is not solely carried out by the author who often is primarily concerned with the composition. This also reflects the idea that it is sensible to separate composition and transcription in the various stages of the writing process.

Other suggestions that Waugh makes include the use of comic strips and speech bubbles which can then be converted to text only. Reading aloud can be useful and punctuation can be read by giving the name of the mark when it is read or by having different sounds for different marks. Waugh also suggests 'walking and reading' where the reader has to stop walking at a punctuation mark. One of the main uses of punctuation is to avoid ambiguity, and some useful examples are offered where children can change the punctuation to create different meanings:

PRIVATE. NO SWIMMING ALLOWED.

PRIVATE? NO! SWIMMING ALLOWED.

This kind of ambiguity also features in a useful BBC video (BBC Education, 1998) which is a compilation of English Express programmes. For the programme on punctuation the scene is 'Sentence City' which is in dire straits so the skills of the internationally famous crime fighters the 'punctuation posse' are called upon to impose some semantic order. During the historical drama, which is a feature of all the programmes, the point is made that a long time ago English had no punctuation. Ambiguity was rife, so that a letter read to Queen Elizabeth I which commenced 'My royal lady with the wind in our sails . . . ' leads to queries over flatulence and the need for punctuation after 'lady'!

Practice points

- Children should be taught that one of the main reasons for punctuation is to improve clarity and avoid ambiguity.
- As teachers you should be clear that punctuation is more about meaning than about pauses when reading aloud.
- The use of the full stop and the comma require complex knowledge, but they should be the first priority.

Glossary

Conjunction – a type of word that is used mainly to link clauses in a sentence, e.g. She was very happy *because* John asked for help with his maths.

References

BBC Education (1998) *The Grammar Video (2)*. Produced by BBC Education. 100 mins. BBC Worldwide (Educational publishing), videocassette.

Burchfield, R. W. (ed.) (1996) *The New Fowler's Modern English Usage.* Oxford: Oxford University Press.

Burningham, J. (1977) *Come Away from the Water Shirley!* London: Cape.

Hall, N. (1998) *Punctuation in the Primary School.* Reading: University of Reading; Reading and Language Information Centre.

Hutchinson, D. (1987) 'Developing concepts of sentence structure and punctuation'. *Curriculum*, 8 (3): 13–16.

Waugh, D. (1998) 'Practical approaches to teaching punctuation in the primary school'. *Reading*, 32 (2): 14–17.

Annotated bibliography

BBC Education (1998) *The Grammar Video (2).* Produced by BBC Education. 100 mins. BBC Worldwide (Educational publishing), videocassette.
A lively, amusing and informative series of programmes that look at spelling, punctuation and sentences.
L1 *

Hall, N. and Robinson, A. (1996) *Learning About Punctuation.* Clevedon: Multilingual Matters.
A range of contributors offer their thoughts on the teaching of punctuation. Includes a study that looked at the development of a group of 8 and 9 year-old children.
L2 **

Hall, Nigel, and Robinson, Anne. Manchester Metropolitan University. The Punctuation Project. [online – cited 26-6-00] Available from:
http://www.partnership.mmu.ac.uk/punctuation/
Information about the punctuation research that Hall and Robinson carried out. Includes a series of reference lists related to punctuation.
L1 ***

Kress, G. (1982) *Learning to Write.* London: Routledge and Kegan Paul.
An important text that looks closely at the differences between speech and writing. Also contains well thought out views on children's 'errors'.
L3 **

Chapter 18

Grammar

Grammar has been given a new emphasis in the Framework for Teaching. This section reminds us that questions about grammar teaching have been around for some time. We outline the difference between 'descriptive' grammar and 'prescriptive' grammar. An examination of the important idea of 'knowledge about language' is followed by reflections on the approach adopted by the Framework for Teaching.

The word 'grammar' itself is used in two very distinct ways: prescriptively and descriptively. Prescriptively, the term is used to prescribe how language should be used; descriptively the term is used to describe how the language actually is used. Prescriptive grammarians (☞) believe that English grammar is a fixed and unchanging series of rules which should be applied to the language. For prescriptive grammarians expressions like: *I ain't done nothing wrong*, or *We was going to the supermarket*, are quite simply wrong. To understand this a bit better it is necessary to consider two other related questions that often get muddled up with grammar in the public discourse (☞), and they are the question of style and the question of Standard English

Many complaints about incorrect grammar are actually complaints about style. Split infinitives (☞) are a case in point. There is nothing *grammatically* wrong with a sentence like: *I am hoping to quickly finish writing this paragraph.* It makes perfect sense, but it might be thought stylistically preferable to write: *I am hoping to finish writing this paragraph quickly*, or even to write: *I am hoping quickly to finish writing this paragraph.* However, if I were to write: *Hoping writing I paragraph finish to quickly am*, there would be something grammatically wrong with that!

So far as Standard English is concerned, an accident of history meant that, when printing developed, it was the Anglian regional dialect that was written down (➡ Chapter 1, 'The History of English, language and literacy'). Because it was written it became the 'standard'. It would thus be more accurate to describe Standard English as the standard *dialect*. Other dialects are then described as 'non-standard'. Standard English is distinguished from non-standard dialects by features of vocabulary and features of grammar. In addition middle-class speech tends to keep some of the grammatical features of the written form, particularly with regard to the use of negatives and the use of some verb forms. Thus matters of class and matters of dialect have come to be linked.

From the point of view of *prescriptive* grammarians, the grammar of Standard English is 'good' or 'correct' grammar, and the grammar of non-standard dialects is 'bad' or 'incorrect' grammar. So, for example, children who say *I ain't done nothing*, often have their language 'corrected' by their teachers, and even by their own parents, on the ground that it is 'bad' grammar, or indeed, more generally, that it is just 'bad' English.

Descriptive grammarians are interested in describing how the language actually is used rather than how it ought to be used. Thus a descriptive grammarian will note that a middle-class speaker, using the standard dialect known as Standard English, may say: *We were pleased to see you*, and that a working-class speaker using a working-class cockney dialect may say: *We was pleased to see you*. Both examples are grammatical within their own dialects, both examples make perfect sense, and in neither example is there any ambiguity. The idea that a plural subject takes a plural verb is true only of the middle-class standard dialect, not of the working class Cockney dialect. To put it another way, the plural form of the verb in middle class standard is *were*, while the plural form of the verb in working class Cockney is *was*.

Let us now offer this simple working definition: *Grammar is an account of the relationship between words in a sentence.* In the light of this definition what the grammarian has to do is to look for regular patterns of word use in the language, and give labels to them. However, some of the relationships are pretty complicated, and describing them is not easy. The definitions many of us half remember from our own primary school days – 'a noun is a naming word', 'a verb is a doing word' – are at best unhelpful and at worst downright misleading. Though meaning has a part to play in determining the relationship between words, parts of speech are not defined in terms of word meaning, they are defined, rather, in terms of the function of the words within the sentence. As an example of what we mean, think about the word *present*.

> *Present* can be a verb:

> I **present** you with this tennis racket as a reward for your services.

> or a noun:

> Thank you for my birthday **present**, I've always wanted socks!

> or an adjective:

> In the **present** circumstances I feel unable to proceed.

It will be clear, then, that teaching grammar has its problems. Confusion can occur at a number of levels: between prescriptive and descriptive approaches, between questions of grammar proper and questions of style, and around issues of variation between standard and non-standard dialects.

GRAMMAR OR KNOWLEDGE ABOUT LANGUAGE (KAL)?

Even before the literacy hour, effective primary teachers had always drawn children's attention to many of the practical aspects of language use. The teaching of reading and writing, of spelling and punctuation required the continual use of everyday language about language; language so everyday that we tend to forget that words such as *alphabet, letter, word, spelling, sentence, full stop* are all language about language. In addition many teachers took the opportunities offered by reading and writing to draw children's attention to specific items of vocabulary. Much of this specific attention to language itself was at the word and sentence level.

The proposal to teach children explicitly about language raises some questions:

- What are the reasons for teaching primary children about language?
- What are the benefits to be gained?
- What should be taught, and at what ages?
- How should it be taught?
- What is the place of terminology?
- Where does grammar fit into all of this?

Cox (1991) suggests that there are two justifications for teaching children explicitly about language. The first is that it will be beneficial to their language use in general. The second is that it is essential to children's understanding of their social and cultural environment, given the role language plays in society. A third suggestion, related to the second, is that 'language should be studied in its own right as a rich and fascinating example of human behaviour' (LINC, 1991: 1).

The LINC project made cautious claims:

> Language study can influence use, but development of the relationship between learning about language and learning how to use it is not a linear one but rather a recursive, cyclical and mutually informing relationship.
>
> (Carter, 1990: 4)

The National Literacy Strategy is founded on similar ideas:

> The relationship between literacy learning and the use of an associated meta-language of technical terms is a complex one. Both are likely to assist the other.
>
> (Beard, 1999: 28)

While it looks possible that the right sort of detailed attention to language itself may be more widely beneficial, there is, as yet, no substantial research evidence to show that this is the case. We must look, therefore, to the other justification for language study: that it is a subject of inherent interest both in its own right and in the role that it plays in wider social and cultural life. The question immediately arises as to the appropriate age range for language study and, while earlier reports delayed any *systematic* attention to language until the later primary years, in the current orders for English in the National Curriculum explicit attention to language is seen as appropriate from the reception year.

If we next consider the approach to be taken, the classroom activities that were developed within the LINC project started from the basis that children should be encouraged to discuss language use in meaningful contexts that engaged their interest. Here are some examples of work done in primary schools under the auspices of the LINC project, all of which were extremely productive in getting children to think and talk about language itself (all examples from Bain et al, 1992):

- Making word lists
- Compiling dictionaries including slang and dialect dictionaries
- Discussing language variation and social context
- Discussing accent, and standard English
- Compiling personal language histories and language profiles
- Capitalising on the language resource of the multilingual classroom
- Role play
- The history and use of language in the local environment
- Collecting and writing jokes
- Writing a class book about books
- Collaborative writing
- Writing in different genres
- Media work
- Book making
- A Dr Xargle project (Willis, 1988; 1990).

Many of the examples in the above list could be and indeed were done with the youngest children, and terminology was learned in context as and when the children needed it in their work.

GRAMMAR AND THE FRAMEWORK FOR TEACHING

The Framework for Teaching incorporates a skills approach to language learning with some 800 separately listed objectives. The word-level objectives that concern us here are those found in the section called 'vocabulary extension'. The earlier objectives in the section do reflect previous effective primary practice. One recurring objective, for instance, involves children making lists of words of personal interest to them or around specific topic areas. These are then to be used in their writing. As the children get older, however, the vocabulary extension work involves much more focused word study: antonyms, and synonyms for instance, homonyms, onomatopoeia, foreign derivations, word change over time, dictionary and thesaurus work, slang and dialect words, and by the time they are in the third term of year 6 they are inventing words and doing crosswords.

The objectives in the sentence-level strand are grouped into two sections: 'grammatical awareness', and 'sentence construction and punctuation'. The sections overlap somewhat. Under the 'grammatical awareness' heading children move progressively from deploying their implicit knowledge of grammar to explicitly identifying parts of speech, and to using the grammar of standard English. Under the 'sentence construction and punctuation' heading the objectives develop from basic punctuation in the early years to simple clause analysis in year 6.

At both word and sentence level, as the children get older the work is generally more and more decontextualised: one looks in vain, for instance, for objectives that incorporate the word-level work in the children's writing at text-level. At sentence level, to take a glaring example from year 5 term 1, the children are required to learn the differences between direct and indirect speech, but none of this is translated through to text level work by way of getting the children to write a conversation or a report. Instead, at sentence level, they have to turn direct into indirect speech. More positive examples can be found but, by and large, the learning of terminology is not contextualised in the children's other work. There are some early indications that grammatical knowledge learned as part of sentence-level work is not transferring to children's extended writing.

Effective grammar teaching will involve pupils playing with language, and exploring language in ways that are meaningful and fun. Teachers will need both to understand the issues and to be confident in naming terms themselves, so that they can then use them with confidence in everyday discussion with pupils. If teachers use the terms correctly with the children all the time, the children will learn what the terms refer to, even if they are not able to define them to the satisfaction of a linguistics expert until they are older. Dry as dust decontextualised old fashioned grammar exercises of the *underline the noun* variety do not work and put more children off than they help. In addition, textbooks that do not discuss dialect variation, that confuse matters of style with matters of grammar, and that take a prescriptive 'correct English' approach throughout are to be avoided.

Practice points

- Wherever possible link your grammar teaching with text-level work.
- Engage children's curiosity about language through work on, for example, accent and dialect.
- Use appropriate terminology frequently and in the context of daily work.

Glossary

Grammarian – someone who studies grammar.
Infinitive – part of a verb that is used with 'to': e.g. to *go* boldly.
Public discourse – discussions and debates in the public domain particularly seen through the media.

References

Bain, R., Fitzgerald, B. and Taylor, M. (1992) *Looking into Language: Classroom Approaches to Knowledge about Language*. Sevenoaks: Hodder & Stoughton.

Beard, R. (1999) *National Literacy Strategy Review of Research and Other Related Evidence*. London: DfEE.

Carter, R. (ed.) (1990) *Knowledge about Language and the Curriculum: The LINC Reader*. London: Hodder & Stoughton.

Cox, B. (1991) *Cox on Cox. An English Curriculum for the 1990s*. London: Hodder & Stoughton.

Language in the National Curriculum (LINC) (1992) 'Materials for professional development'. Unpublished.

Willis, J. (1988) *Dr. Xargle's book of Earthlets: An Alien's View of Earth Babies*. London: Anderson Press.

Willis, J. (1990) *Dr. Xargle's book of Earth Tiggers*. London: Anderson Press.

Annotated bibliography

Bain, R. and Bridgewood, M. (1998) *The Primary Grammar Book: Finding Patterns Making Sense*. Sheffield: National Association for the Teaching of English (NATE).
The activities in this pack encourage children to collect examples of word usage, to make lists, to produce their own examples, and to explore language use in the context of their own work to see how it all works.
L1 *

Bain, R., Fitzgerald, B. and Taylor, M. (1992) *Looking into Language: Classroom Approaches to Knowledge about Language*. Sevenoaks: Hodder & Stoughton.
This is the book that describes some of the classroom activities that arose out of the LINC project. There are lots of excellent ideas here, some of which could even be adapted for use within the literacy hour, but others of which would be more suitable for language and literacy work outside the literacy hour.
L2 **

Crystal, D. (1988) *Rediscover Grammar*. Harlow: Longman.
The best book of its kind if you want to learn about grammatical terms and concepts. Succinct and as straightforward as possible.
L1

Qualifications and Curriculum Authority (QCA) (1998) *The Grammar Papers: Perspectives on the Teaching of Grammar in the National Curriculum.* London: QCA Publications.

A collection of six papers from unnamed writers. In the examples they give there is an emphasis on the pupils' production of language in meaningful situations, and the sixth paper is a useful review of the research evidence about teaching grammar.

L3 ***

The Survey of English Usage: University College London (1996–98). *The Internet Grammar of English.* [online – cited 26-6-00] Available from: http://www.ucl.ac.uk/internet-grammar/home.htm

This is an online course in English grammar written primarily for university undergraduates.

L2

Chapter 19

Assessing writing

The main purpose of assessment is to feed into decisions about future teaching. We start by considering marking as a sometimes forgotten assessment tool. This is followed by thoughts on the vital job of formative assessment (☞). The section on summative assessment (☞) includes reflections on national tests and target setting. This chapter should be read in conjunction with Chapter 11, 'Assessing reading' and Chapter 25, 'Assessing talk', as some strategies – such as diaries of observations – are applicable to all three modes and other strategies are specific to one mode.

Some of the most important assessment of children's writing is carried out orally during the process of writing when the teacher sits with the child and offers advice. This kind of advice is likely to be most effective if the teacher has a clear idea of how children's writing should develop (➡ Chapter 12, 'The development of writing') and has a clear idea about how to intervene. The other day-to-day activity that can be a vital assessment tool is marking: either with the child or after the event.

One of the ideas about responding to children's work is that every single piece of written work should be marked. If we pause to consider the volume of writing that children produce in school, we quickly realise that this is not a realistic or manageable idea. If we take a class of 30 children and conservatively estimate that they might generate four pieces of writing every day, that would total 600 pieces of writing in one week alone. If you gave only 2 minutes to each piece of writing, that would mean 20 hours marking per week. The practical reality of these figures means that decisions need to be made on which work should be sampled for marking. Ideally these decisions should be agreed as part of a whole school marking policy.

The choice of writing for written feedback depends on the nature of the writing and your approach to assessment. It is worth remembering that appropriate written comments can be collected together to form the basis of an assessment profile for a child. One of the ways to select writing for written feedback can be on the basis of range. So if on the last occasion you marked a story, then a piece of non-fiction might be appropriate the next time. Or if on the previous occasion you had commented on the presentation of a final draft, you might want to comment on an early draft.

One of the difficult aspects of marking children's work relates to the range of choices that are available for your response. One possible way to account for these choices might be to have a three point marking system:

1 A specific positive comment about the writing.
2 A specific point about improving something that is individual to the child.
3 A specific point about improving something that relates to the class target.

One of the common criticisms made by inspectors about marking is if ticks, stars, smiley faces, scores out of 10, etc., are used too much. These give no information to the child about what in particular they did well or specifically how they could improve next time. However, for young children the extrinsic rewards such as stickers, smiley faces or merit awards can be an important way of rewarding hard work. As a teacher you need to be clear about the pros and cons of the different strategies. A tick at the end of a piece of work should perhaps only be used to indicate that you have checked that the child completed the work and it indicates that you have skim read the piece. A reward such as a sticker could be used to indicate that the child has worked particularly hard and ideally should accompany longhand comments which are the most important kind of marking.

FORMATIVE ASSESSMENT

The Centre for Language in Primary Education (CLPE) has developed some of the most thoroughly trialled and thoughtful record-keeping systems in recent years. Their Primary Language Record (PLR) featured pro formas for formative reading and writing observations, along with summative documents which supported reporting to parents and information for the next teacher, etc. One of the important hallmarks of the record was the requirement to take account of the parents' and child's views of language development. Parts of the report also require understanding of the particular issues for ethnic-minority and multi-lingual (☞) children. There have been some reservations about the PLR, primarily about its time-consuming nature, but these often resulted from teachers not understanding the philosophy of the record. These reservations were compounded by the growing paperwork required by the National Curriculum and its assessment. In spite of the high quality of the PLR continual government initiatives in primary education have made the use of records like the PLR very difficult.

Formative assessment methods often use the teacher's skills as perceptive observers of children's development something that Yetta Goodman memorably called 'kid watching'. But in recent years inspectors have pushed for assessment that is closely linked to the learning objectives for a particular lesson or activity. Box 19.1 gives an idea of this.

It is important to remember that much short-term or day-to-day assessment is not written down. As the Qualifications and Curriculum Authority (QCA) document 'Target Setting and Assessment in the National Literacy

Objectives:
1. To construct an argument in note form or full text to persuade others of a point of view and:
2. Present the case to the class or a group
3. Evaluate its effectiveness

Names	1.	2.	3.	Observations
James Boyd	△	△	\	Strong key points and presentation but found evaluation difficult
Yasmin Akhbar	△	L	△	Not enough points made to convince the class but was able to recognise this when evaluating
Gemma Corkhill	△	△	L	Struggled with sequence of ideas but presentation was convincing
Etc.				

Key: △ = objective achieved; L = further teaching required; \ = objective not achieved

Box 19.1

Strategy' points out: 'Not all assessment information needs to be formally recorded for others. Many specific, short term and informal assessments are made by the teacher on a day-to-day basis and are unrecorded' (QCA, 1999a: 9). The assessments that teachers make of children while working with them are used to inform the setting of future tasks. Sometimes tasks may be deliberately structured to provide specific opportunities to assess progress, but it should be remembered that it is not necessary to assess all lessons and activities. The guiding principle is that the assessments that are made should be of a high quality and should lead to more effective teaching and learning. The teacher's skills in questioning, observing, interacting and offering feedback (oral and written) are all opportunities for short-term assessments.

The introduction of the National Literacy Strategy was accompanied by the idea of target setting. The assessment of writing can be closely linked with medium-term target setting. The QCA document suggests some medium term learning targets that reflect clusters of objectives from the Framework for Teaching (Box 19.2).

One of the most useful methods for recording children's progress is a simple notebook with a page for each child. In the past these have been used to note particularly significant moments of development, to celebrate success and to note areas for development or areas of concern. The QCA suggest that

Year 5 Term 2	Understand the differences between spoken and written forms, recognising how writing is adapted for different audiences and purposes.	Recognise the characteristic language, structures and themes of different types of writing, adopting these features in their own writing.

Box 19.2

medium-term targets such as the one Box 19.2 can be stuck to the top of each page to remind the teacher to focus their observations around the progress that has been made towards achieving the target. Although this kind of assessment is clearly linked to the objectives in the Framework for Teaching, the national target setting is measured through success in the SATs (☞). Unfortunately the level descriptions (☞) that are associated with SATs and statutory teacher assessment (☞) do not necessarily match simply with the expectations of the Framework.

SUMMATIVE ASSESSMENT

The evidence to show that national targets have been achieved is measured by children's performance in the SATs at 7 and 11 in the primary school. As the pressure to hit the targets is so great it is not surprising that teachers – particularly for year 6 children – feel that they have to prepare children very carefully for the tests, sometimes at the expense of other important areas of the curriculum. Although national 'teacher assessment' and the SATs are only required at the end of each key stage, it is important that all teachers contribute to the assessment information that is available concerning all children. The statutory requirement is that schools must update their records at least once a year; this is necessary for written reports to parents. All teachers will need to monitor the progress of their children towards the targets and one of the ways they can do this is by levelling children's work.

When teachers decide on the National Curriculum level descriptions that best fit their children's writing they need to consider a range of writing. This often means that annotated portfolios (☞) of writing are kept and used as the basis of the teacher's judgements. The teacher's own written records can also usefully contribute to the judgement. One of the challenges for all assessment processes, including the SATs, is to make sure that the assessments are fair for all children: this requires moderation (☞). However, many people believe that true comparability of assessment is not achievable because of the radically different contexts that exist in all classrooms. If this is the case, child-centred formative assessments (like the PLR) must remain an important strategy because they are more useful in practice.

Levelling work

A publication by what was the School Curriculum and Assessment Authority (SCAA) called *Exemplification of Standards* is a useful tool for improving judgements. As far as writing is concerned the SCAA document features case studies of individual children and collections of their work. For example the writing of a child called Bethan is featured. The collection includes a nature diary entry; 'My Life on a Canal Barge, two drafts of a poem about autumn, a reading diary, a book review, a historically based letter and a science report. The document suggests the following judgement:

> In this selection of writing, Bethan successfully attempts a range of forms which includes poetry, letter, diary entry and explanation. The selection includes passages of extended writing which contain sentences of varying length and complexity, and the appropriate use of notes and short sentences in other work. Throughout this range, ideas and explanation are sustained, and the reader's interest is held. Other organisational features are used appropriately in the work 'The Finders', though the only evidence of paragraphing is in the letter written after reading 'Carrie's War'. Bethan's spelling is usually accurate, and her use of punctuation, including full stops, commas, question marks and inverted commas, is generally correct. In general, vocabulary choices tend to rely on the familiar, although there is evidence of more confident selection in the poem. Some Level 5 qualities are apparent in her use of punctuation and control of a range of forms, but there is insufficient evidence to fully justify Level 5. On balance, a secure judgement can be made that Bethan's performance best fits Level 4 in Writing.
>
> (SCAA, 1995: 59)

Although this example represents a high quality of assessment, it also shows the amount of work that is involved. Nearly every sentence of the quote would require careful consideration by the teacher. It must be remembered that this assessment is only for writing and that the primary teacher has many other subjects and areas to assess. Once again it is important to reiterate that the best assessment has to be manageable and of a high quality.

Although the teacher assessment at the end of key stages is claimed to be as important as the SATs, it is obvious from government comment and inspection reports that the SATs are more influential. In 1998 the SAT writing test included four options to choose from: an interview, a newsletter, and two short stories. Helpfully the tests offer a context for the writing including a suggested audience. They also have some minimal suggestions for things to think about. The newsletter task involved the information shown in Box 19.3.

The marking criteria for this task were published in the QCA document 'English Tests Mark Schemes' which includes examples of writing at different levels. The highest marks for purpose and organisation were to be awarded if

2. The School Trip
A school is planning a trip for next year's year 6.
The headteacher wants to give the children a newsletter to take home.
The newsletter will explain all about the trip and how to prepare for it.
Write the newsletter for next year's Year 6 children to take home.
You can write the newsletter using information from a real school trip

or

you can make up the information.

Remember you are trying to give **useful information** about the trip, and to make it sound **interesting** and **worthwhile**.

Box 19.3

the following criteria were met:

High Level 5
The piece is well written. Detail and sequence are confidently managed throughout to engage and sustain the reader's interest, in that points are well chosen and well ordered, and the full range of information about the trip is covered in appropriate detail. Sustained awareness of the reader is shown through such features as an introduction which establishes the voice and role of the writer and a final paragraph which offers an overview of the task, summarising the value of the trip or indicating what action the reader should take. Ideas are organised appropriately using paragraphs or other layout features. **21 marks**

(QCA, 1998a: 24)

Teachers' assessments of their children should result in changes to future teaching and learning and this is one of the most important reasons for assessment. However, the need to reach the SATs targets means that schools also need to analyse the areas where children are weakest and offer more support in those areas. At a national level QCA publish reports which can contribute to schools decisions on further support.

National reports

The report on the 1998 national assessments for 11-year-olds highlighted some key issues. One of these was a concern that boys were not improving their scores as quickly as girls. An interesting suggestion put forward was that boys should be given opportunities to 'write about their interests' (QCA, 1998b: 5). We agree with this but feel that it is important that all children should be given this opportunity (➡ Chapter 14, 'Genre and the Process of Writing').

As far as writing was concerned a number of weaknesses were commented on by the QCA report. Boys narrative (☞) writing tended to focus on action rather than description or character and they needed to be encouraged to extend their writing into areas such as description and discussion. There were also problems for all children who achieved lower levels of attainment in their understanding of the structures of different kinds of writing. It was also claimed that spelling performance was made weaker by children's lack of knowledge of the conventions and 'rules'. This conclusion perhaps needs more thought in the light of the fact that children's spelling difficulties are often individual. Attempts to teach general rules to all children may only be partially successful if they are not complimented by individualised spelling approaches and a wider range of strategies (➡ Chapter 15, 'Spelling').

The 1999 report (QCA, 1999b) suggested that boys performed better in questions requiring short answers. Girls outperformed boys 'on more open-ended questions involving the interpretation of information, language features and underlying themes' (p8). Overall, the 5% increase in children achieving level 4 in 1999 showed that boys still lagged behind girls and that reading had improved but writing had remained fairly static.

Gipps and Murphy's award winning work on assessment and equity raised gender issues in relation to the original SATs as early as 1990:

> A general picture emerges at ages 7 (in 1990 and 1991) and 14 (in 1991) of girls scoring higher than boys particularly in English and maths; more boys scoring at the extremes; minority ethnic groups scoring lower than 'white' children; those whose home language is not English scoring significantly less well; teacher assessment lower than the SAT score for children from ethnic minorities and/or whose home language is not English.
>
> (Gipps and Murphy, 1994: 205)

The original SATs were carried out in normal classrooms and involved typical classroom activities which were assessed by teachers. At the time many teachers took industrial action, as the tests were too time-consuming and disruptive. It may have been that the general dissatisfaction with government directives caused teachers to choose an issue that they felt was a common concern. This was certainly a politically effective choice, but the government of the day used this as the reason for producing much more narrowly focused 'pencil-and-paper' tests which were to be marked independently. Ironically it is possible that the original style of activity-based test, despite boys initial lack of success, may have been more appropriate for boys. The lower status given to teacher's own assessments may also be a problem in relation to raising the achievements of boys.

Practice points

- Improve your interaction with children to enhance informal assessment skills.
- Keep diaries of observations of children's English development.
- Ensure a high quality of objective focused assessments rather than a large quantity.

Glossary

Formative assessment – ongoing assessment that is used to inform intervention and planning.

Level descriptions – short paragraphs in the National Curriculum that describe the understanding that children should have gained in order to attain a particular level.

Moderation – the process of agreeing assessment judgements with other people

Multi-lingual – speaking two or more languages

Narrative – a text which retells events; stories are narratives.

Portfolio – a collection of children's work that often includes forms for teachers' comments

SATs – Standard Assessment Tasks (like exams) that are taken by all children at ages 7, 11 and 14.

Summative assessment – assessment taken at a particular time that enables the teacher to make a judgement about progress.

Teacher assessment – a statutory process where teachers decide National Curriculum levels for children at 7, 11 and 14.

References

Filer, A. (1993) 'Contents of assessment in a primary classroom', *British Educational Research Journal*, 19: 95–108.

Gipps, C. and Murphy, P. (1994) *A Fair Test? Assessment and Equity*. Buckingham: Open University Press.

Qualifications and Curriculum Authority (QCA) (1998a) *English Tests Mark Schemes*. London: QCA.

Qualifications and Curriculum Authority (QCA) (1998b) *Standards at Key Stage 2: English, Mathematics and Science: Report on the 1998 National Curriculum assessments for 11-year-olds*. London: QCA.

Qualifications and Curriculum Authority (QCA) (1999a) *Target Setting and Assessment in the National Literacy Strategy*. London: QCA.

Qualifications and Curriculum Authority (QCA) (1999b). *Standards at Key Stage 2: English, Mathematics and Science: Report on the 1999 National Curriculum Assessments for 11-year-olds*. London: QCA.

School Curriculum and Assessment Authority (SCAA) (1995) *Exemplification of Standards: English*. London: SCAA.

Annotated bibliography

Bearne, E. and Farrow, C. (1991) *Writing Policy in Action*. Buckingham: Open University Press.

Chapter 4 'A Year's Progress' looks in depth at the links between the writing curriculum and assessment and record-keeping for writing.
L2 **

Gipps, C. and Murphy, P. (1994) *A Fair Test? Assessment, Achievement and Equity*. Buckingham: Open University Press.
This award winning book looks in detail at some of the issues that underpin assessment. Gipps has developed great expertise in this field so any of her publications are worth reading.
L3 ***

Qualifications and Curriculum Authority (QCA) (1999) *Target Setting and Assessment in the National Literacy Strategy*. London: QCA.
Like many other QCA publications on assessment this manages to put forward realistic guidance on assessment. Particularly welcome is the reminder that not all assessment has to be written down.
L1 *

Part IV

Speaking and listening

Chapter 20

The development of talk

The stages of language acquisition are outlined. Links are established between speaking and listening and the subsequent development of reading and writing. Speaking and listening in the National Curriculum and National Literacy Strategy are examined. The balance between speaking and listening, reading and writing is a key issue for this chapter.

People who have 'conversations' with their pet cats are often parodied or ridiculed, but this 'talk' is not so strange as it might at first appear, and in some ways it mirrors human language interaction in the earliest stages. A cat's owner learns that different sounds are invested with different meanings, for example the sound a hungry cat makes can be quite different to the cry made for attention or to be let outside the house. In much the same way, parents learn to 'read' the cries of their new-born children and quickly understand the distinction between a cry of distress and a cry for attention. It has also been known for cats to learn the turn-taking process which characterises conversation. The owner speaks (typically in a warm and comforting way) to the animal, the cat waits for a pause in the proceedings and then contributes a sound. The owner replies and the 'conversation' continues. While this is not a very sophisticated piece of communication, it does constitute the transference of sounds and meaning, and animals can keep up this turn taking game for some time. Babies learn to take turns in conversation in much the same way. The child learns to anticipate silence, and their conversational noises then slot into the spaces left by the adult. The noises themselves do not necessarily represent meaning at this stage: gurgles, chuckles and repetitive sounds merely serve to punctuate the conversation taking place, acknowledging the nature of turn taking and maintaining the shared pattern of contribution. Babies soon learn, however, that they are able to use these noises to greater effect, that some noises are more powerful than others and (eventually) that some sounds represent external objects.

In all societies across the world children face the task of mastering a language system which is historically well established and rooted within their own culture. The vocabularies and grammatical systems of all cultures are complicated and yet children seem to be able to almost magically learn them in order to communicate.

STAGES OF LANGUAGE ACQUISITION

While there are still disputes over the precise stages of language acquisition, it remains possible to outline broad sequential features which indicate the process.

Birth–6 months

At this stage the noises that babies make are not culturally distinctive: despite different languages they initially make the same sounds in all societies. The typical sounds made range between those which represent hunger or distress, and those which represent contentment. Sounds made at this stage are nasal, formed at the back of the mouth and are reminiscent of consonants. Gradually, words start to be formed closer to the front of the mouth and the baby gains greater control over speech mechanisms. By the end of this stage, babies begin to 'babble', and appear to enjoy finding out what sounds they are capable of generating. They also enjoy the response these sounds generate from adults.

6 months–12 months

During this stage, the noises that represented urgency (cries) or well-being (cooing) become gradually replaced by the rhythm and tone of the child's distinctive voice. Inflections and patterns within the babble take on greater significance. This is the first indication that the child is learning to organise sounds into identifiable patterns (the beginnings of grammar and sentence structure). As the babble becomes more organised, other linguistic features begin to appear. These include the first words, which are often duplicated syllables (such as 'dada', 'mama', 'baba'). The phonemes usually heard at this time are /p/, /b/ and /m/, and it is typically some time before the child starts to use some others such as /v/, /f/, and /s/. Inflections in the child's words take on extra significance at this time. The child who is able to use the word 'mama' develops a variety of pronunciations to express different needs: for example by changing the inflection at the end of the word the child turns it into a question, and 'mama?' conveys the question 'Where is my mother?'.

1 year–2 years

The crossover from babble to recognisable talk continues. Often the child's speech contains features of both, but increasingly there are key words and phrases which appear on a regular basis. Speech is less likely to be duplicated and there is a greater variety to the babble that takes place. Typically sentences are contracted so that the main meaning is invested in two words (described as 'two-word utterances'). Sometimes these two words are able to convey a simple message (such as 'all gone'), but at other times they may take on a variety of potential meanings (for example *mum car* which could mean mummy is in the car, mummy has got a car, mummy where is the car? etc.).

2–3 years

Gradually more verbs and adjectives are added to speech. Sentences begin to take on greater length and complexity. Sentence structure may still appear shaky, but typically there are enough words and enough contextual and grammatical clues present to convey meaning. The repetition of nursery rhymes and songs is an important feature of language development in the early stages and children use these memorised snippets of meaning to help them understand the language use taking place all around them. Stories take on extra significance, and children become aware of the ways in which the voice can be controlled, so that a whispered section of a story has quite different meaning to a section which is shouted in a booming tone. These linguistic behaviours are often re-enacted through play with dolls and other toys.

3 years onwards

The ability to be able to ask questions becomes increasingly important, and every parent has had to deal with the child who asks a question, receives a reply and then asks another question. This process is invariably repeated until the parent is frustrated or exhausted! Suffixes (☞) become a noticeable feature of language acquisition at this time and are another early indicator of the child's attempts to grapple with the intricacies of grammatical structures. A common example of this is a noticeable inflection on the suffix 'ed'. Children begin to acknowledge that verbs are given the suffix 'ed' to place them in the past tense, but the process of doing this is sometimes over emphasised, almost pointing out the process in action. The 'ed' will be pronounced as though it rhymes with 'bed', and 'kick-ed', 'show-ed' and 'drink-ed' are examples. By about the age of 4, the child has begun to develop a wider range of verbs, and greater grammatical variations become more apparent in everyday speech.

The range of development from 3 years onwards varies greatly, but it is generally accepted that spoken language acquisition is in place by the age of 5, leaving more sophisticated features to be acquired by the age of 7. Maggie MacLure constructed a 'Communicative Inventory at Age Five' which might prove enlightening at this point. She suggested that by the age of five, many children will:

- Draw on a vocabulary of several thousand words
- Control many of the major grammatical constructions of their language – though some aspects of grammar will not be acquired until later
- Speak with a regular, adult-like pronunciation, adopting the speech patterns of their community
- Talk for a range of purposes – including many 'higher-order' ones such as hypothesising, speculating, predicting
- Use talk to further their own learning
- Express their feelings through talk, and understand the feelings of others

- Disconnect talk from the 'here-and-now' where appropriate
- Assess other people's background knowledge and adjust their own talk in the light of this
- Assume joint responsibility for the meanings that are produced through talk
- Know (or quickly learn) many of the cultural and procedural rules for talking with different kinds of people – peers, parents, teachers, strangers
- Engage in role play, and experiment with different interactional 'identities'
- Deploy a range of rhetorical (☞) and persuasive tactics for increasing the likelihood of securing their own goals, avoiding blame or trouble etc.
- Have some metalinguistic (☞) knowledge, i.e. be able to reflect on, and talk about, talk itself
- Get some pleasure out of playing with, and through, language
- Have a developing sense of genres of talk, e.g. jokes, stories, 'news' etc.

(NOP, 1992 :23–4)

PRE-SCHOOL LANGUAGE INTERACTION

By examining the stages of language acquisition and beginning to understand the theories of how and why this process takes place, it becomes clear that pre-school experience of social interaction is a desperately important factor in the child's ongoing language development. The significance of the adults around the child at this time should not be underestimated. It has been acknowledged that they provide a number of important conditions for the child as they:

- Provide access to an environment where talk has high status
- Provide access to competent users of language
- Provide opportunities to engage in talk
- Provide responses which acknowledge the child as a competent language user.

(Wray et al, 1989 :39)

From this short list it will be apparent to you that if adults provide these key features to support language development in the early years, then some children are likely to be better skilled in these areas than others as a direct result of their home environment. Even having accepted that children have LAD and LASS capabilities (➡Chapter 2, 'Theories of Learning') which enable them to construct the rules of language engagement, it is clear that there are other features of language acquisition (such as encouragement, positive questioning, status and opportunity to develop as speakers) which are dependent upon the quality of interaction with adults. The degree to which a rich language environment assists language development has been well documented; see the work of Tizard and Hughes (1984) for more information in this area.

Even though most of the language acquisition process is complete as children enter school, there is much that the teacher can do in the early years to consolidate and develop these skills. Children's language acquisition is likely to be stronger if they are encouraged to become active participants in conversation, if they are encouraged to be questioning (despite how frustrating this can be for some adults to deal with), to hypothesise, imagine, wonder, project and dream out loud, to hear stories and to tell stories to others, experiencing a range of telling techniques which illustrate the potential power of the spoken word. The social and cultural aspects of language development are equally important at this time, as children learn, through talk, to place themselves within a specific social context, and in this way the development of language and identity are closely linked.

The quality of social experience and interaction will vary greatly between children, and during the early years teachers need to be aware that some children will arrive at school appearing to be confident, articulate masters of the English language, whereas others seem less comfortable language users. Beginning teachers should be aware of deficit models (➡Chapter 2, 'Theories of Learning') and remember that it is too easy to label a child's spoken language as 'poor' without sufficient thought. Bearne, for example, offers a transcription of a discussion including Sonnyboy, a 6-year-old boy from a Traveller community, demonstrating his ability to 'translate' language for other children:

Emily:	I loves them little things.
Sonnyboy:	Yeah . . . I loves the little things – that tiny wee spade . . . And this little bucket . . .
Teacher:	Do you think it would be a good idea to ask Cathy to get some? (Cathy runs a playgroup for the Traveller children on their site.)
Emily:	What for?
Teacher:	So that you'd have some at home.
Sonnyboy:	And who'd pay for them? Would Cathy pay?
Teacher:	No, it would be part of the kit.
Emily:	I don't know what you mean. Kit – who's Kit? Me Da's called Kit – would me Da have to pay?
Sonnyboy:	Not your Da – it's not that sort of kit, Emily. It's the sort a box with things in that you play with . . . like toys and things for the little ones.

(Bearne, 1998 :154)

It is important then that the teacher understands about language diversity and the ways in which judgements are made about speakers in the classroom. From this perspective it is equally important that teachers recognise their own histories and status as language users, and resist the temptation to impose their own social criteria on the child's ongoing language development. As Bearne goes on to point out:

Language diversity is . . . deeply involved with social and cultural judgements about what is valuable or worthy . . . Judgements are often made about intelligence, social status, trustworthiness and potential for future employment on the basis of how people speak – not the content of what they say, but their pronunciation, choice of vocabulary and tone of voice. Such attitudes can have an impact on later learning.

(Bearne, 1998 :155).

There is a relationship between the development of the spoken word and the development of the written word. If the child feels that their spoken language is in some way inadequate, this has implications for aspects of literacy development. All approaches to the teaching of both reading and writing acknowledge the important links with talking. It is therefore important that teachers in the early years acknowledge that children have different starting points within speaking and listening, are sensitive to the notion of language diversity, and actively work towards supporting the child's attempts to establish bridges between speaking and listening and reading and writing.

SPEAKING AND LISTENING IN THE 1988/1995 NATIONAL CURRICULUM

The introduction of the 1988 National Curriculum brought with it many changes, one of which was to allocate a more prominent role to speaking and listening in primary classrooms. Prior to the publication of the orders for speaking and listening, it was clear that the profile of this area of language development had begun to take on wider significance in schools (through the experience of initiatives such as the National Oracy Project), and the Cox Committee was established as part of a statutory consultation process in the writing of the English National Curriculum proposals. The first draft set of proposals stated:

> The overriding aim of the English curriculum is to enable all pupils to develop to their full ability to use and understand English. Since language can be both spoken and written, this means the fullest possible development of abilities in speaking, listening, reading and writing.
>
> (DES, 1988: para 3.12).

The second draft set of proposals begin with the unequivocal statement that:

> Our inclusion of speaking and listening as a separate profile component in our recommendations is a reflection of our conviction that they are of central importance to children's development
>
> (DES, 1989: para 15.1)

The structure of the original National Curriculum orders and the subsequent revision orders (DFE, 1995) both clearly placed speaking and listening on an equal plane with writing and reading. The committees and consultation processes which resulted in these documents acknowledged the centrality of speaking and listening to the learning of English, and placed speaking and listening as the very first aspect of both the general requirements and the programmes of study in each of the documents. Whereas the consultation documents were of a more philosophical, discursive nature and the final orders were far more direct in terms of ground to be covered, both documents firmly established the primacy of speaking and listening in the primary curriculum.

Teachers at the time of the first National Curriculum were encouraged to look for ways in which specific speaking and listening teaching could be enhanced through work in other areas of the curriculum, so (for example), the language of hypothesising might be a natural feature of a typical primary science lesson, and it was seen as good practice to develop a cross-curricular approach.

From the character of early National Curriculum documentation, it is possible to recognise the wide-ranging role of speaking and listening. It read as though speaking and listening were to be exploratory, investigative and developmental. For example, the National Curriculum Council published an introductory pack which (among other things) talked about:

- Collaboration with other children
- Discussion of books and ideas with teachers and other children
- Commenting in thoughtful ways
- Participating orally in imaginative play
- Discussing language progress with teachers
- Listening to other children's stories
- Taking part in formal oral presentations.

(NCC, 1989, Primary English 1 and 2)

These kinds of statement again establish speaking and listening as vital, lively aspects of primary classrooms, offering teachers exciting opportunities for the teaching of English.

SPEAKING AND LISTENING IN THE FRAMEWORK FOR TEACHING

There can be little doubt that the place of speaking and listening has been challenged by the National Literacy Strategy Framework for Teaching. Whereas the Cox Reports and the two forms of National Curriculum located speaking and listening within a strong philosophy of whole language development, there are different philosophies (➡ Chapter 2, 'Theories of learning') at work within the structure of the framework.

The Framework for Teaching acknowledges that speaking and listening are aspects of wider literacy, but follows this belief by compiling a list of features that together make up a 'literate primary pupil', of which only the need for a 'technical vocabulary through which to understand and discuss their reading and writing' mentions speaking and listening at all (DFEE, 1998 :3). This list is immediately followed by outline requirements for reading and writing.

Of course it is possible to locate areas of the Framework for Teaching where speaking and listening *are* promoted. For example; 'Split familiar oral and written compound words (☞) into their component parts' (year 2 term 2), 'Discuss the merits and limitations of particular instructional texts' (year 3 term 2) and 'Summarise orally in one sentence the context of a passage or text and the point it is making' (year 3 term 3). While these are clearly speaking and listening activities, they are significantly different in a number of ways from the original National Curriculum orders.

Firstly, the structure of the Framework for Teaching is predominantly reliant on the development of reading and writing. Hence the final example offered above appears as an activity under the heading 'Non-fiction Reading Comprehension'. Speaking and listening activities are located as subsidiary within wider work on reading and writing. Secondly, the nature of the work itself is different. Again, the examples offered above are hardly likely to be described as exploratory, investigative or developmental forms of talk. Speaking and listening takes on a functional quality; a means by which the skills of reading and writing may be enhanced. Thirdly, there is an implicit suggestion that speaking and listening activities are more suited (as literacy activities) to Key Stage 1. When scanning the Framework for Teaching for examples of speaking and listening activities, it becomes noticeably more difficult after year 3, suggesting that as an aspect of literacy development, speaking and listening's combined importance wanes as children get older. This is in direct opposition to research evidence which suggests that speaking and listening tasks involving 11-year-olds brings in greater opportunity for higher language skills such as speculation, sustained argument, cohesion (Wilkinson 1991).

It bears repeating that there has been no legislation which deprioritises speaking and listening, in fact the National Curriculum 2000 states that:

> In teaching the literacy framework some aspects of speaking and listening are also covered. As well as implementing fully the literacy Framework for teaching, schools must take care to cover the whole of the speaking and listening section of the English programmes of study for Key Stages 1 and 2.
>
> (DfEE/QCA, 1999: 23)

There has, however, been a sea change in recent years which effectively ensures that speaking and listening is seen as less of a priority by many policy-makers. Teaching has changed towards a tighter transmission model (☞), and as the emphasis for the teacher shifts towards teaching that which is demonstrable and measurable, there are inevitably fewer opportunities for speaking and listening to develop as natural activities. The primary school day is dominated by the Literacy and Numeracy Strategies, leaving little opportunity for creative and unpredictable aspects of development such as talk. The nature of speaking and listening tasks have changed so that they are no longer exploratory, investigative or developmental; they serve the purpose of supporting reading and writing, which are now the key indicators of literacy.

WORKING BEYOND THE NLS FRAMEWORK

Recent research evidence highlights a commitment towards the development of speaking and listening particularly amongst recently qualified teachers, who understand the value this has towards cognitive development (Lyle,

1997), and it is important that the NLS's emphasis on reading and writing should not diminish this positive practice. Teachers intending to develop speaking and listening beyond the brief established by the Framework for Teaching need to build conscious opportunities for oracy into their work, and it is perhaps fruitful to begin by looking at some aspects of the study which are best addressed in this way.

The National Curriculum 2000 directs that children should be offered opportunities to talk for a range of purposes, including planning, predicting and investigating:

> *Group discussion and interaction*
> 10. The range of purposes should include:
> a)   investigating, selecting, sorting
> b)   planning, predicting, exploring
> c)   explaining, reporting, evaluating.
>
> *Drama activities*
> 11. The range should include:
> a)   improvisation and working in role
> b)   scripting and performing in plays
> c)   responding to performances.
>
> (DfEE/QCA, 1999: 52)

Some of these features of spoken language are ideally suited to mathematical and scientific study. By asking the children to hypothesise, to predict, to project into the future, the teacher not only encourages healthy mathematical and scientific practices, this also brings into being a range of associated language features. By asking children to discuss and share their predictions they are also required to defend their positions, to see other people's viewpoints, to balance different hypotheses, to apply a stated idea to their own prediction and so on.

To take a different kind of example, there is clear documentary evidence of the development of historical understanding coming about as a direct result of talk (De-Fountain and Lowe, 1992, Fairclough, 1994, Redfern 1996). Educationalists and historians alike have found it a relatively easy task to capture historical understanding taking place in the classroom through directed discussion and observation. The use of historical artefacts and visits to sites of historical interest allow teachers the opportunity to establish exploratory talk which actually facilitates deeper understanding. Similarly, there is much to be gained through open discussion centred around fiction, music and art. These areas of study are meant to be discussed, they invite individual interpretation which requires subsequent discussion. This is not fruitless talk (if such a commodity should exist!), it actively and directly enhances the child's learning.

If these kinds of opportunities are restricted in the primary classroom, then there are clear implications for the nature of (for example) scientific and historical knowledge. If the teacher's planning is focused on demonstrable and measurable knowledge with predictable outcomes, it is unrealistic to expect the associated talk to rise above the closed, descriptive, repetitive or the functional. If, however, the teacher introduces an element of unpredictability, of interpretation, of negotiation, then the nature of the associated talk changes, and instead becomes open, exploratory, tentative, questioning, insightful and collaborative. To build a classroom which encourages a range of speaking and listening activities for a range of purposes is to accept that there are different kinds of knowledge, different kinds of teaching and different kinds of learning. To restrict opportunities for this kind of interaction in the Primary classroom is to restrict the kinds of understandings they help generate.

Practice points

- Plan specific opportunities for cross-curricular speaking and listening work including creative arts.
- Develop a range of teacher/pupil interaction styles in order to develop a high quality of speaking and listening.
- Enjoy and celebrate opportunities for regular structured and exploratory drama work.

Glossary

Compound words – a word made up of two other words: e.g. cupboard.
Metalinguistic – technical vocabulary used to describe language: e.g. word, sentence, verb, bilingual, etc.
Rhetorical – skills of speech used for particular effects.
Suffix – letter or letters (known as a 'morpheme') added to the end of a word which change the meaning.
Transmission models – models of teaching which emphasise instruction of knowledge above independent learning.

References

Bearne, E. (1998) *Making Progress in English*. London: Routledge.
Bruner, J. S. (1983) *Child's Talk: Learning to Use Language*. Oxford: Oxford University Press.
De-Fountain, J. and Lowe, A. (1992) 'Pupils working together on understanding in NOP'. *Thinking Voices: The Work of the National Oracy Project*. London: Hodder & Stoughton.
Department of Education and Science and the Welsh Office (DES) (1988) *English for Ages 5–11 (The First Cox Report)*. London: HMSO.
Department of Education and Science and The Welsh Office (DES) (1989) *English for Ages 5–16 (The Second Cox Report)*. York: National Curriculum Council.
Department for Education (DFE) (1995) *Key Stages 1 and 2 of the National Curriculum*. London: HMSO.

Department for Education and Employment (DfEE) (1998) *The National Literacy Strategy Framework for Teaching*. London: HMSO.

Department for Education and Employment/Qualifications and Curriculum Authority (DfEE/QCA) (1999) *The National Curriculum: Handbook for Primary Teachers in England: Key Stages 1 and 2*. London: DfEE/QCA.

Fairclough, J. (1994) *Role Up*. Produced by English Heritage. English Heritage, videocassette.

Lyle, S. (1997) 'An investigation into the attitudes of teachers at Key Stage 2 to speaking and listening in the national curriculum in Wales', *Educational Studies*, 23 (1): 39–53.

National Curriculum Council(NCC) (1989) *An Introduction to the National Curriculum*. York: NCC/Open University.

National Oracy Project (NOP) (1990) *Teaching Talking and Learning in Key Stage 1*. York: National Curriculum Council.

National Oracy Project (NOP) (1992) *Thinking Voices: The Work of the National Oracy Project*. London: Hodder & Stoughton.

Redfern, A. (1996) *Talking in Class: Oral History and the National Curriculum* Colchester: Oral History Society.

Tizard, B. and Hughes, M. (1984) *Young Children Learning*. London: Fontana.

Wilkinson, A. (1991) 'Evaluating group discussion', *Educational Review*, 43 (2): 131–141.

Wray, D., Bloom, W. and Hall, N. (1989) *Literacy in Action*. Barcombe: Falmer.

Annotated bibliography

Bearne, E. (1998) *Making Progress in English*. London: Routledge.
While this is not purely a book about speaking and listening, it contains wonderful examples of children's talk (often with teachers) and provides keen insight into the way in which this talk is related to reading and writing development.
L2 **

Maclure, M., Phillips, T. and Wilkinson, A. (eds) (1988) *Oracy Matters*. Milton Keynes: Open University Press.
Andrew Wilkinson coined the term 'oracy' and this collection is an important record of the work that was done before and during the National Oracy Project.
L2 **

Norman, K. (ed.) (1992) *Thinking Voices: The Work of the National Oracy Project*. London: Hodder & Stoughton.
A collection of voices which includes children, teachers, project coordinators, LEA advisers, academics and researchers, combining to present a readable and comprehensive introduction to speaking and listening issues.
L2 **

Chapter 21

Accent, dialect and Standard English

The emphasis in this chapter is on accent and dialect (☞) as rich resources of the English language. A discussion on standard English (☞) flags up the political factors that are at work. We conclude with some thoughts on language and identity.

Some people insist that the use of regional accents represent inferior intellect. The following extract from a poem by William Wordsworth sheds some light on this matter:

The Jay makes answer as the Magpie chatters;
And all the air is filled with pleasant noise of waters.
(Wordsworth, 1807: 270)

Wordsworth's own regional accent meant that water would have been pronounced 'watter', meaning that 'chatter' and 'water' represent a natural rhyme.

One of the reasons why the English language is considered to be so rich is because of the many intriguing and fascinating variations it has to offer. These variations reveal themselves in many ways including through accent and dialect. While there are many people in society who regard accents and dialects as a rich source of language, there is sometimes a tendency to treat them differently in schools. Some teachers feel that they are obliged to correct children's 'mispronunciations' because of the National Curriculum's insistence on the use of Standard English. It is not difficult to become confused about the differences between accent, dialect, standard English, Queen's English, etc. The whole business of the child's language can seem like a linguistic minefield. A strong understanding of some of the terms can help you to know when it is appropriate to correct a child and when it may be inappropriate.

All speakers of English use a dialect. Dialect refers to a specific vocabulary and grammar which is influenced by geographical factors. It does not refer to the ways in which words are pronounced. Regional dialect includes particular words that are special to the locality. For example, a flat, circular slice of potato cooked in a fish and chip shop has a large range of names across the country: in Warrington it is a *scallop*, in South Wales it is a *patty*, in

Liverpool it is a *fritter*, in West Bromwich it is a *klandike* and in Crewe it is a *smack*. Dialect also contains grammatical differences: for example in Stoke the phrase 'Her's not coming until tomorrow' is an example of the ways in which regional dialect alters the grammatical structure of the sentence while maintaining meaning.

Just as all speakers of English are users of dialect, all speakers of English use an accent. Accent is the way in which the language is spoken. Some accents are geographical, others are related to social characteristics, but in all cases accent refers to the ways in which the language sounds. Some accents have characteristic inflections and pronunciations which typify them and allow the listener to make guesses about the speaker's geographical origin. You cannot guess this about speakers who use received pronunciation.

Received pronunciation (RP) (☞) is sometimes referred to as 'the Queen's English' or 'BBC English'. It is the 'posh' accent with which we have come to associate public schools, 'high society' and radio broadcasters from 50 years ago. It is different to other accents because it denies the listener any indication of the speaker's geographical origin. It is primarily a socially influenced accent rather than a geographically influenced one, and it locates the speaker in a particular social group.

STANDARD ENGLISH

The question of spoken 'Standard English' is one that has also been particularly influenced by political factors. It is a complex issue that is centrally about the social context of language use, and it is bedevilled by prejudice and misunderstanding. The Cox Report contained a sensible discussion of the issue (DES, 1989) and the 1990 National Curriculum orders required only that older primary pupils should have opportunity to use spoken Standard English 'in appropriate contexts' (DES, 1990: 25) and that knowledge should rise out of the pupil's 'own linguistic competence' (DES, 1989: 6.11). The 1995 National Curriculum highlighted the issue of Standard English in a separate section which included the misleading requirement that 'To develop effective speaking and listening pupils should be taught to use the vocabulary and grammar of Standard English' (DFE, 1995: 2,3) but otherwise left the Cox approach intact. The statement is misleading because effective speaking and listening develops in all dialects not just Standard English.

The literacy hour has shifted the ground radically with its requirement that children should be taught 'to use standard forms of verbs in speaking and writing' from year 2 onwards with no reference to appropriateness of context. The absurdity of such a requirement had already been expounded by Katherine Perera (Cox, 1995: 66–73) and no subsequent evidence is offered in the literacy strategy's own review of research (Beard, 1999) to support such a change of approach. The lack of distinction between Standard English for writing and Standard English for talking also means that such a requirement is questionable.

The National Curriculum attempts to bypass some of the difficulties concerning prejudicial assumptions about dialect by referring to appropriateness. The documentation guides teachers towards getting children to understand that different language forms require different degrees of formality. Children are encouraged to see the differences between, for example, the spoken language of the playground and spoken language in a formal interview.

There have been numerous debates about the role and status of accent, dialect, Standard English and RP, and the advent of the National Curriculum and the National Literacy Strategy have merely added to the debate. Standard English is presumed to be the superior dialect, but this is to presume that the language itself can be standardised. This seems to imply that poetic language and the language of a chemistry textbook are two forms of the same dialect.

LANGUAGE AND IDENTITY

Trudgill (1975) offers a pyramid of social variation, at the peak of which are those who use Standard English and speak with the accent of RP, resulting in high social status. The base of the pyramid is made up of a wide range of regional accents and dialects which are afforded low social status. This may seem a crude generalisation, but if accents and dialects carry social baggage with them, then there are issues for teachers to consider when one form of dialect is accepted as superior in the classroom.

> There is a particular danger that, if standard English is held up as a superior dialect which ought to replace the child's own, the child will come to resent and reject anything that has to do with standard English – especially reading . . . there is evidence to suggest that some children at least may not learn to read because they do not want to: and that they do not want to for reasons which have to do with group identity and cultural conflict, in both of which dialect certainly plays a role.
>
> (Trudgill, 1975: 67).

As an example of identity and conflict we offer the following anecdote. When one of the authors of this chapter was completing his initial teacher training he was told by a supervising tutor that he could not be a teacher until he had lost his 'working-class accent'. Over 10 years later, while completing classroom-based research the author watched a lesson given by a student teacher in a classroom where she, the teacher and the children all shared the same strong Potteries accent and dialect. Despite the fact that the lesson had progressed perfectly well, and the children had achieved the aims of the lesson, the student was failed outright by the university tutor who 'could not understand a word that was said'. The student reported that 'I was told I can't speak. I'm common'.

These examples illustrate the close connection between accent, dialect and personal identity. The insensitive correction of regional dialects runs the risk of upsetting people, whether they are children or adults. It is for this reason that activities which encourage reflection on language in different contexts (such as role play for different degrees of formality and looking at the differences between speech and writing) are preferable to continual correction.

There have been arguments to suggest that non-standard dialects should be purged from the classroom and teachers have resorted to all kinds of tactics to attempt to ensure this takes place:

> Generations of teachers have employed persuasion, exhortation, punishment, scorn and ridicule in attempts to prevent children from using non-standard dialects – and all of them without success. And there is no reason to suppose that they will be any more successful in the future.
>
> (Trudgill, 1975: 66).

The issue for the teacher therefore is how to achieve the balance between using the child's own language as a motivational and cultural tool for development while at the same time illustrating that certain language forms are more appropriate than others at certain times and in certain social situations. Much of this is achievable by establishing particular audiences and contexts for talk activities. However, although children have to be aware that Standard English is the norm in formal situations they also need to be aware that there is considerable prejudice against regional accents and dialects.

Practice points

- Regional dialects should be respected and seen as a rich language resource.
- Standard English is often best discussed in the context of writing.
- Sometimes correction is necessary, but this always needs to be done sensitively.

Glossary

Dialect – regional variations of grammar and vocabulary in language.
Received pronunciation – a particular accent often called 'BBC English'.
Standard English – the formal language of written communication in particular. Many people call this 'correct' English.

References

Beard, R. (1999) *National Literacy Strategy Review of Research and Other Related Evidence*. Suffolk: DfEE Publications.

Cox, B. (1995) *Cox on the Battle for the English Curriculum*. London: Hodder & Stoughton.

Department of Education and Science and The Welsh Office (DES) (1989) *English for Ages 5–16 (The second Cox Report)*. York: National Curriculum Council.

Department of Education and Science and The Welsh Office (DES) (1990) *English in the National Curriculum*. London: HMSO.

Department for Education (DFE) (1995) *English in the National Curriculum.* London: HMSO.

Trudgill, P. (1975) *Accent, Dialect and the School.* London: Open University Press.

Wordsworth, W. (1807) 'Resolution and independence', in *Oxford Library of English Poetry, Volume 2.* Bungay: Book Club Associates.

Annotated bibliography

Dutton, Dave. Completely Lanky: Lancashire Dialect Book. The Lancashire Webring. [online – cited 26-6-00]. Available from:
   http://www.nyt.co.uk/lancashire.htm#WE'VE%20SUPPED%20SOME%20STUFF!
Lighthearted revelations about Lancashire dialect. This includes the option to listen to dialect phrases being spoken.

Milroy, J. and Milroy, L. (1985) *Authority in Language.* London: Routledge.
A mainly theoretical, but lively, examination of attitudes towards 'correct' and 'incorrect' uses of English. The third (1999) edition of this book addresses the increasing debate about Standard English in schools.
L3 ***

Trudgill, P. (1975) *Accent, Dialect and the School.* London: Open University Press.
This book remains the primary text in its field. It is short, readable and very informative about a complicated area of language development.
L2 **

Chapter 22

Planning for talk

The reasons for systematic planning for talk are followed by an example of some children talking about an exciting display in their classroom. The chapter concludes with some examples of classroom strategies.

A man follows the same routine each day. He gets up in the morning, leaves his flat on the 19th floor and gets into the lift. He descends to the ground floor, catches the number 28 bus and goes to work in a public library. At the end of the day he returns on the 28 bus, but he always travels to the 8th floor then uses the stairs up to his flat on the 19th floor. Why does he always proceed from the ground floor to his flat in this way at night? *(Answer at the end)*

Box 22.1

Solving this kind of lateral thinking (☞) problem can be one of many ways to engage children in collaborative thinking and talking. As you saw in Chapter 20, 'The development of talk' it is important that talk is systematically planned just like other areas of the curriculum.

There is an expectation that opportunities to plan for talk should arise out of language planning across the curriculum:

> Time and space for speaking and listening may often be found in the course of reviewing the language requirements and demands of work which are already in place.
>
> (QCA, 1999: 7)

But while this is often the case, teachers need to plan effectively so that these opportunities are fully exploited. OFSTED's summary of inspection findings from 1994–1998 clearly states that good literacy teaching needs focused English work outside the structure of the literacy hour:

> Teachers need to plan carefully their coverage of the whole of the English Curriculum, including speaking and listening, extended writing and

drama; the literacy hour is a basic minimum and is likely to need reinforcing at other times in the school day and by giving more attention to
those aspects of literacy which feature in other subjects.

(Ofsted, 1999: para 12.1)

At the same time, teachers are advised that planning for the National Literacy
Strategy should be designed to develop these opportunities. A regional director of the National Literacy Strategy wrote:

> Because the reading and writing activities during the Literacy Hour will
> be built up in oral contexts, you will be able to maintain a rigorous and
> continuing emphasis on the spoken word. Through such teaching you
> will be able to develop the quality of thinking and the discussion skills of
> the pupils by involving them in interpreting, evaluating and speculating
> on the teaching material that you present.

(Hughes, 1999: 3)

In order to facilitate this, model planning documents to enhance opportunities for speaking and listening identified from the National Literacy Strategy
weekly plan have been produced as guidance [Hughes, 1999: (Untitled insert)
Number 7, Table 5]. Other observers have noted that the greater emphasis on
the use of CD-ROMs has created an environment where children (typically in
pairs) naturally discuss their progress, their ideas and their concerns.

Planning for talk begins with the conviction that talk is a valuable exercise; if
it were not, then we would experience far more primary classrooms where children were 'seen and not heard'. Many teachers believe that talk focuses children's attention learning and understanding in ways which are largely
unavailable to other activities. By planning lessons which offer overt opportunities for open talk, these teachers acknowledge that children discuss tasks differently with their peers, and are less likely to be intimidated by this than by the
act of searching for the correct answer in the teacher's head.

EXAMPLES OF CHILDREN TALKING

In the two examples of exploratory talk which follow, a group of children
discuss what they see in a snailery. In the first extract they are working
alone, in the second extract the teacher has arrived and begins to focus their
discussion:

> Three children (6 and 7 years old) discuss snails in a snailery without
> their teacher present.
> Susan: Yes, look at this one, it's come ever so far. This one's stopped
>   for a little rest . . .
> Jason: It's going again!
> Susan: Mmmm . . . good!
> Emma: This one's smoothing . . . slowly
> Jason: Look, they've bumped into each other (laughter)
> Emma: It's sort of got four antlers.

Susan: Where?

Emma: Look! I can see their eyes.

Susan: Well, they're not exactly eyes . . . they're a second load of feelers really aren't they? They grow bigger you know, and at first you couldn't hardly see the feelers and then they start to grow bigger, look.

Emma: Look, look at this one. He's really come . . . out . . . now.

Jason: It's got water on it when they move.

Susan: Yes, they make a trail, no . . . let him move and we see the trail afterwards.

Emma: I think it's oil from the skin . . .

Jason: Mmm . . . it's probably . . . moisture. See, he's making a little trail where he's been. They . . . walk . . . very . . . slowly.

Susan: Yes, Jason, this one's doing the same, that's why they say 'slow as a snail'.

Emma: Ooh look, see if it can move the pot.

Jason: Doesn't seem to . . .

Susan: Doesn't like it in the p . . . when it moves in the pot . . . look, get him out.

Jason: Don't you dare pull its . . . shell off.

Emma: You'll pull its thing off . . . shell off . . . ooh it's horrible!

Jason: Oh look . . . all this water.

(Grudgeon et al, 1998: 2)

Three children (6 and 7 years old) discuss snails in a snailery with their teacher.

Teacher: Can you tell me how you think they move?

Emma: Very slowly.

Teacher: Jason, you tell me, how are they moving?

Jason: They're pushing themselves along.

Teacher: How many feet can you see?

Susan: Don't think they have got any feet really.

Teacher: None at all?

Susan: No.

Emma: I should say they've got . . . can't see 'em. No.

Susan: Haven't exactly got any feet.

Emma: Slide . . . the bottom . . . so it slides . . . they can go along.

Teacher: Doesn't it look like one big foot?

All: Yes . . . yes (murmur hesitantly).

Teacher: Where do you think its eyes are?

Emma: On those little bits.

Susan: I can see . . . little.

Teacher: Which little bits?

Susan: You see those little bits at the bottom.

Teacher: Yes? You think the top bits? Which ones do you think Susan?

Susan: I think the bottom one.

Teacher: You think the bottom . . . well, have a close look at the bottom horns. What is the snail doing with the bottom horns?

Susan: He is feeling along the ground.

Teacher:	He's feeling along, so what would you call the bottom horns, Jason?
Susan:	Arms? No . . . sort of . . .
Emma:	Legs?
Teacher:	You think they're legs, you think they're arms. What do you think they are Jason, if he's feeling with them?
Jason:	Feelers?

(Grudgeon et al, 1998: 2)

From these transcripts several learning points are clear:

- The children are unafraid to hypothesise ('I think it's moisture').
- The children generate more creative, descriptive and insightful observations *without* their teacher.
- The children operate as a group, they share their ideas, they listen to one another and they respond positively to new suggestions.
- They look for opportunities to draw one another into the task, typically using 'tag' questions (☞).

Although the teacher probably has the best of intentions there are a number of ways that talk is less productive in the second extract than in the first.

- Typically, the teacher asked closed questions which necessitated single word, 'correct' answers.
- The teacher was keen to draw in all members of the group (especially Jason). It would appear to the teacher that following their discussion, Jason has learned the word 'feelers', but Susan already used the word in context in the previous transcript.
- The structure of the discussion shifts when the teacher arrives so that short questions are followed by short answers which lead to further short questions.
- The existence of exploratory, supportive and hypothetical talk becomes non-existent as a response to the teacher's questioning.

These extracts serve as a reminder that direct instruction and intervention can only achieve so much. In spite of the current trends we must remember that the teacher's ability to plan exciting learning opportunities and to sometimes *leave* children to talk is an important skill in itself. Guidance (such as QCA, 1999: 9) often stresses the need for teachers to model features of speaking and listening, but it is important to remember that there are times when good teaching also consists of planning which allows children to explore and interact. The new National Curriculum supports this kind of planning quite clearly (DfEE, 1999: 50 section 3), and teachers need to feel confident that their planning for talk meets these requirements. Once again the issue is one of balance and as a teacher of English it is up to you to decided when direct intervention as opposed to facilitation is appropriate.

CLASSROOM STRATEGIES

Given that children are capable of using high-order language skills in their discussions and debates, it is the responsibility of the teacher to plan for opportunities where these skills can be exploited to the full. One way of ensuring that genuine collaboration takes place – and therefore talk – is to insist that if there is a written outcome for a talk session it should be on a single shared piece of paper. This may sound simple, but if there is a single written outcome, then the children involved are pushed towards a period of negotiation and agreement, aiming for a document which reflects all the findings, feelings and ideas of the group.

Other ways of enhancing the quality of talk in the primary classroom rest heavily on the teacher's planning skills. Numerous talk activities were identified by the National Oracy Project including drama activities (➡ Chapter 24, 'Drama'). Here is a brief selection:

Twos to fours

The teacher sets a particular problem for a pair to discuss. After discussion, the pair meet with another pair who have been given *exactly the same task* in order to compare and elaborate on their findings. This is a good idea to use with maths and science problems.

Envoying

When working in groups, one member of each group is allocated the role of envoy. The envoy has the responsibility of gathering further information and resources as required, reporting progress to the teacher and seeking further clarification for the group. This is a particularly effective way of managing practical group activities as the teacher can focus attention on a much smaller number of children in order to maintain progress.

Jigsawing

This technique is a straightforward idea which is complicated to explain, but which offers considerable learning opportunities. Children are organised into 'home' groups (of four to six children) to begin to solve a particular problem or to work on a collaborative activity. Each child in the group then has the responsibility of finding out more about one particular aspect of the problem. These children gather together in 'expert' groups in order to gather as much information as possible to then take back and share with their 'home' group. Once each child in the group has given their expert opinion to their home group the problem solving continues until an end point is reached.

Children as researchers

A more time consuming, but equally valuable, method of planning for talk is to build in opportunities for working groups to diverge from the central core of study and begin a period of collaborative research. For example, if the children are studying Roman Britain, there will be core content that the teacher plans to cover with all the class. Beyond this, groups of children could be offered opportunities for further study of an area within this subject which particularly interested them. If necessary the teacher could control the pool of suggested topics, so in the example above, optional study areas could be law, food, housing, stories, art and so on. Each group of children could be given the task of researching their chosen subject in detail, and the outcome might be a mini lesson given to their peers.

Each group is encouraged to use resources and materials they can find to enhance their lesson. This would then be followed up with an activity devised and delivered by the group which they would administer and mark. The kind of work might include a cloze (☞) procedure, or a comprehension (☞) passage for example. The benefits of this way of working are that:

- The children feel some ownership over their area of study and are consequently better motivated
- The teacher has the potential to focus in more closely on particular groups of children because they are working independently
- The work demands a high level of negotiation and cooperation.

Practice points

- Talk based activities require as much thought and planning as reading and writing activities.
- The absence of a written outcome can sometimes result in a higher level of learning.
- Talk activities inevitably result in a noisier working environment, but this is often the product of a high level of engagement and thought.

Glossary

Cloze – activities that involve filling in missing sections of text, usually words.

Comprehension – A series of questions centred around a particular text extract.

Lateral thinking – a way of thinking that involves people establishing creative, imaginative and alternative solutions to problems. Popularised by Edward de Bono.

Tag questions – questions that are added onto the end of a statement, e.g. ' . . . isn't it?' or ' . . . aren't they?'

References

Baddeley, G. (1992) *Learning Together Through Talk*. London: Hodder & Stoughton

Department of Education and Science (DES) (1975) *A Language For Life (The Bullock Report)*. London: HMSO.

Department for Education and Employment Qualifications and Curriculum Authority (DfEE/QCA) (1999) *The National Curriculum: Handbook for Primary Teachers in England: Key Stages 1 and 2*. London: DfEE/QCA.

Furlong, T. (1999) 'True talk in the literacy hour'. *The Primary English Magazine*, 5 (1).

Grudgeon, E., Hubbard, L., Smith, C. and Dawes, L. (1998) *Teaching Speaking and Listening in the Primary School*. London: David Fulton.

Hughes, M. (1999) 'Oracy within the National Literacy Strategy'. *English Four to Eleven*, 7, 1–3.

Office for Standards in Education (OFSTED) (1999) *Primary Education: A Review of Primary Schools in England 1994–1998*. The Stationery Office [online - cited 29-2-00]. Available from:
http://www.official-documents.co.uk/document/ofsted/ped/ped-00.htm.

Qualifications and Curriculum Authority (QCA) (1999) *Teaching Speaking and Listening in Key Stages 1 and 2*. London: QCA.

Annotated bibliography

Baddeley, G. (1992) *Learning Together Through Talk*. London: Hodder & Stoughton.
Pack that includes a range of classroom strategies in text and video. Another influential project from the National Oracy Project.
L1 *

Qualifications and Curriculum Authority (QCA) (1999) *Teaching Speaking and Listening in Key Stages 1 and 2*. London: QCA.
This document has a specific section on planning for talk which outlines key philosophical and organizational issues, but it also provides interesting and realistic examples of specific talk related activities throughout Key Stages 1 and 2.
L1 *

Answer to problem: The man is not very tall so he can't reach the button for the 19th floor: he can only reach the number 8.

Chapter 23

Play and language

Learning is sometimes best achieved through opportunities for play. It is suggested that the most productive language environments for children stimulate wordplay, role-play and experiments with language. Teachers also have opportunities to enhance their formal language teaching through different kinds of play.

It is far too simplistic to imagine that play is something that only happens pre-school, or only during the early years of primary. The reality is that play is a vitally important aspect of literacy at all levels, including for adults. Professional writers understand this: novelists, dramatists and poets are regularly praised for their ability to play with language. Advertisers and journalists continually play with words in order to achieve effective wordplay and puns. Playing with words is a creative act and it teaches us a great deal about the language and its structure.

Early years educators in particular have traditionally recognised the value of play. The constraints of the National Curriculum and the recent imposition of national targets for literacy have meant that there are fewer spaces in the curriculum where teachers feel play is justified. Play does, however, have a valid and important role in the curriculum:

> Play is a key process whereby children will gain their knowledge and understanding of science, maths, history and any other of the National Curriculum subjects. The quality of learning experiences if play is of high quality should be all the greater.
>
> (Fisher, 1996: 107)

Speaking and listening are commonly understood to benefit through play, but there are other major benefits too. For example, the teaching of writing can be supported by role-play areas:

> The sort of writing that might emerge from setting up a post office in the classroom could include: filling in forms, keeping records of money deposited and distributed, notices, signs, posters, advertisements, stamp design, making passports, writing addresses.
>
> (Browne, 1996: 7)

It is important that you plan time so that children can learn at their own pace through first-hand experiences. When you organise science experiments or maths problems children need opportunities to explore.They need the time to handle materials, to discuss ideas, to hypothesise, to reflect, and to test ideas. This can help children develop a sense of purpose and a sense of motivation for such activities.

TEACHERS OBSERVING PLAY

When teachers observe their pupils at play they begin to see the learning process in detail. The early years teacher can often explain aspects of children's individual language, social and emotional development in detail because they have watched the children at play in the 'shop corner', or have listened to the tales they have to tell. These are not worthless moments, they are the times when children begin to demonstrate mastery over their own language, their own stories and their own lives.

Similarly, in the playground, teachers gain different insights when witnessing their pupils at play. Children who are reluctant to take part in class contexts become superheroes in the playground and children who seem supremely confident become introspective and can spend hours talking and exploring by themselves. It is important that teachers understand these dimensions of development because they enable teachers to plan more effectively for the needs of their children.

The purposes for play are not just about revealing development at that moment in time. There are excellent opportunities to *generate* knowledge and understanding through play. The example of the snailery in the previous chapter is a good example of this in action, the children play with language, unsupervised, watching snails in a snailery, and in so doing generate new understandings about the creatures they observe. For teachers the challenge is to construct learning opportunities for children through play which will help both formal and informal learning.

FEATURES OF PLAY IN THE CURRICULUM

Play is an important feature of most English work. During creative writing children are encouraged to 'use their imagination'. Teachers rely on an imagination which needs to be developed through the art of play. To take an example, if the child is asked to imagine life on a remote planet, the teacher implicitly accepts that such imaginings have been part of the child's socialisation process. If we ask a child to empathise with a character from a novel, this requires children to pretend they are that character: 'let's pretend' is a regular feature of children's play. The more we look at the language curriculum the more we see opportunities for play, or activities which rely on the experience of play for successful completion. Drama is now a statutory part of the speaking and listening section in the National Curriculum 2000, and this – like some of the objectives from the Framework for Teaching –

requires sustained periods of play in order to develop the necessary skills and understandings.

Drama

4. To participate in a wide range of drama activities and to evaluate their own and others' contributions, pupils should be taught to:
   a) create, adapt and sustain different roles, individually and in groups
   b) use character, action and narrative to convey story, themes, emotions, ideas in plays they devise and script

(DfEE/QCA, 1999: 51)

Pupils should be taught to compare forms or types of humour, e.g . . . word play, joke poems, word games, absurdities . . . poetry that plays with language . . .

(DfEE, 1998: 36: Year 3 Term 2)

Similarly, in the *Exemplification of Standards for English* (☞), the assessment of children's progress is tightly related to the business of play:

Throughout this dramatisation, Sarti sustains her chosen role, adapting some of what she says to make it more appropriate for the context . . . she listens intently to what her 'colleagues' are saying . . . she is the one who ensures that they reach a consensus . . . her work in the dramatised activity and her evident determination to learn the words of her story book, reveal more about her capabilities in English than might be apparent in less structured oral activities.

(SCAA, 1995: 14)

The ability to imagine, to respond sensitively and creatively to others, to sustain an idea over time, to be adventurous with the use of language are all attributes which would be difficult to achieve if the child had never been allowed the space for creative play in the early years and beyond.

Practice points

- Play should be planned for both Key Stage 1 and Key Stage 2.
- Planning for play should be balanced between structured and more open forms of play
- Opportunities for play can be used as a way of assessing speaking and listening

Glossary

Exemplification of Standards – materials that illustrate children's work and compare them with level descriptions.

References

Browne, A. (1996) *Developing Language and Literacy 3–8*. London: Paul Chapman.

Department for Education and Employment/Qualifications and Curriculum Authority (DfEE/QCA) (1999 The National Curriculum: Handbook for Primary Teachers in England: *Key Stages 1 and 2*. London: DfEE/QCA.

Department for Education and Employment (DfEE) (1998) *The National Literacy Strategy Framework for Teaching*. London: DfEE Publications.

Fisher, J. (1996) *Starting from the Child?* Buckingham, Open University Press

Grudgeon, E., Hubbard, L., Smith, C. and Dawes, L. (1998) *Teaching Speaking and Listening in the Primary School*. London: David Fulton.

School Curriculum and Assessment Authority (SCAA) (1995) *Exemplification of Standards: English – Speaking and Listening*. London: SCAA.

Annotated bibliography

Fisher, J. (1996) *Starting From the Child?* Buckingham: Open University Press.
Chapter Five (The Place of Play: The Status of Child-Initiated Experiences)
A more philosophical exploration of the nature and value of play. Deeply committed to the notion that teachers need to understand far more about play in order to plan and assess teaching and learning effectively.
L2 ***

Hall, N. and Robinson, A. (1988) *Exploring Writing and Play in the Early Years*. London: David Fulton.
A book full of rich examples of children's development through play balanced with sensitive commentaries.
L1 *

Holland, P. (1999) 'Just pretending'. *Language Matters*, Spring 1999: 2–5.
Reports research into managing boy's play in the nursery. Insightful and clearly linked to professional issues in the classroom.
L2 ***

Chapter 24

Drama

Reasons for teaching drama are outlined. Drama is linked to play in the early years and to story across the primary curriculum. A theoretical model of the 'building blocks of drama' is provided and some practical ideas are presented as starting points.

Drama is one of the richest and rewarding areas of language study yet it remains an underused medium in many classrooms. The National Curriculum 2000 has clarified the place of drama documenting the requirements separately, one of the few progressive ideas behind the new curriculum. Some teachers feel intimidated by the subject, claiming that drama is like teaching without a 'safety net', others find it the most liberating and invigorating part of their job. Drama sessions can provide some of the most memorable, challenging, enjoyable and rigorous moments of the child's time at school, yet for some this potential is reduced to a predictable and pedestrian Christmas nativity.

Drama is often overlooked for a variety of reasons: lack of suitable space, inability to book hall times, the sense of not feeling 'arty' enough, etc. Similarly, a lack of teacher confidence and the sense of a 'loss of control' in teaching situations tend to dissuade some teachers from taking 'risks' with the subject. Consequently the place of drama on the primary curriculum is often synonymous with uncertainty, introspection and apprehension, yet this need not be the case. Effective primary teaching acknowledges the 'problems' and 'dangers', but understands that these are actually key features of drama teaching. Good drama teaching acknowledges the shifts in control and the changing nature of knowledge during the sessions. It builds on positive relationships and trusting interaction between teachers and learners.

WHY TEACH DRAMA?

- Drama promotes an awareness of the self which is difficult to achieve in any other area of the curriculum.
- Drama helps children to understand their world more deeply and allows them an opportunity to find ways to explore and share that understanding.

- Drama helps children to cooperate and collaborate with their peers. It encourages them also to see themselves in a wider social context and should help them become more sensitive to others
- Relationships between the teacher, the child and their shared language are different in drama sessions. Expectations change, negotiated progress is a more prominent feature and there is a greater sense of active participation for the child
- Drama creates direct links across the curriculum into other areas of study
- Drama can be highly motivating for children and highly productive for teachers as learning becomes a more dynamic process
- Drama offers the primary teacher a route into language study that is not covered by any other form of teaching
- Drama offers an element of negotiation and unpredictability in an increasingly rigid curriculum
- Drama is an art form which has played a central part in our cultural heritage
- It encourages self-expression and focuses the child on the art of communication.

There are two broad schools of thought concerning the promotion of drama in the primary classroom. For some, the priority is to make links with the foundation subjects of the National Curriculum in order to integrate drama. Winston and Tandy (1998) for example offer carefully designed drama sessions that link in with science (materials and their properties), history (Anglo-Saxon settlements) and geography (the coming of a reservoir).

Others offer the argument that drama is important for its own sake, and that it should be taught in primary schools as such. The National Curriculum 2000 has moved towards this position by prescribing drama as a separate section in the speaking and listening requirements. The welcome increased emphasis on drama means that both schools of thought are important, opening up a form of language-based study which is beneficial for the child not just educationally, but also spiritually, morally and socially. Teachers should plan accordingly, encouraging children to use the richness of the experience in a multitude of ways.

THE EARLY YEARS

Both perspectives would acknowledge that the presence of drama is noticeably stronger in the early years. When children first come to school they are not bound by the formal conventions of learning, and for them play is an intrinsic part of the process by which they come to know about the world and by which they then come to refine and communicate their knowledge. Early years teachers recognise the importance of play and provide a wealth of opportunity for the child to explore a variety of roles and social situations. This should never be perceived as 'mere' play. 'Dressing-up' boxes, shop corners, cafés and carefully selected toys offer children crucial opportunities to enact, to imitate, to imagine, to confront, to review and to understand the social world they inhabit. Good drama teaching builds on this understanding, acknowledging that play is part of the way in which children come to make sense of their world.

Early drama teaching builds on the child's natural inclination for play and usually develops into two areas. Firstly, there are a variety of drama 'games' which often involve walking and clapping games, mime and movement activities which tend towards protecting or invading invisible spaces. These activities introduce some structure to drama times and establish the position of the teacher within a specific exploratory context. Secondly, and more importantly, there is a movement towards the provision of structured imaginative play, allowing the teacher to plan more carefully and encouraging the child to use their intrinsic sense of participation to explore some issues in greater detail.

Story regularly provides a natural and productive initiation for more detailed drama sessions. Story is a familiar and important feature of early years classrooms, and there are clear links between the thematic features of children's stories (finding/losing, friends/enemies, deception, hiding, escaping, etc.) and early explorations into movement and drama. Stories also serve as a perfect medium through which the teacher can begin to introduce the productive language associated with drama: What would happen if? Let's suppose that . . . , Perhaps there might be . . . , Have you ever wondered what would happen if . . . ? By using familiar characters and story settings a new discourse opens through which children can explore possibilities. These can be discussed, debated, transformed into a turn-taking game with the teacher controlling the narrative and children providing dialogue, or re-enacted using class toys.

Airs and Ball (1997: 42–53), for example, use established children's stories such as *Goldilocks* and Janet and Allan Ahlberg's *Burglar Bill*, to investigate a range of dilemmas through drama. Using the familiar story of the *Three Little Pigs*, the authors suggest that children work on a different ending, where the pigs have constructed 'Fortress Pork' and the wolf retires to the forest only to discover a bag containing a walking stick, a grandmother's shawl and a skirt (left over from another story!). Using the 'Grandma' disguise, the wolf now has all kinds of new possibilities which children can structure, discuss, practice, re-enact and finally reflect upon, assessing the wisdom of 'judging by appearances'.

UNDERSTANDING DRAMA

The movement towards more formally planned drama work with older children needs to be capable of being both spontaneous and well structured. Brian Woolland suggests that the building blocks for music are *pitch*, *melody*, *harmony, tempo, rhythm* and *texture*, and asks 'What are the raw materials of drama?' His answer begins to indicate a conceptual route for intending drama teachers:

- **Role or character**
  Acting as if you were someone else.
  Placing yourself in another situation.

- **Narrative**
  Ordering a sequence of events or images in such a way that their order creates meaning.
  The way in which the drama is moved forward – withholding information; sudden turn of events; surprise ending or beginning, etc.

- **Language**
  Verbal (This may include: naturalistic dialogue; a formal, heightened style of language such as a proclamation, or the beginning of a ritual; a direct address to an audience; characters talking to themselves; choral speech).
  Non-verbal (This may include symbols; body language; facial expression; the use of space; ritual).

Finally, Role or character, Narrative and Language all operate within a particular

- **Context**
  Where does the action of the drama occur?
  Is it set in a particular historical period?
  What are the relevant social / political conditions?

(Woolland, 1993)

Teachers therefore need to know how to use these 'building blocks' to construct meaningful and valuable drama. One method which is cited by almost all drama books is that of 'Teacher-in-role'. At its most basic, this involves the teacher adopting the role of another person (typically historical, fictional or imagined) for the purposes of questioning and answering. Often this is a technique used to explore the motivation of historical figures or to generate debate about current (perhaps local) social issues. More importantly, as Bolton (1992: 32). argues 'The main purpose of Teacher-in-Role is to do with ownership of knowledge'. While the teacher (in this simplified version) is potentially in control at all times, the nature and origin of knowledge begin to shift, so that children become instrumental not only in generating new understandings, but also (and most importantly) in understanding the process of social interaction. As children learn how to interact within this context they, of course, become capable of reversing roles and assuming the 'mantle of the expert'. This is a term originally devised by Heathcote and Bolton (1995) with its origins firmly in drama but has now come to have meaning across the curriculum. It is a process which is often 'watered-down' and deserves much greater study from those intending to make drama part of their classroom.

Practice points

- Drama often requires large spaces although 'pushing back the desks' in the classroom is sometimes necessary and important.
- Use children's natural creativity by giving them the chance to invent their own collaborative drama at times.
- Use the observation of drama experiences as an opportunity to plan for new skills/subject matter.

References

Airs, J. and Ball, C. (1997) *Key Ideas: Drama*. Dunstable: Folens.

Bolton, G. (1992) *New Perspectives on Classroom Drama*. Hemel Hempstead: Simon & Schuster.

Heathcote, D. and Bolton, G. (1995) *Drama for Learning: Dorothy Heathcote's Mantle of the Expert Approach to Education*. Portsmouth, NH: Heinemann.

O'Sullivan, C. and Williams, G. (1998) *Building Bridges: Laying the Foundations for a Child-Centred Curriculum in Drama and Education*. Birmingham: National Association for the Teaching of Drama (NATD).

Winston, J. and Tandy, M. (1998) *Beginning Drama 4–11*. London: David Fulton.

Woolland, B. (1993) *The Teaching of Drama in the Primary School*. Harlow: Longman.

Annotated bibliography

Airs, J. and Ball, C. (1997) *Key Ideas: Drama*. Dunstable: Folens.
A valuable guide with lively, practical ideas for the non-drama specialist.
L1 *

Heathcote, D. and Bolton, G. (1995) *Drama for Learning: Dorothy Heathcote's Mantle of the Expert Approach to Education* Portsmouth, NH: Heinemann.
This is not intended as a National Curriculum handbook, it concerns itself primarily with the study and promotion of drama. It provides an excellent link between theories of drama education and their application in primary education.
L3 ***

Clipson-Boyles, S. (1998) *Drama in Primary English Teaching*. London: David Fulton.

Winston, J. and Tandy, M. (1998) *Beginning Drama 4–11*. London: David Fulton.
Both usefully structured for the non-specialist, offering advice for developing drama into other areas of literacy, and providing example cross-curricular lesson plans.
L2 **

Chapter 25

Assessing talk

We start by outlining some features of talk then offer guidance on principles for the assessment of talk. The chapter concludes by examining ways in which these principles may be put into practice with the help of a transcribed conversation between a teacher and pupil. This chapter should be read in conjunction with Chapter 11, 'Assessing reading' and Chapter 19, 'Assessing writing', as some strategies – such as diaries of observations – are applicable to all three modes and other strategies are specific to one mode.

There are practical problems when attempting to assess talk in the primary classroom mainly because it is more difficult to *record* than other curriculum areas. In order to assess talk, three questions need to be answered: 'How do I record talk?', 'How do I measure talk?' and 'How do I compare talk?'.

Assessment of talk serves two primary functions. Firstly, it allows the teacher to make judgements about the development of talk itself and at times this is a statutory requirement. Secondly, it affords the teacher an opportunity to assess other forms of understanding which are communicated through that talk:

> A child who feels confident with her or his knowledge in a particular area is more likely to be fluent, at ease, capable of communicating information, making explanations or being persuasive, than a child who has no particular expertise in that area. On the other hand, a child might know a great deal yet not wish to voice that knowledge publicly, or show the ability to use particular talk strategies on any given occasion.
>
> (Bearne, 1998: 174).

So, different forms of assessment are needed at different stages of development and in order to record different features of talk. In the early years, the assessment of talk usually takes the form of observable features such as:

- Does the child initiate and carry on conversations?
- Does the child listen carefully?
- Can the child's talk be easily understood?
- Does the child describe experiences?
- Does the child give instructions?
- Does the child follow verbal instructions?

- Does the child ask questions?
- Can the child contribute to a working group?
- Does the child 'think aloud'?
- Does the child modify talk for different audiences?

(Grugeon et al, 1998: 104)

At later stages, other features of talk will take greater significance in the assessment process. Teachers will find that they begin to look for evidence where the child is seen to be hypothesising, imagining, directing, exploring, practising, recalling, developing critical responses, explaining and sustaining talk.

It is essential that teachers in the early years understand that talk has a different function outside the classroom. Research evidence suggests that children's talk in fantasy play is significantly different to classroom interaction. For example, it has been reported that: ' . . . utterances (☞) were longer, they used more adverbs and used modal auxiliary verbs more frequently than when they were engaged in non-fantasy sessions' (Hutt, 1989: 123). Put simply, when teachers observe children in play contexts they often see a very different language user. Some children, freed of the pressures of performance in front of the teacher, begin to demonstrate skills as language users and a preparedness to explore and experiment which teachers would otherwise never witness. Experienced teachers at Key Stage 2 will be only too ready to add that this kind of evidence is equally applicable among older children who perceive themselves as poor users in the classroom, yet seem to be perfectly articulate and imaginative when outside at play. The point here is that teachers who intend to assess talk and who grow concerned about a child's development in this area should look to that same child at play for further evidence of language use.

PRINCIPLES OF TALK ASSESSMENT

The National Oracy Project (NOP) established six principles of assessment which were applicable to speaking and listening:

- **Planning** – the groupings, the activities, the learning environment
- **Observing and gathering information** – through notes, children's talk-diaries, file-cards, hand-held tape recording, etc.
- **Recording** – on observation sheets, audio and video tape, to build evidence of talk cumulatively for each child
- **Summarising** – by reviewing the collected evidence and considering the main areas of achievement and needs
- **Making judgements** – about the progress of each child, linked closely to your summaries
- **Reporting** to parents, to children, to the school.

(Baddeley, 1992: 65)

This framework offers a detailed route through which talk can be formally assessed in primary classrooms, but it has to be remembered that the more recent implementation of the Framework for Teaching has changed the possibilities for and nature of talk assessment. The work of the NOP was carried out at a time when *language* teaching not literacy teaching was the norm. Teachers discussed 'talk environments' (☞) and established lessons where structured sustained discussion and open-ended exploratory talk were commonplace.

Teachers are now encouraged to build opportunities for talk into their planning for the Literacy Hour, and to look for further opportunities across the rest of the primary curriculum. The current QCA recommendations are helpful as they offer guidance related to building assessment into curriculum planning. It is suggested that the following points are guiding principles for teachers:

- **Focusing on two or three children each week** (to ensure systematic coverage of the whole class)
- **Using objectives for whole class monitoring** (developing whole class lists of which children meet specific teaching objectives)
- **Integrating speaking and listening assessment with other records** (possibly building a page-per-pupil record which incorporates talk).
- **Termly checks** (looking for patterns, omissions etc.)
- **Annual review** (to provide feedback for children, target setting and future planning).

(QCA, 1999: 13)

A short case-study

The example below is an extract from a fully transcribed conversation between a teacher and a year 4 child called Stephen. The teacher was a newly qualified teacher and inexperienced in the significance, development and the assessment of talk. Stephen was a boy who wrote very little and, over the previous three months, had offered the teacher little evidence of his ability. The task set by the teacher was to investigate 'What is a poem?', and a number of questions had been established to focus ideas along the lines of 'what colour is a poem?', 'what season is a poem?', etc. Stephen arrived late for the lesson after a visit to the dentist and missed the focused introduction. He discussed the task with some of his peers, worked for some 20 minutes and then arrived at the teacher's desk with an indecipherable piece of writing. The teacher was taping a conversation with another child as Stephen arrived (as part of an Oracy Project investigation) and the tape was left running as Stephen began to explain his ideas.

The extract below begins to indicate that the teacher's initial assessment of the child's reasoning and language skills were inadequate. Yet it also indicates the ways in which Stephen began to sharpen and consolidate his ideas in response to the teacher's inexperienced questioning. It is clear that Stephen had not been intimidated by the challenging nature of the task, nor by his lack of ability in writing. The extract shows that he had clear ideas and wanted to be able to clarify and communicate them effectively:

TEACHER Let's find out what you've got. What colour is a poem?

STEPHEN I put 'white and innocent' because it's ready for your thoughts to . . . (inaudible) the paper.

TEACHER I'm sorry Stephen, it's for your thoughts to *what* the paper?

STEPHEN Sweep. Or dazzle.

TEACHER That's a nice picture in my mind. Why did you use the word 'sweep'?

STEPHEN Well I just thought it sounded right. It does sweep across the paper really. As you write it. It just goes across the paper. That's what I think.

TEACHER How did you answer 'What does a poem taste like?'?

STEPHEN I put 'It tastes like a lemon because when you bite into it, it stings'. Like when you get into the actual poem it tingles in your head. Sometimes it stings. Sometimes it makes you go all excited.

TEACHER So how is that like a lemon?

STEPHEN Well the lemon stings and the poem kind of stings.

At this point, there is already clear evidence that Stephen has responded thoughtfully to the task, that he is still clarifying his responses (he is unsure whether to use 'sweep' or 'dazzle'), but that he is engaged in a challenging process of sifting through his own ideas, searching for the most appropriate responses. It is interesting that sometimes he thinks about the physical comparisons he is drawing, and at other times he is thinking carefully about the *sounds* that the words make; in both cases providing evidence of poetic thought at a high level. However, he went on to develop a larger idea he had been developing:

TEACHER What was the next question?

STEPHEN 'What season is a poem?'.

STEPHEN I put 'winter' because it's hibernating in your head until you write it down. Then it becomes spring.

TEACHER Oh! After it's written down it becomes spring. Why do you think that is?

STEPHEN Because in spring everything comes out new, and with a poem it's brand new to everybody else.

TEACHER That's a really nice way of thinking about it.

STEPHEN The next question was 'What sound is a poem?' and that is to do with winter as well, because in winter it's muffled.

TEACHER Why does it sound muffled?

STEPHEN Because it's in a deep sleep.

TEACHER The poem is?

STEPHEN Yes, until it comes out you don't hear it that well in your mind. Then it's been unblocked. Or unmuffled.

TEACHER 'Unmuffled'! What a lovely word. What's the next question?

STEPHEN 'Where is a poem?'. Again it's in the mind of the author until it's written down, and then it starts to grow up.

TEACHER Say that again slowly.

STEPHEN A poem is in the mind of the author until you get it written down, and then it starts to grow up.

TEACHER Why does a poem start to grow up once it's written down?

STEPHEN Well it's like a human, because when a human leaves home it's kind of like a sign of growing up and finding it's own way around in the world by itself. Stuff like that.

Stephen went on to develop his ideas throughout the conversation and was extremely pleased with his results.

If you compare this case-study with the NOP assessment framework at the beginning of this chapter you will see that this description addressed four of the categories:

> **Planning** – the poetry activity.
>
> **Observing and gathering information** – noting that Stephen arrived late and that he asked his peers about the activity.
>
> **Recording** – literally, on a tape-recorder.
>
> **Summarising** – revealed by our analysis in this section.

There is sufficient evidence in these short extracts to indicate that had Stephen's talk not been part of an ongoing assessment process, the teacher would not have been able to establish valid statements about Stephen's language abilities. Space restricts further extracts, but an examination of the full transcription (☞) would indicate that Stephen *does* think aloud, he *does* ask questions, he continually modifies his idea using talk as a vehicle, he tests the ways that words sound out loud, he thinks about his audience, he is confident in his own ability, he is prepared to take chances with words he has invented to communicate his ideas. It is worth repeating that this is a child whose prior language assessments had been meagre to say the least.

Practice points

- Be sufficiently confident to allow times when children can explain their ideas fully without being hurried. Always seeking the simple, correct answer does not allow children opportunities for you to assess their understanding and progress.
- Look for opportunities to build written assessment of talk into other areas of the curriculum (i.e. collaboration during a group science experiment).
- Assessment of speaking and listening should (like all effective assessment) build into clear targets for the child and planned objectives for the teacher.

Glossary

Talk environment – Typically a way of describing a classroom or specific lesson where talk was the main feature, and where a variety of forms of talk were encouraged, planned for, resourced and encouraged.
Transcription – The written form of a recorded conversation
Utterance – Any verbal expression intended to carry meaning

References

Baddeley, G. (ed.) (1992) *Learning Together Through Talk: Key Stages 1 and 2.* London: Hodder & Stoughton.
Bearne, E. (1998) *Making Progress in English.* London: Routledge.
Godwin, G. and Perkins, M. (1998) *Teaching Language and Literacy in the Early Years.* London: David Fulton.
Grugeon, E., Hubbard, L., Smith, C. and Dawes, L. (1998) *Teaching Speaking and Listening in the Primary School.* London: David Fulton.
Hutt, S. J. (1989) *Play, Exploration and Learning.* Quoted in Grugeon, E., Hubbard, L., Smith, C. and Dawes, L. (1998) *Teaching Speaking and Listening in the Primary School.* London: David Fulton.
Qualifications and Curriculum Authority (QCA) (1999) *Teaching Speaking and Listening in Key Stages 1 and 2.* London: QCA.

Annotated reading

Bearne, E. (1998) *Making Progress in English.* London: Routledge.
Chapter Four ('Speaking and Listening') offers a broad overview of this area of language development with an emphasis on organising and planning for talk activities in the classroom which lead to assessment opportunities.
L2 **
Grugeon, E., Hubbard, L., Smith, C. and Dawes, L. (1998) *Teaching Speaking and Listening in the Primary School.* London: David Fulton.
L1 **
Qualifications and Curriculum Authority (QCA) (1999) *Teaching Speaking and Listening in Key Stages 1 and 2.* London: QCA.
Both deal with monitoring and assessing talk and both offer simple observational assessment grids which could be adapted for individual use in the classroom.
L1 *

Part V

General issues

Chapter 26

Planning

Recent national curriculum developments have resulted in new forms of planning. This chapter explores some of the key planning issues by reflecting on examples of planning for literacy, and English outside of the literacy hour.

Prior to the advent of the National Curriculum in 1988–9, the nature of teachers' planning was quite different to what is expected today. As students, before we started our teaching carreers, we would carry out detailed lesson plans for each activity that we planned. These activities would be generated from an original 'topic web' (☞) that would have a central theme or 'topic' that would unite all the activities for that half term or term. It was expected that the children's responses to the activities would enable the teacher to respond to their interests and needs by changing the initial planning. Once we qualified as teachers, the detailed lesson plans were not required and the main planning requirement was the topic web and a weekly plan that listed the activities to be carried out. The negative aspect of this was that children could cover the same topic several times in their primary school career, in a way that was unplanned, simply because teachers cooincidently chose the same topic. Although in the better schools these topics were mapped to avoid unnecessary repetition.

In spite of some negative aspects there were at least two positive advantages of this style of planning. The first was that teachers' main priority was to spend their time preparing resources and activities that would motivate children. From the child's point of view activities are more important than objectives because it is the activities that determine what the child will actually be doing on a particular day, whereas objectives tend to be of particular relevance to the teacher. The second positive aspect of the old systems of planning was the greater levels of flexibility which allowed teachers to tap into children's interests. I am sure you will also have realised that the amount of paperwork required was much less than current expectations and this has been a serious and unresolved problem over the last decade.

The National Curriculum brings with it the requirement to ensure that you are covering all the programmes of study. In the past this meant that various methods were devised to 'tick off' or 'shade in' the programmes of study to record the fact that they had been covered. The advent of the National Literacy Strategy (NLS) has brought with it even more monitoring and planning. Prior to the NLS the programmes of study for English would have been planned the same as all the other National Curriculum subjects but the new requirements for one hour of 'literacy' every day specified particular medium-term and short-term planning formats. Thankfully there is not a requirement for teachers to complete individual lesson plans for each activity of the literacy hour!

EXAMPLES OF PLANNING

In order to reflect on some of the issues for planning literacy and English we have created some examples of planning. The medium-term plan and the weekly grid shown in Tables 26.1 and 26.2 are taken directly from the Framework for Teaching; the formats are well thought-out and we see no reason not to use them. The short-term lesson plan is a format that we have used with trainee teachers. The medium-term plan requires you to select objectives from the Framework and organise them into a coherent sequence for the half term. One of the early decisions that has to be made is which objectives are continuous and which are blocked: blocked objectives will be achieved in a set timescale, whereas continuous objectives will be addressed throughout the half term. At this stage, decisions about the kinds of text that you use will be made. It is important to remember that the literacy hour should be built on the use of high-quality 'real' texts wherever possible (➡Chapter 4, 'Texts for children').

Teachers next complete the weekly grid which indicates the kinds of activity that they will use in order to address the appropriate objectives from their medium-term plan. It was quite a surprise to see the suggestion for a 'carousel' of activities following the previous criticisms of the influential 'three wise men' report (Alexander et al, 1992) which suggested that 'Group work may quickly become counterproductive if teachers try to manage too many groups of pupils within the same class and/or have pupils working on too many different activities or subjects simultaneously' (1992: 29). Despite this there is an expectation that up to four independent activities will take place at the same time as the guided read or guided write where the teacher should be based. As far as teachers' planning – as opposed to students' planning – is concerned, the weekly grid should usually indicate how differentiation will be achieved, but in our examples the differentiation is indicated in our lesson plan and is not repeated on the weekly grid.

The lesson plan

The lesson plans in Figures 26.1 and 26.2 raise a number of more general issues that you need to be aware of when planning your literacy hours. In recent years there has been a growing emphasis on learning objectives; this emphasis has been pushed by Her Majesty's Inspectorate (HMI) and The

Table 26.1 NLS Medium Term Plan

National Literacy Strategy
Medium Term Planning Half Termly Planner
School

Class 4W	Year Group(s)	Year 4	Term 1	1st Half/2nd Half	Teacher	Wk
Phonics, Spelling and Vocabulary	*Grammar and Puctuation*		*Comprehensive and Composition*		*Texts*	
Continuous work:	Continuous work:		Continuous work:		Range:	
1 to read and spell words through: 2 identifying phonemes in speech and writing 2 using phonic/spelling knowledge as a cue, together with graphic, grammatical and contextual knowledge, when reading unfamiliar texts	1 to re-read own writing to check for grammatical sense (coherence) and accuracy (agreement); to identify errors and to suggest alternative constructions; 5 to practise using commas to mark grammatical boundaries within sentences; link to workon editing and revising own writing		8 to find out more about popular authors, poets, etc. and use this information to move onto more books by favourite writers;		Fiction and Poetry: Historical stories and short novels . . .	
Blocked work:	Blocked work:		Blocked work:		titles:	Wk
1 to distinguish between the spelling and meanings of common homophones, e.g. to/two/too; they're/their/there; piece/peace	3 identify the use of powerful verbs		1 to investigate how settings and characters are built up from small detials, and how the reader responds to them.		*The Iron Man* – Ted Hughes. *Shaggy and Spotty* – Ted Hughes. *The Sheep-Pig* – Dick King-Smith.	1
						2
						3
						4
						5
						6
						7
						8

Table 26.2 NLS Weekly Plan

National Literacy Strategy Teaching Objectives

Weekly Plan
Name of School

Class:
Year Group(s):
Term:
Week Beg:
Teacher:

	Whole class – Shared reading And writing	Whole class – Phonics, spelling, vocabulary and grammar	Guided Group Tasks (reading or writing):	Independent Group Task	Independent Group Tasks			Plenary
Mon	Discuss first page of 'Iron Man'. Details of setting.	Discuss meaning of homophone. Write children's examples on flipchart.	Read first chapter of 'Iron Man' and discuss children's response. e.g. description of the mending of the 'Iron Man'. 2 T	Work with a partner to complete amended 'NATE' activity on setting. 3 OA I	Match homophones in set of cards and write into sentence context. 4 OA I	Use Dorling Kindersley 'Test for Success' programme to work on verbs. 5 OA I	Use the ideas of 'falling', 'breaking' and 'mending' to create own story opening. 1 OA I	Examples of powerful verbs.
Tues	Discuss first page of 'The Sheep Pig'. Details of setting.	Discuss 'to/two/too': spelling and meanings in context. Given context children offer correct spelling.	Read 'Shaggy and Spotty' and discuss children's response. e.g. reflections on fairgrounds. 5 T	'NATE' activity. Include complete paragraph with description to make 3 predictions. 1 OA I	Match homophones in set of cards and write into sentence context. 2 OA I	Use Dorling Kindersley 'Test for Success' programme to work on verbs. 3 OA I	Use the ideas of 'falling', 'breaking' and 'mending' to create own story opening. 4 OA I	Examples from story openings.

Table 26.2 – continued

Day								
Wed	Watch first 10 minutes of 'Sheep-Pig' video. Compare with book opening for types of detail.	Discuss 'they're/their/there': spelling and meanings in context. Given context children offer correct spelling.	Read first chapter of 'Iron Man' and discuss children's response. 3 T	Work with a partner to complete amended 'NATE' activity on setting 4 OA I	Match homophones in set of cards and discuss meanings. 5 OA I	Use Dorling Kindersley 'Test for Success' programme to work on 1 OA I	Use the ideas of 'falling', 'breaking' and 'mending' to create own story opening. 2 OA I	Examples of homophones.
Thur	Discuss importance of illustrations for the setting of 'Shaggy and Spotty' text.	Discuss 'piece/peace': spelling and meanings in context. Given context children offer correct spelling.	Read first section of 'The Sheep Pig'. 1 T	Work with a partner to complete amended 'NATE' activity on setting 2 OA I	Match homophones in set of cards and write each word into sentence context. 3 OA I	Use Dorling Kindersley 'Test for Success' programme to work on verbs. 4 OA I	Draw three pictures that show the Iron Man 'falling', 'breaking' and 'mending' and provide captions. 5 OA I	Examples from NATE activity.
Fri	Discuss some of the powerful verbs used in the first chapter of the Iron Man.	Consolidate meaning of homophone. Write children's examples on flipchart.	Read first chapter of 'Iron Man' and discuss children's response. 4 T	'NATE' activity. Write 3 distances, 3 place names, and three short sentences for creation. 5 OA I	Find other homophones with help of dictionaries. 1 OA I	Use Dorling Kindersley 'Test for Success' programme to work on verbs. 2 OA I	Use the ideas of 'falling', 'breaking' and 'mending' to create own story opening. 3 OA I	Discuss popular authors.

Liverpool John Moores University: **School of Education and Community Studies**

LESSON PLAN

Trainee teacher: .... *Course:* .... *Year:* ....

Subject: English	Date & time: Monday	Class/group: Y4	Number of pupils:
		SEN pupils:	

Lesson description: Term 1, first half term: Literacy Hour

Learning Objective(s)   Based on Skills, Attitudes, Concepts, Knowledge

1. To distinguish between the spelling and meaning of common homophones.
2. To investigate how setting and characters are built up from small details, and how the reader responds to them.
3. To identify the use of powerful verbs.

National Documentation Reference
Y4 T1 Word level 6; Sentence level 3; Text level 1.

Use of ICT	**SMSC Opportunities**
Dorling Kindersley 'Test for Success' package.	

Continuity and Progression

Word level work extends previous work on homonyms. Sentence level work continues work on the functions of words. Text level work develops understanding of narrative structure.

Differentiation Summary *(please circle):*
By Activity:	Outcome	Different activities	Open-ended activity	Stepped activity	Extension activity
By Support:	Pupil collaboration	Teacher	Classroom assistant		
By Organisation:	Streamed group	Subject set group	Individualised learning	Resource	Pupil choice

Assessment Summary *(please circle):*
Type:	Formative	Summative	Diagnostic		
Strategy:	Pupil self-evaluation	Interaction and observation	Structured observation	Work samples	National test
	Standardised test	Teacher designed activity	Practical task		
Record keeping:	**Pupil Record:**	Pupil profile Portfolio	**Class record:** Mark book Checklist		

Organisation including **Risk Assessment -** Hazard/Risk/Control	**Resources:**
Groupings and timings as suggested by National Literacy Strategy.	Enlarge first page of 'Iron Man'. Flipchart or blackboard for second segment. 6 copies of NATE shared reading booklet. Approximately 50 Laminated word cards with a range of homophones. 2/3 PCs and Dorling Kindersley 'Test for Success' CD ROM. Writing resources.

Figure 26.1 Literacy Hour, Lesson Plan

Time	Learning Activity Indicate what pupils will be doing *(include differentiation issues)*	Teaching Agenda Highlight key teaching points/questions *(include differentiation issues)*	Learning outcomes/Assessment Indicate what you expect pupils to be able to do, and your strategies for checking this *(include differentiation issues)*
15	Whole class shared reading of 'The Coming of the Iron Man' (P1).	Why does Ted Hughes use questions to help set the scene? How does he use the senses to aid the description?	Pupils should understand more about the techniques of setting the scene in narrative and specifically how this is done at the beginning of the Iron Man. Understanding will be checked through interaction.
20	Discuss the meaning of the term 'homophone'. Ask the children to suggest examples and invite them to write them on the flipchart.	'Words which sound the same but have different meaning or different spelling' (NLSFFT: 81) Check that the children understand that the examples should sound the same. Explain the significance of the 'homo' and 'phone'.	Children should be able to give examples of homophones and should know the definition. Understanding will be checked through interaction.
20	**Group work** Guided Read: Discuss the techniques Hughes uses to describe the reassembly of the Iron Man.	Where does the section on the reassembly begin? give evidence from the text. Whose perspective is the beginning of this section written from?	Understand the first chapter and specifically some of the techniques used to set the scene.
	Independent work Activity 1: Work in partners; one person does the writing. Write down three predictions for each of the following questions: How far had he walked?; Where had he come from?; How was he made?	Encourage creativity in the answers but based on the limited information given in the text. Differentiation: peer support for children with low attainment (LA); more depth of description with fewer examples for children with high attainment (HA).	Experience the importance of imagination when responding to narrative.
	Activity 2: Find homophones from a set of cards and write a sentence that includes each one.	Ensure meaning is understood and spelling is appropriate. LA: matching and oral work. HA: Locate other homophones	Put homophone into meaningful context.
	Activity 3: Work through 'Test for Success' exercise on verbs.	Check children understand menu system on CD ROM. Differentiation through pre-set levels in package.	Understand function of verbs and that writers can choose verbs for effect. Compile Checklist of test scores and identify those children who are struggling.
	Activity 4: Write opening to a story that includes a character who falls, breaks up, and reassembles.	Encourage use of imagination but get children to justify how the writing relates to the brief. Differentiation by outcome.	Lively, imaginative opening with clear justification of decisions.
10	**Plenary** Group 5 to explain work done on computer and to give examples of verbs. Other children to give similar verbs that are more 'powerful'.	Check understanding of function of verb.	Understand function of verbs and that writers can choose verbs for effect.

Figure 26.1 – continued

LESSON PLAN

Trainee teacher: .... Course: .... Year: ....

Subject: English	Date & time: Monday	Class/group: Y4 Number of pupils:
		SEN pupils:

Lesson description: Term 1, first half term: Literacy Hour - **Shared reading segment**

Learning Objective(s)   Based on Skills, Attitudes, Concepts, Knowledge

1. To investigate how setting and characters are built up from small details, and how the reader responds to them.

National Documentation Reference
Y4 T1 Text level 1.

Use of ICT	SMSC Opportunities

Continuity and Progression

Text level work develops understanding of narrative structure.

Differentiation Summary (please circle):

By Activity:	Outcome	Different activities	Open ended activity	Stepped activity	Extension activity
By Support:	Pupil collaboration	Teacher	Classroom assistant		
By Organisation:	Streamed group	Subject set group	Individualised learning	Resource	Pupil choice

Assessment Summary (please circle):

Type:	Formative	Summative	Diagnostic		
Strategy:	Self evaluation	Informal observation	Formal observation	Interaction and observation	Work samples
	National test	Standardised test	Teacher designed activity	Practical task	
Record keeping:	Pupil Record:	Pupil profile Portfolio	Class record: Mark book	Checklist	

Organisation including **Risk Assessment -** Hazard/Risk/Control	**Resources:**
Whole class interactive discussion.	Enlarge first page of 'Iron Man'.

Time	**Learning Activity** Indicate what pupils will be doing (include differentiation issues)	**Teaching Agenda** Highlight key teaching points/questions (include differentiation issues)	**Learning outcomes/Assessment** Indicate what you expect pupils to be able to do, and your strategies for checking this (include differentiation issues)
15	The pupils will be sitting on the carpet and an enlarged version of the Coming of the Iron Man' (P1) will be visible on the OHP or flipchart. Initially the children will be encouraged to read the extract with the teacher. This will be followed by discussion of various issues.	Ensure all the children can clearly see the extract and that they have enough space to sit. Encourage a wide range of children to contribute and avoid some children dominating the discussion. Ask if any of the children already know the story. Why does Ted Hughes use questions to help set the scene? How does he use the senses to aid the description? How effective is this opening compared to others? What is significant about the position of the end of this first page?	Pupils should understand more about the techniques of setting the scene in narrative and specifically how this is done at the beginning of the Iron Man. Understanding will be checked through interaction.

Figure 26.2 Shared Reading, Lesson Plan

Office for Standards in Education (OFSTED). The advantage of objectives is that they provide a clear focus for the lesson and should inform activity selection, the nature of the teacher's interaction and the nature of assessment. The disadvantage is that they restrict the teacher's ability to respond flexibly to the interests of the children. In the past it was deemed to be good practice to deviate from lesson planning where appropriate in order to relate more closely to children's observed development, needs and interests. However, as the Framework prescribes a large number of objectives that must be followed it is sensible to use these word-for-word when writing lesson plans. One possible exception to this might be if a particularly broad or challenging objective needs subdividing into smaller, more manageable objectives. Usually objectives will be taken from the year that the children's class corresponds with, but teachers are sometimes finding that children's development means that they have to select from earlier or later objectives. You have to be very careful that such decisions are based on a genuine understanding of children's development and not on low expectations.

Continuity and progression is another area that, as you realise from the introduction to this chapter, has grown in importance. Ideally this part of the lesson plan should note the outcome of assessment as the basis for further work. As the examples we have given are fictitious it was not possible to indicate a link between some assessment that we had carried out and the lesson plan. Homework opportunities could also be indicated in the continuity and progression box.

There are many strategies for differentiating the learning that children undertake. Prior to the literacy strategy, mixed ability teaching was an option that some teachers used effectively. However, there is an expectation that the literacy hour will be planned using literacy ability groups. In growing numbers of schools whole yeargroups are being organised into two, three or four ability classes where the children move to work with another teacher for the hour. Three of the questions you should ask if this is happening in your school:

- Are there *frequent* opportunities for the children to be assessed and unlimited opportunities to change groups if the assessment indicates that this is necessary?
- Is the work that the different groups carry out genuinely different?
- Is the use of sets being monitored to make sure that it is having a positive effect on achievement?

Unless these conditions are met one of the dangers is that the lower attainment groups will suffer from self-fulfilling-prophecy (➡Chapter 2, 'Theories of learning') and low self-esteem.

As we described in Chapter 19, 'Assessing writing', it is important to remember that not all assessment is written down nor is it necessary or possible to assess every lesson. The guiding principle for assessment has to be to aim for the highest quality of assessment which can genuinely feed into future planning. If this is the case, then you will need to decide the level of ongoing written assessment that is manageable and productive.

The planning of the activities themselves raise a few more issues. One of the independent group activities in the example involves children using a CD ROM. The particular package that is suggested was unusual at the time of its design in that it was one of the first to base its underlying structure on the Framework for Teaching. It was also unusual in that the exercises were designed by teachers. However, as a knowledge-based package with a particular focus it also represents only one possible kind of software. As we indicate in Chapter 28, applications packages offer powerful opportunities for the spiral development of skills and knowledge. For example, the use of a multimedia authoring package could include children's own digital photographs, digitally recorded sound, a wide range of text effects, appropriate writing, and hypertext links. A project like this needs plenty of time over a sustained period, something that does not necessarily fit easily within 20 minute slots in the literacy hour. Although the advantages of ICT are frequently overstated we remain convinced that it is still underused in many classrooms.

The use of published schemes is an issue that has caused considerable debate over the years. The worst kinds of schemes involved children individually ploughing through decontextualised activities. But even modern and appropriate schemes have to be used with much thought by teachers. If they are being used to support the literacy hour, it is important – although this may sound obvious – that the suggested activities genuinely meet the learning objectives of the Framework; too often this is not the case. One obvious place of support is the standards site (http://www.standards.dfee.gov.uk/literacy) where activity resource sheets are available to be downloaded and used as the basis for activities to support the literacy hour. However, like all resources, they need to be carefully and critically evaluated to ensure that they will meet the particular needs of your class. In the example we have given – in order to illustrate that published schemes can be used – we modified a National Association of Teachers of English (NATE) pack. The decision to use the pack was based on an evaluation of its quality and the recognition that it was underpinned by some important philosophies which are typical of NATE's reputation as a teacher-centred organisation with many years of experience.

Planning English outside of the literacy hour

The Framework for Teaching meant that teachers were required to come to terms with a radically new system of teaching English. Along with the different kinds of subject knowledge came different planning systems. For many teachers the requirement to ensure that one hour of each day was devoted to literacy meant that the idea that any other English might be taking place as

ENGLISH OUTSIDE OF THE LITERACY HOUR

MEDIUM TERM PLAN

Overview

A sustained period of creative artwork germinating from chosen poetry. Children will be encouraged to reflect on the links that exist between the arts and the way that the different disciplines can influence each other.

Objectives

Children should learn:
- To make choices on the basis of poetry that they prefer.
- Develop their performance skills in order to work towards what they consider to be an effective and powerful performance.
- Appreciate that some links between poetry and other arts are more effective than others.
- Communicate effectively to a range of audiences.

Possible activities

1. Share a collection of poetry books and encourage the children to browse. Children should begin to locate poems that they like with a partner. At the end of the session encourage children to read aloud their poems and say why they liked the poem.
2. Each group should choose one poem as the basis for a sustained period of work. They should prepare this to be performed to the whole class, possibly from memory. Groups should decide how to allocate the various parts of the poem to different speakers.
3. Pairs should introduce some kind of movement/drama to their reading of the poem.
4. One large image should be planned as a backdrop to each poem. If possible this image should be created on OHT to be projected onto an appropriate surface.
5. A range of percussion instruments should be selected by each group and decisions made on the best ways that sound could be used to enhance the performances.
6. Each pair should now join forces with another pair and explain their ideas for a poetry performance so that they can perform each other's poems.
7. A 'dress rehearsal' will include a video camera to record the rehearsal. The recording will be used as the basis for making final improvements.
8. Final performances for other people in the school community: e.g. another class, parents, etc.

Outcomes

- Experience the power of poetry and reflect on the experience of performance.
- Development of preferences for poetry.
- Greater awareness of the enjoyment and importance of the creative arts.

Points to note

This unit of work is perhaps best undertaken over half a term and should be a timetabled session at least once a week.

Figure 26.3 English outside the Literacy Hour

well was difficult to accept. However, one key area of the National Curriculum that is not catered for by the literacy hour is speaking and listening (➡Chapter 22, 'Planning for Talk').

One of the other difficulties with the prescribed literacy hour relates to the opportunity to develop extended work on reading and writing. The short timeslots that characterise the hour may offer a different pace, but they are not satisfactory for developing extended pieces of writing where young writers make important decisions about their writing sometimes resulting in outstanding artistic products. Another significant omission is the opportunity for cross-curricular work which at its best can provide a more meaningful context for English which is viewed by many as an arts subject, not just the learning of a set of skills. Indeed, this more holistic view of English arguably contributes positively to skill development.

In the example in Figure 26.3, we have used the headings for medium term planning which are suggested by the example schemes of work for other subjects given at the standards site (http://www.standards.gov.uk). There are numerous possible areas for units of work that could have been chosen, such as a range of speaking and listening, creative writing, writing workshop, collaborative problem solving, self-chosen research projects, local environment work, critical literacy projects, media study, festivals and celebrations, etc. In the end we chose some poetry work that we had successfully carried out in a school which seemed to motivate the children. The idea to link this with other creative arts came from the children themselves who, when given regular opportunities to choose and share poetry, spontaneously used music, movement and drama to enliven their poetry readings.

Practice points

- Where possible use the objectives from the Framework for Teaching word-for-word.
- Use the planning frameworks suggested by the Framework for Teaching rather than waste time designing your own.
- Think carefully about English planning outside the literacy hour.

Glossary

Topic web – planning diagram consisting of a central title with related ideas linked through lines and boxes. The National Literacy Strategy has renamed this a 'concept map' or 'brainstorm'.

References

Alexander, R., Rose, J., and Woodhead, C. (1992) *Curriculum Organisation and Classroom Practice in Primary Schools: A Discussion Paper, (The 'Three Wise Men' Report)*. London: Department of Education and Science (DES).

Wyse, D. (1999a) 'Teachers' resources'. *Literacy and Learning*, Issue 7: 42–44.
Wyse, D. (1999b) 'Teachers' Resources'. *Literacy and Learning*, Issue 8: 54–56.

Annotated reading

Barker, R. and Fidge, L. (1998) *Key Stage 2 Literacy Activity Book – Year 3*.
London: Letts Educational.
An example of one of the pupil books from the Letts literacy scheme
designed to support the teaching of the literacy hour. Like a number of
other schemes this offers text extracts and activities which it is claimed link
with the Framework for Teaching. (See Wyse (1999a) for a more detailed
review of this package.)
L1 *

Department for Education and Employment (DfEE). Standards and
Effectiveness Unit. The Standards Site [online – cited 22-6-00]. Available
from:
    http://www.standards.dfec.gov.uk/literacy
This site includes the option to select a learning objective from the
Framework for Teaching and it will offer an activity resource sheet. Very use-
ful for finding ideas for activities and has the benefit of being officially
approved. The activities also feature in the training materials for the National
Literacy Strategy.
L1 *

Laar, B. (2000) *Primary Literacy Anthology: Year 6*. Cheltenham: Stanley
Thornes.
One of a wealth of resources from a literacy scheme. This anthology for year
6 has a range of text extracts to support the literacy hour. The scheme
includes photocopiable resource sheets and lesson plan collections. (➡
Chapter 4, 'Texts for Children' for a list of potential problems with using
published schemes.)
L1 *

Webster, C. (1998) *100 Literacy Hours: Year 6*. Leamington Spa: Scholastic.
This book from the '100 Literacy Hours' series includes photocopiable
resources and lesson plans. Useful as ideas for activities. (See Wyse (1999b)
for a more detailed review of this package.)
L1 *

Chapter 27

Home/school links

Some of the differences between learning at home and learning at school are discussed. The setting of homework is related to home-reading and home-school agreements. The chapter concludes with some ideas from research on working with families.

In the past there was a tendency to think that children were like 'empty vessels' who knew nothing until they were filled with knowledge by schools. In the worst cases this meant that parents and children felt intimidated by schools: the schools suggested that they knew best and that parents were not really much to do with education. The Bullock Report signalled that a change in such attitudes was necessary.

> No child should be expected to cast off the language and culture of the home as he [sic] crosses the school threshold, nor to live and act as though home and school represent two totally separate and different cultures which have to be kept firmly apart. The curriculum should reflect many elements of that part of his life which a child lives outside school.
>
> (DES 1975: S20.5)

In order to turn the fine words of the Bullock report into practice, some schools worked very hard to involve parents more in their children's education. Schools began to see themselves as very much part of the local community. In recent times the National Literacy Strategy Framework for Teaching has laid down challenging requirements for which highly trained teachers are needed. This might give the idea that because the Framework is complex there is nothing that parents can offer in support of their children's literacy development; this is not the case.

LEARNING AT HOME AND AT SCHOOL

Direct evidence of the importance of the home environment in supporting children's learning comes from a range of research. Barbara Tizard and Martin Hughes's early work looked at the differences between talking and thinking at home and at school. They argued forcefully that the home was a 'very powerful learning environment' (1984: 249) and that school nurseries were not aware of this.

> Our observations of children at home showed them displaying a range of interest and linguistic skills which enabled them to be powerful learners. Yet observations of the same children at school showed a fundamental lack of awareness by the nursery staff of these skills and interests. There is no doubt that, in the world of the school, the child appears to be a much less active thinker than is the case at home. We do not believe that the schools can possibly be meeting their goals in the most efficient manner if they are unable to make use of so many of the children's skills.
>
> (Tizzard and Hughes, 1984: 264)

Since this research Hughes has continued to work in the area of home and school but his emphasis has changed. In a recent study Greenhough and Hughes (1999) have hinted that the 'conversing' (☞) of parents may be generally weaker than the conversing of teachers. They tentatively suggest that there might be a link between the amount of meaningful conversation about books at home, and the child's reading progress at school.

One part of their research is an illustration of the different ways that four schools tried to improve the level of conversing in the home: (a) a workshop for parents; (b) a modified version of the home-school reading diary; (c) introductory talk by the class teacher and a modified diary; (d) use of a 'visitors' comments' book for each reading. They conclude that these strategies only had limited success and argue that changing parents' approaches with their children may be similar to changing teacher's practice; often a gradual and sophisticated process. One aspect that Greenhough and Hughes did not seem to address was the child's own perspective. It is possible that some children might have wanted a different kind of reading experience at home – such as 'just' listening to a story – after a day at school that was full of a high level of conversing.

Another important piece of research was Margaret Clark's study of young fluent readers: that is children who could read before they started school. In her conclusions to the study she made an important point about reading development, hinting that it may not be a simple developmental sequence as many people had suggested (➡ Chapter 3, 'The development of reading'). In addition Clark pointed towards the importance of the experiences that the children had at home.

> That the attributes of the particular child were an important aspect of the situation is not denied but the crucial role of the environment, the experiences which the child obtained, their relevance to his interest and the readiness of adults to encourage and to build upon these, should not be underestimated.
>
> (Clark, 1976: 106)

A recent replication (☞) of Clarke's study by Stainthorp and Hughes (1999) also illustrates the kinds of home experiences that young fluent readers have. What is striking about the experiences that are documented is the meaningful and varied literate activities that were supporting the children: looking at road signs; reading newspapers; sharing texts with older family members; visits to the library; using computers; writing lists, birthday cards, messages; playing games; etc. There was very little evidence that 'direct instruction' in reading was part of these children's pre-school experiences, yet they all learned to read before they started school. This does not imply that other children do not need to be *taught* to read, but it does mean that schools need to use a range of approaches in order to ensure that young fluent readers continue to be motivated and challenged once they arrive at school.

SENDING 'WORK' HOME

One of the most common strategies to support home/school links in recent years has been through 'bookbag' schemes. Each child has a durable bag that contains books, often a reading scheme book and a free choice book, and the child takes this home on a regular basis. Often a reading diary accompanies the books and parents are expected to note the date, title of the book and to make a comment about their child's reading. Table 27.1 shows an example of a parent's comments (➡ Chapter 11, 'Assessing reading' for more discussion):

The Basic Skills Agency has taken the idea of bookbags a step further. In collaboration with Swindon Borough Council, it set up a National Support Project to promote 'storysacks' throughout England and Wales. Storysacks, containing a good children's book and supporting materials, were designed to stimulate reading activities. The sacks and the soft toys of the book characters they contained were made by parents and other volunteers. These, along with other related items such as an audio tape, language game and a card of activities, were used by parents at home to bring reading to life and develop the child's language skills. Storysacks were sent out on a library basis to pre-school and reception age children and aimed to give parents the confidence to enjoy sharing books with their children.

Since September 1999 all schools had to have 'home–school agreements'. Bastiani and Wyse (1999) look beyond the legal requirement (that such an agreement must be in place) to the hard work that is involved in setting up a meaningful home–school agreement. One of the interesting points they make

Table 27.1   A parent's comments on a child's reading

Date	Book and Page Number	Comments
7/5	Roll over	Well read.
14/5	Better than you	Fluent reading.
17/5	Big fish	Well read. Why no punctuation, i.e. question marks, speech marks? Esther commented on this. [Teacher:] I don't know. I will check.
21/5	Sam's book	Well read.
28/5	Lion is ill	Well read.

is that parents are not obliged to sign such agreements nor should there by any punitive consequence if they do not. It is suggested that if parents have reservations these should be used as a basis for discussion and a possibility for greater understanding of families' needs. They also stress the vital importance of genuine consultation.

> A key ingredient in the process of consultation with parents, which is a formal requirement in the introduction of agreements, is genuineness. Unfortunately educational practice is littered with the debris of glossy rhetoric (☞), phoney consultation and unfilled promises. Schools may, for example, consult but only hear what they want to hear; they may listen to some parents and ignore others; they may hear, but do nothing.
>
> Bastiani and Wyse, 1999: 10)

Most home–school agreements include statements about homework. The government recommendation is that children as young as 6 should do 1 hour a week of homework and that children in years 5 and 6 should do 30 minutes a day. The idea that children of 9 should be required to do 30 minutes a day is highly questionable and seen by some as an infringement of their family's freedom to engage with their children in ways that are more interesting than the kind of homework that schools are likely to send home. Nevertheless, popular opinion would seem to suggest that homework is a good thing and that parents' concerns are more about how they can help rather than whether it should be done. A survey in the *Guardian* reported that 85% of the 1000 parents who took part in a Mori poll agreed with the government's guidelines on homework. However, as Marshall (1999) suggests, the decision to set more homework is often a politically popular one because most people equate more work with higher standards. The limited research that is available on this issues would suggest that this is not the case. In fact more homework can sometimes result in lower standards as the *Times Educational Supplement* reported (Cassidy, 1999).

As schools are required to set homework it is important that they encourage children to engage in interesting activities. For example, one of our children's teachers suggested that they phone up a grandparent and ask them about the time when they were children. This activity inspired Esther to write one of her longest pieces of writing at home.

> My grabad [grandad] and gramar didn't have a tely. they did hav a rabyo [radio]. they had a metul Ian [iron]. they had sum bens [beans] and vegtbuls. thee wa lots ov boms in the war. the shoos were brawn and blac Thay had long dresis. Thay had shurt trawsis and long socs.

There is always the danger that the pressures of time for teachers can result in photocopied homeworksheets that are uninteresting and of questionable value. As is the case with many things in teaching it is better to organise a limited number of really exciting homework tasks, that are genuinely built on in the classroom, than to set too many tasks where it is difficult for the teacher to monitor them all.

WORKING WITH PARENTS IN THE CLASSROOM

The National Literacy Strategy clearly recognises the importance of community and parental involvement in raising standards of literacy. The National Year of Reading in 1998 was an attempt to involve the wider community in the promotion of reading for pleasure and learning. As far as the Framework for Teaching is concerned the weekly planning grid (see Table 26.2) includes 'other adult[s]' (OA) as one of the considerations. As a teacher you may have the opportunity to work with parents who have volunteered to help in the classroom. These parents volunteer to support schools in their own time and are a precious resource.

One of the most important things to remember is that schools and teachers need to offer guidance to people who are supporting literacy in the classroom. The Framework for Teaching includes complex ideas which will need to be explained to parents. Parental help is often invaluable in the groupwork section of the literacy hour. They can also support struggling readers either individually or in groups, but again it should be remembered that this is a skilled task and they will require the chance to discuss how things are going and how they can best help the children.

Knowsley local education authority carried out a project that included the recruitment and training of large numbers of adult volunteers who helped primary pupils with their reading on a regular basis. An evaluation by Brooks et. al (1996: 3) concluded that the training for parents and other volunteers was one of the most important components of the project and 'it seemed to make the most significant difference to raising reading standards'. The idea of training parents is one that the Basic Skills Agency has also been involved in. Their family literacy initiatives had different aims from the Knowsley project in that their main purpose was to raise the basic skills of both parents and children together. For parents the emphasis was mainly on helping them to understand more about what happened in schools and how they could support this. The children's sessions involved hands-on motivational activities. Joint sessions were also held where parents were encouraged to enjoy a natural interaction with their children during joint tasks. Brooks et al (1999) found that these family literacy programmes – with some modifications – worked as well for ethnic minority families as for other families.

Practice points

- Involve and support parents who work in your classroom as much as possible.
- Talking to the parents of children who have special education needs should be one of your priorities.
- Genuinely seek information from parents about their views of their child's development and progress.

Glossary

Conversing – a broad range and high quality of talk related to a book or other text.

Replication –the repeat of a piece of research to check that the results are the same.

Rhetoric – literally the skills of speech used for particular effects, but in this case fine sounding words not reflected by the day-to-day reality.

References

Bastiani, J. and Wyse, B. (1999) *Introducing Your Home–School Agreement*. London: Royal Society of Arts (RSA).

Brooks, G., Cato, V., Fernandes, C. and Tregenza, A. (1996) *The Knowsley Reading Project: Using Trained Reading Helpers Effectively*. Slough: The National Fundation for Educational Research (NFER).

Brooks, G., Harman, J., Hutchison, D., Kendall, S. and Wilkin, A. (1999) *Family Literacy for New Groups*. London: The Basic Skills Agency.

Cassidy, S. (1999) 'Startling findings on primary homework'. *Times Educational Supplement*. News and Opinion. July 2 [online – cited 2-2-2000]. Available from:
    http://www.tes.co.uk/tp/900000/PRN/teshome.html

Clark, M. M. (1976) *Young Fluent Readers*. London: Heinemann Educational Books.

DES (Department of Education and Science) (1975) *A Language for Life (The Bullock Report)*. London: HMSO.

Greenhough, P. and Hughes, M. (1999) 'Encouraging conversing: trying to change what parents do when their children read with them'. *Reading*, 98–105.

Marshall, B. (1999) 'How anxiety makes for a lot of homework'. *Times Educational Supplement*. News and Opinion. December 17 [online – cited 2-2-2000]. Available from:
    http://www.tes.co.uk/tp/900000/PRN/teshome.html

Stainthorp, R. and Hughes, D. (1999) *Learning from Children Who Read at an Early Age*. London: Routledge.

Tizard, B. and Hughes, M. (1984) *Young Children Learning: Talking and Thinking at Home and at School*. London: Fontana Press.

Annotated bibliography

Bastiani, J. and Wyse, B. (1999) *Introducing Your Home–School Agreement*. London: RSA.
A useful guide to introducing home–school agreements. Informed by good practice in secondary schools but relevant to all phases.
L1 *

Greenhough, P. and Hughes, M. (1998) 'Parents' and teachers' interventions in children's reading'. *British Educational Research Journal*, 24 (4): 283–398.

A fuller version of the research that we refer to in this section. This was included in a special edition of the journal where all the articles are concerned with 'families and education'.
L3 ***

Tizard, B. and Hughes, M. (1984) *Young Children Learning: Talking and Thinking at Home and at School.* London: Fontana Press.
An important text that asks awkward questions about schools' approaches to parents. Interesting comparison with Hughes's more recent work.
L2 **

Chapter 28

Information and communications technology

Information and communications technology (ICT) is something that most people will use during their working life and increasingly during their leisure time. This chapter looks at some of the issues that the new technology raises for teachers. The significant role of applications software and the internet form the main focus.

The establishment of the World Wide Web in the last few years marks a very important development in the history of human communication: as significant as the printing press. However, periodic explosions of technological development have resulted in regular claims about 'revolution' in the primary curriculum. Yet at the time of writing it was still not uncommon to see some schools sharing the old 'BBC' personal computers or to see more advanced computers in classrooms rarely being used. This chapter is underpinned by the assumption that IT hardware in schools should always be in use.

One of the challenges for the teaching and learning of ICT is the dramatic differences that exist in relation to resources and knowledge. Consequently in some schools classes have to share computers, but in others they have several per classroom or have well-equipped dedicated rooms. Some teachers are expert and use technology all the time in order to make them more efficient at their job, others have almost a fear of technology. As far as children are concerned there are a minority who sell their own products and compete aggressively in adult markets: for example, the 15-year-old Irish girl who developed a much quicker algorithm (☞) for coding and encoding security codes for credit transactions. There are also many children who quickly develop a high level of expertise at home, but at the opposite end of the spectrum there are others who either lack the interest or opportunities to develop such knowledge. In the light of the problems with resources and knowledge the government has set challenging targets:

By 1999
All newly qualified teachers should be ICT literate

By 2002
Serving teachers should be using ICT in the curriculum confidently

Most school leavers should have a good understanding of ICT and there should be measures in place to assess their competence
(Times Educational Supplement, 1999)

There has been a tendency to see the main role of technology to reinforce basic skills and drills. Examples include the use of maths packages to develop simple number skills in Key Stage 1 or more sophisticated packages that offer exercises on basic skills and will carry out analyses of answers in order to diagnose weaknesses. Currently there are a range of packages that are tackling skills in more imaginative and interactive ways: one excellent example is Dorling Kindersley's 'Now I'm Reading'. While good skills packages can be used in limited ways to enhance other classroom work, it is our view that applications are much more important and beneficial for developing English.

APPLICATIONS

The scope for the 'spiral' development of knowledge, skills and understanding using applications packages is vast. Applications are tools that allow us to carry out various jobs quicker and more efficiently. Examples include: word processing, desk-top publishing, spreadsheets, web authoring packages, databases, graphics packages. One of the first applications to receive widespread use in primary schools was the word processor. Unfortunately its use has been dogged by two problems. Many schools used word-processors that were cheaper versions of the adult industry standard packages, sometimes under the mistaken impression that software dedicated for use by children would be much easier to use. These packages often lacked key features, such as the ability to construct tables. The second problem, and one that is perhaps more serious, was that word processors tended to be used crudely as a way of providing a neat copy of work for display. Although enhanced presentation clearly is one of the advantages of word-processing packages, it is the opportunities they offer for drafting and revision during the writing process that are vital. If this is the case, it is important that children sometimes start their writing at the computer.

Desktop publishing (DTP) packages started a trend which has reached new heights in web authoring packages. DTP encourages children to 'publish' texts by creating pictures using art packages or by scanning in their own artwork, and combining these with texts that they have created. These packages primarily make the organisation and layout of pages much easier than if you tried to achieve the same result using a word processor.

The software that enables children to design web pages has the added facility to include moving images and sound. The other significant difference that this software has is the ability to link different texts by clicking on an icon, picture or piece of text; these are called hypertext links. These packages challenge us to think about what a 'text' really is. If children are encouraged to record their own sounds, create their own images, develop their own writing, and establish their own links, this really can lead to exciting learning outcomes. There are a number of companies developing web-authoring software specially for children. So as not to repeat the mistakes of the past teachers must ask themselves two key questions about such software: (1) Is it really easier to use than the industry standard versions which are designed to be as user friendly as possible? (2) To what extent will it enable children to achieve their aims? At the time of writing it was possible to download 'AOL Press' free or receive a free copy of an early version of 'Dreamweaver' (two high-quality web-design packages) as part of a magazine offer.

THE INTERNET

The internet represents a mind-boggling information resource for teachers and children alike. We now have unprecedented access to a global information source that was not available five years ago. So, for example, if we are interested in space we can log onto the web site at NASA and look directly at photographs taken by space probes and save these for use in the creation of texts. In the past such images would initially have been unavailable and only published through books at a later date. The internet therefore, offers great potential for supporting the learning of English. First of all it is worth examining some of the sites that are available to support children's learning.

We have already suggested the huge breadth of information that is available. However the learning of English is also crucially supported by 'doing' and through interaction. So it is important that teachers look carefully at the nature of learning that might be taking place if children access particular sites. There is growing recognition that technology alone will not offer better learning experiences than conventional practice unless its design is enhanced by sound underlying principles and philosophies: a high quality of interaction is one of these principles. The BBC has been one of the leading players in terms of educational web sites (http://www.bbc.co.uk/education/home/), an early example was their 'Teletubbies' site which encouraged young children to investigate 'Who spilled the Tubby custard?'. The site included visual images, speech and sound and the main interactive element involved selecting the correct path to discover the culprit. Another example for older children 'An animated history of books' was lively and informative, but limited in terms of interaction.

Schools themselves have also developed their own interactive sites with an early award winner including a primary school in Suttton-on-Sea. At the time of writing I whizzed over to their site to remind myself what was available. A trip to the on-line discussion 'gossip' area revealed the following jokes that had been left as part of a discussion:

> Yes your jokes are really funny, and we have some too . . .
> What do you call a fly with no wings? A walk.
> Where is the best place to have a school canteen? Next to the sick room.

What do you call a budgie that's just been run over by a lawnmower? Shredded tweet.
What animal is born to succeed? A canary with no teeth.
What do you call a donkey with three legs? A wonkey.
What do you find in the middle of MARSH? The letter R.

There is also a weather area where people from around the world can add details of their weather to a database. The database then allows you to ask questions about various aspects of weather such as 'Have wind-speeds of force 9 been recorded by anyone?' The site also includes various basic quizzes such as spelling and numbers and these will tell you how many answers were answered correctly.

There are also a growing number of sites which can help teachers with their work. Early in the development of the National Literacy Strategy an activity resource was made available so that teachers could search for an activity that would fulfil a particular objective from the Framework for Teaching (unfortunately suggested texts were sometimes not offered in that particular section of the activity resource sheet). The National Grid for Learning (NGFL) is another interesting development that offers various support sites for teachers in addition to its work with schools that includes supplying much better hardware facilities. One of the NGFL sites is called 'Literacy Time' which includes various options. 'Children's choice' initially looked promising but had a rather boring presentation of suggested activities. 'See a School' was better (by coincidence this happened to be Sutton-on-Sea primary school again) with a portrait of one teacher's work implementing the literacy hour including some photos. 'Literacy Time' also includes a useful CD ROM section with reviews by teachers, for example: *Storymaker* – 'create visually stimulating animated stories which incorporate recorded speech', or *Funday Times Timmy the Dream Hunter* – 'Very high quality animated story with activities. Not appropriate for curriculum support but good home purchase'; an interesting comment in relation to the kind of curricula that is deemed suitable for schools.

RESEARCH

The British Educational Communications and Technology Agency (BECTa) have produced some useful materials that cover a range of issues including research evidence. One of the publications (Shreeve, 1997) includes a range of case-studies illustrating the use of ICT. Jane Mitra an IT Coordinator from Hertfordshire describes the production of a multimedia (☞) guidebook called 'The Bones'. This cross-curricular project was sparked by a visit from an osteopath who brought in a skeleton and this was followed by visits from other health workers. The multimedia authoring software allowed the children to link together artwork, recorded sounds, scanned images and text. The final product gave the school a useful information resource that was owned by the young authors. Another featured case-study involved a structured internet task where Key Stage 2 children were encouraged to locate a map, interesting information and pictures from a geographical site called 'Citynet'. These case-studies support a point made by one of the other BECTa publications (Kuhn and Stannard, 1997) which also forms the central theme for Tweddle et al (1997), and that is that conventional definitions of literacy are undoubtedly being challenged by the new technologies. The boundaries between text, image and sound are much less pronounced.

Miller and Olson (1994) pointed out that IT in education has often created powerful but opposed views. ICT is seen by some to be the solution to all the world's problems and this has created a backlash from others who suggest that claims for brave new worlds are frequently overstated: we still look forward to the robot that will do the housework! Their research found that the personal pedagogy of teachers could not be easily separated from the use they made of ICT and that ICT did not seem to drive practice, if anything, previous practice determined the nature of ICT use. This is important because it suggests that 'revolutions' are unlikely but nevertheless ICT is an important part of the development of learning and teaching.

Questions about the extent to which ICT developments will have a lasting effect can only be addressed by reflecting on their use over time. On this basis there can be no doubt that e-mail and the internet have permanently added to the range of language and literacy processes. As far as CD ROMs are concerned they may in time be replaced by faster and more efficient on-line facilities, but at present they do offer ways of consolidating the development of literacy skills. There is no danger that new technology will replace books, pens and paper, but it does mean that we have to extend the range of our teaching to enable children to have confidence to understand, access and control such technology.

Practice points

- ICT should be used constantly in the classroom.
- The choice of software needs to be planned for each full year to ensure appropariate opportunities for children.
- Emphasis should be on the use of applications packages for meaningful purposes.

Glossary

Algorithm – mathematical routine which quickens the time taken to reach the solution to a problem.

Multimedia – texts that use a range of media in their production including: text, pictures, links, moving images, sounds.

References

Kuhn, S. and Stannard, R. (1997) *IT in English Literature Review*. Coventry: National Council for Educational Technology (now BECTa).

Miller, L. and Olson, J. (1994) 'Putting the computer in its place: a study of teaching with technology'. *Journal of Curriculum Studies*, 26 (2): 121–141.

Shreeve, A. (ed.) (1997) *IT in English: Case Studies and Materials*. Coventry: National Council for Educational Technology (now BECTa).

Times Educational Supplement (1999) 'National grid for learning timeline'. 15 October.

Tweddle, S., Adams, A., Clarke, S., Scrimshaw, P. and Walton, S. (1997) *English for Tomorrow*. Buckingham: Open University Press.

Annotated bibliography

Homerton College Cambridge. 'Teachers Evaluating Educational Multimedia'. [online – cited 2-2-00] Available from:
> http://www.teem.org.uk/

Very useful site that includes evaluations of packages to support the teaching of English and literacy.
L1 *

Literacy Time.
> http://www.vtc.ngfl.gov.uk/resource/literacy/index.html

This web site is part of the National Grid For Learning site and has a range of useful pages including links to other sites that may be of interest to English teachers.
L1 *

Shreeve, A. (ed.) (1997) *IT in English: Case Studies and Materials*. Coventry: National Council for Educational Technology (now BECTa).
Features a range of informative and interesting case studies of ICT work carried out in Key Stage 2 and Key Stage 3 classrooms.
L2 **

Tweddle, S., Adams, A., Clarke, S., Scrimshaw, P. and Walton, S. (1997) *English for Tomorrow*. Buckingham: Open University Press.
Very well written account that focuses on the possibilities for ICT now and in the future. Somewhat biased in favour of secondary examples, but these can be adapted for use in primary schools. Features a fascinating extract from a child's short story that includes a fictional chatline script.
L3 ***

Chapter 29

Supporting black and multilingual children

Issues related to ethnic minority children and multilingual (☞) classrooms are covered in this chapter, but particular emphasis is given to classroom environments which are exclusively or predominantly white. In both cases, intending teachers should be aware of the language needs of the children in relation to their cultural development. A recent research study on equal opportunities in higher education/school partnerships will be outlined to raise awareness of a number of related issues. Readers will be offered practical classroom guidance to support multilingual children.

The issue of 'race' (☞) and multilingualism remains a sensitive area for many teachers. Over two hundred languages are spoken by children in British schools and the number of young bilingual speakers continues to rise, but these facts are rarely addressed by those who work within initial teacher education. At the same time, it is clear that underachievement (for a variety of reasons) is a recurring factor for many children from ethnic minority backgrounds (Gillborn and Gipps, 1996) and that much work needs to be done to create language teaching which adequately reflects the academic potential they possess.

All teachers are necessarily involved in the promotion and development of language work in schools, but some remain unfamiliar with the particular needs of the multilingual child. It is extremely important that *all* children become competent and confident users of the English language as soon as possible in order to maximise their life chances through examinations and assessment processes (which are primarily carried out in English). However, this should never mean that the teacher expects children to surrender their own first languages in order to achieve academic success.

LINGUISTIC DIVERSITY

The potential of linguistic diversity in the multilingual classroom can easily be overlooked by students and more experienced teachers alike who insist on the exclusive use of English in their language work. Where attempts have been made to use English to the exclusion of other first languages considerable problems have arisen and there remains significant dispute. Some parents have raised objections to bilingual teaching (Schnaiberg, 1996) while educators have been quick to point out the ways in which the processes of single language teaching excludes some children from the routes to success (Schnaiberg, 1995). Others argue that the practice of supporting bilingual children more openly provides a stronger language culture within the classroom, meaning that there are potential linguistic benefits for white, monolingual children.

The teacher who sees only difficulties in dealing with multilingual children conveniently forgets that they are proven experts in handling language and in many ways could be more proficient than the teacher. As such, these children have considerable language skills on which the teacher can build, and they are likely to have much to offer others, particularly with regards to the subject of language study. Having said this, even if the child may be skilled in language use, he or she will still need particular support and guidance to develop greater proficiency in the use of English at school.

The language development of multilingual children often highlights a considerable gulf between the rate of oral language acquisition and the equivalent in reading and writing. Consequently, the beginning teacher needs to be aware of the need to apply greater sensitivity to these children; on the one hand the child should be encouraged to use spoken English at every possible opportunity, on the other, the teacher needs to employ teaching strategies which ensure that the same child does not begin to lose confidence in their language use because they perceive themselves as failed readers and writers.

Beginning teachers also need to understand that it is unhelpful to conceive of 'multilingual children' as some kind of homogeneous group. Some children will have been born in this country and their parents may have insisted on a different first language in order to retain the child's sense of ethnic identity and community (this is sometimes the case with Italian families, for instance). It is important to acknowledge that there are social and cultural differences which have direct relevance for the teacher of English. Black and Asian minority parents may have different perceptions of their relationship to and role within the perceived 'host' white community. Some will encourage their children to embrace British customs, language, codes, etc. as fully and as unproblematically as possible, others will seek to resist such moves and instead promote and defend their own cultural beliefs, languages and practices in order to maintain their cultural identity as distinct within British society. It would be unwise for the beginning teacher to begin to enter into a debate which meant that one side or another would be seen as preferable; it is more important to acknowledge that the child's own role within these two cultures can be difficult to negotiate. It is professionally important, therefore, to be aware of the child's set of cultural beliefs, to make every effort to understand and respect the position of the parents and to ensure that the child is not placed in a position whereby he or she is required to make qualitative judgements between the school and the home.

THE PROMOTION OF STANDARD ENGLISH

Standard English is the required language form of the National Curriculum, but teachers should be wary of promoting this to the detriment or exclusion of the bilingual child's first language. To adhere rigidly to Standard English with multilingual children is to deny those children aspects of their own identity, their skills as language users and their access to self-expression. It affects their confidence, their perception of themselves as speakers, listeners, readers and writers, and therefore has a potentially negative affect on the child's self-esteem. As one writer points out:

> If English is to replace rather than add to the languages of the children we teach, we must ask what is the effect of such a programme on their cultural identity, their self-esteem and sense of place in the community
> (Blackledge, 1994: 46)

There is evidence to show that the least successful way to deliver English teaching to a multilingual child with a poor grounding in English is to remove them from the classroom setting and provide short sharp bursts of tuition in isolation. More effective is the practice of resourcing the multilingual classroom with bilingual texts (including big books), dual language CD-ROMs, stories taped (often by parents) in other languages, etc. Teachers who develop practices which ignore or exclude the needs of bilingual pupils in order to serve a perceived need of the white majority in the class should be aware of recent research into this area which reported the success of 204 'two-way bilingual' schools, demonstrating through achievement data that *all* pupils benefited from such approaches and not, as might be expected, only the bilingual children themselves (Thomas and Collier, 1998).

CLASSSROOM APPROACHES

Many teachers find themselves developing their own resources in response to the challenge of multilingual children. While this may initially stem from a lack of suitable resources, more effectively it stems from the teacher's overt recognition of the child's needs, and the production of such materials helps to consolidate the positive approach to language work that the child will need to develop. Such materials also communicate an equally positive message to parents, who can be encouraged to use them either in the school or at home.

It has been pointed out that dual language books are not always as immediately helpful as may be presumed (Gravelle, 1996). One language may be given greater status than another, cultural subtleties in translation are not always successful and there are difficulties when written languages which are read from right to left are placed next to English as the starting points for the child could become confusing. However, the construction of dual language books are a popular way forward in many multilingual classrooms as children often find the process supportive and beneficial. Language issues should be less problematic when children are allowed to create dual language books for themselves, and when parents are encouraged to take part in this process. Walker et al, (1998: 18) offers particularly interesting and intricate designs for dual language book making, and it should be remembered that once these books are made, they can serve the purpose of recording the child's personal development and later provide an immediate and personal starting point for other children who need similar support.

Cross-curricular and thematic approaches in primary classrooms often offer opportunities to acknowledge multicultural dimensions to study. Teachers can acknowledge consciously the monocultural (☞) way in which many primary school themes are conceived, and open this planning up to more accurately reflect a multicultural society. Themes such as 'Ourselves', 'Food', 'Shelter', 'Sacred Places' and 'Journeys' all offer links across the National Curriculum and possibilities for multicultural work to emerge (Hix, 1992).

Story telling can be another particularly successful method of encouraging the multilingual child to negotiate between more than one language. There is evidence that story telling has been a particularly important strategy with bilingual learners in the early years (MacLean, 1996). All cultures have their own histories, myths, legends and stories which are passed on through generations of children. These stories cross cultural boundaries; some are recognisably similar with subtle shades of difference, others will be particular within a specific cultural context. In either case, the story itself becomes a powerful, shared experience and the telling, the retelling, the writing and reading of the range of possible stories opens a rich vein of language study for the teacher to exploit. Again, parents should be seen as a valuable and authoritative resource in this area.

It is important to recognise that the black or Asian child whose first language *is* English may still need particular support. It should hardly need stating that if the black, Asian or multilingual child is isolated in a predominantly white context it is important that they are not perceived in any way as a novelty. Research repeatedly reports that teachers have different relationships with children from ethnic minorities. For example, it has been claimed that teachers spend less individual time with ethnic minority children, they are more likely to misinterpret black boys' language use as aggressive or confrontational (Nehaul, 1996; Sewell, 1997) and statistics suggest that in some parts of the country black boys are now 15 times more likely to be expelled than their white peers (Thornton, 1998). Other research indicates significant discrepancies in the ways in which white teachers are prepared to deal with issues of race in general, and ethnic minority children in their classes in particular (Jones, 1999). This kind of evidence needs exploration in greater depth than this space allows, but it is clear that black and white children in British schools experience quite different relationships with the education system that serves them. Recommendations relating to successful practices and strategies for the support of black and multilingual children in British schools have been published to guide teachers in these areas (Blair and Bourne 1998, Jones 1999).

Practice points

- Be particularly aware of the bilingual child's first few weeks in the classroom. Look for opportunities to display your respect for their language through dual language notices and opportunities to share new words and phrases together.
- Make a particular point of learning to pronounce unfamiliar names accurately both as a mark of respect and as a model for the rest of the class.
- Acknowledge that you are unlikely to know everything about every child's culture, but in so doing acknowledge also that it is your responsibility to understand the lives of *all* the children in your class, not just those who share your own cultural background.

Glossary

Bilingualism/multilingualism – Referring to a child who speaks two or more languages.
Monocultural teaching – Teaching which fails to recognise the multicultural nature of society.
Race – a heavily disputed concept which refers to ethnic identity.

References

Blackledge, A. (ed.) (1994) *Teaching Bilingual Children*. Stoke-on-Trent: Trentham Books.
Blair, M. and Bourne, J. (1998) *Making the Difference: Teaching and Learning Strategies in Successful Multi-Ethnic Schools*. London: Department for Education and Employment (DfEE).
Gillborn, A. and Gipps, C. Office for Standards in Education (OFSTED) (1996) *Recent Research on the Achievements of Ethnic Minority Pupils*. London: HMSO.
Gravelle, M. (1996) *Supporting Bilingual Learners in Schools*. Stoke-on-Trent: Trentham
Hix, P. (1992) *Kaleidoscope: Themes and Activities for Developing the Multicultural Dimension in the Primary School*. Crediton: Southgate.
Jones, R. (1999) *Teaching Racism or Tackling it?* Stoke-on-Trent: Trentham Books.
MacLean, K. (1996) 'Supporting the literacy of bilingual learners: storytelling and bookmaking'. *Multicultural Teaching*, (2): 26–29.
Nehaul, K. (1996) *The Schooling of Children of Caribbean Heritage*. Stoke-on-Trent: Trentham Books.
Schnaiberg, L. (1995) 'Bilingual Education'. *Education Week* (newspaper), 1 November.
Schnaiberg, L. (1996) 'Parents worry bilingual education hurts students'. *Education Week* (newspaper), 28 February.
Sewell, T (1997) *Black Masculinities and Schooling: How Black Boys Survive Modern Schooling*. Stoke-on-Trent: Trentham Books.

Thomas, W. P. and Collier, V. P. (1998) 'Two languages are better than one'. *Educational Leadership*, 55: 23–26.

Thornton, K. (1998) 'Blacks 15 times more likely to be excluded'. *Times Educational Supplement*, 11 December.

Walker, S., Edwards, V. and Leonard, H. (1998) *Write Around the World: Producing Bilingual Resources in the Primary Classroom*. University of Reading: Reading and Language Information Centre.

Annotated bibliography

Edwards, V. (1998) *The Power of Babel: Teaching and Learning in Multilingual Classrooms*. Stoke-on-Trent, Trentham Books.
A particularly helpful text in terms of its sensitivity to new arrivals in school and its guidance for teachers with limited experience of children from a range of cultures. Practical advice for the production of dual language cassettes, books, displays, etc.
L1 **

Hix, P. (1992) *Kaleidoscope: Themes and Activities for Developing the Multicultural Dimension in the Primary School*. Crediton: Southgate, Hampshire Education Authority.
Much of this book remains at the multicultural (rather than an anti-racist) level, but the strength of the book is the range of ideas for establishing a multicultural dimension to language development.
L1 *

Jones, R. (1999) *Teaching Racism or Tackling it?* Stoke-on-Trent: Trentham Books.
A book aimed in particular at white teachers working in predominantly or exclusively white classrooms.
L3 ***

Chapter 30

Poetry

The significance of poetry in the primary classroom is discussed and we suggest that it can be a highly motivational method of developing work in language and literacy. Some examples of different approaches to the teaching of poetry are outlined.

Poetry is one of the most important linguistic opportunities for the primary classroom, offering degrees of intensity, subtlety and artistry which are largely unavailable to other areas of study. However, in many primary class-rooms poetry is underused as a tool for language development and for learning. It is sometimes perceived to be unnecessarily complicated, outdated and irrelevant to modern children. The Bullock Report acknowledged that poetry started 'at a disadvantage' and could be 'an object of comic derision' (DES, 1975: para 9.22–23).

THE EARLY YEARS

It is important look back to the early years to see where children's relationships with language develop. Story is an important early influence, but poetry exists as an even earlier feature of many children's first steps towards language acquisition. Nursery rhymes are an early introduction to many features of the English language. They are self-contained, offering the child a (typically humorous) snippet of language that is worth remembering and through repetition the child learns to share the poetic structure with others. Children learn to invest rhyme with emphasis, for example 'Ring-A-Ring-Of-Roses' ends with the phrase 'all fall DOWN', which the child learns to accentuate by intonation and by literally falling down. Similarly, the rhyme:

Round and round the garden
like a teddy bear
one step, two step
and TICKLE HIM UNDER THERE

teaches the child anticipation, turn-taking, humour, the joy of a shared frag-ment of language. There are close links here with communal songs and stories, but poetry has the particularly important feature (at this stage) of brevity: it is manageable and memorable.

Parents of young children know how advertisements and jingles from the radio and television become embedded in much the same way. The child learns that (for whatever reason) this piece of language is worth holding on to, and that it is worth the investment of time and effort needed to capture and then control it. Once sufficient examples are mastered, the child has a common language reserve that can be shared with other children and adults even if they are complete strangers.

Children often arrive at school with a myriad of such examples of captured language under their belts. These become supplemented with skipping games, chants, songs learnt in assembly (typically), and the repertoire grows accordingly. It is all the more depressing therefore to find teachers at Key Stage 2 who are reluctant to use this phenomenal starting point to greater effect in the classroom. Some teachers actively shy away from the development of poetry in their classrooms, others fall back into a 'now write a poem about it' syndrome, when the potential for the development of language study is enormous.

MOVING FORWARD

Word games offer many children a route into poetic observations and allow the teacher to build a range of poetic devices to be called upon at later stages. Shape poems allow the child to arrange appropriate words so that their appearance represents that which is being described (such as a slithering snake, or the tail of a kite). Riddles and rhyming games bring all kinds of phonic and spelling strategies into clear focus, but they also allow the teacher to introduce discussions around regular and irregular rhyming schemes, the power of internal rhymes within creative writing, and so on.

One typical poetry starting point is to create associations with colours. Often the results are along the line of 'Red is Santa at Christmas, Red is the colour of my blood . . . ', but with careful encouragement from the teacher the child can bring more sensitive descriptions to the task and begin to expand each line to incorporate personal and more detailed observations. Using a theme can be a worthwhile process, and moving away from the more predictable limitations of colours, teachers can initiate work on a much wider range of possible starting points such as spells, tortures, animals, and so on. However, poetry need not be restricted to the 'exotic'. Michael Rosen has regularly promoted the concept of 'memorable speech', and suggested that teachers should look to children's everyday contact with language as starting points for their writing:

> Everything we remember, no matter how trivial: the mark on the wall, the joke at luncheon, word games, these like the dance of a stoat or the raven's gamble are equally the subject of poetry.
>
> (Rosen, 1989: 11).

Some teachers begin poetry writing by simply asking children to collect together the language they come across (verbal and written) and use these as starting points for poems about their lives.

Using specific poetic forms based on syllabic patterns (such as the haiku (☞) or the cinquain (☞)) helps children work within particular confines, and returning to such small tasks several times helps them develop self-criticism and the discipline of redrafting. Regular rhythmic patterns such as the limerick provide similar opportunities for children to work within specific poetic structures that are light-hearted and offer reasonably quick returns for their linguistic investment. Other poetic devices such as alliteration (☞) can be enjoyably explored (Sesame Street uses this concept all the time – 'Wanda the Wicked Witch Went to the Well on a Wednesday') and once these devices are learnt they become tools for the child to use in future writing. Teachers should keep careful notes on which poetic devices the children are familiar with and remind them of the strategies they have at their disposal when writing.

Book making, class anthologies and open readings are particularly well received ways of enhancing the profile of poetry. Parents are invariably appreciative of such opportunities to see their child's work 'in print' or to hear them perform. Children should always have audiences in mind for their work, and these kinds of opportunities to share their work with others helps to encourage further reflection on the impact and meanings of their poetry.

EXTENDING THE STUDY OF POETRY

The temptation to move into 'what does the poet really mean?' should be resisted as this is not the point of poetry. A better approach is 'what are the different ways that we all *read* this poem?' It should also be remembered at all times that poetry is meant to be *heard*, and children need opportunities to develop the specific skills required to listen to the relationship between the sounds of the words in poetry. Teachers should also be wary of believing that poetry should always be 'fun': for many children it is cathartic; a way of coming to terms with complex emotions.

Writing poetry can be a liberating and challenging experience for those children who respond to investigative study. For example, the skills of poetic inference (☞) and deduction are comparable to scientific processes, and the experimental, trial and error nature of much writing in this form is equally analogous to scientific enquiry:

> In writing, we as teachers should aim to bring the precision of poetry – that unrelenting, largely conscious search for the right word, and the largely unconscious search for the appropriate sounds, in terms of rhyme, rhythm, assonance and alliteration – to the emotion, the excitement of science.
>
> (Sedgwick, 1997: 2)

Children are capable of extraordinary observations and often make startling conceptual links between what they see, hear, feel, know and imagine and how they compare those understandings. Working on the Northumbrian coastline, a group of children studied one village's fading relationship with the sea. One child looked at the slight film of oil on the surface of the water and wrote:

Anchored kittiwakes bob calmly
on the vinegar water
A bitter scent lingers in the air.
Sweet shards of crystal nuzzle
into the knotted rocks.
A lilted tongue tilts to its side
whispering
tish
tish

The child's perception of the water's surface is something that would have been difficult to predict, and responses such as these become crucial starting points for creative writing as they allow metaphors to be played with, expanded and explored linguistically. At another stormier part of the coast other children variously described the sea as a cobra, a lion, a porpoise and a wolf, developing animal metaphors and similes which were often insightful and occasionally surprising. Waves were variously described as 'carelessly turquoise', 'hypnotising', 'pearl diamonds' and 'silk sheets'. The noise of the water became a lullaby, a quarrel, a whisper, a growl, a lisp and a roar. Observations such as these offer powerful starting points for discussion and for further investigations into poetry. They also provide a forum for reading aloud, opportunities for which should be supported and frequently provided by teachers.

As primary teachers typically spend longer periods of time with the same children it is possible for them to develop methods of writing which build on shared previous experiences. After a period of working on the development of new images to describe observations one of the authors arrived at school one morning after a particularly heavy frost. He took his year 3 class into some woodland adjacent to the playground and one girl wrote:

Sour frost swirls through the air,
mist killing the sun.
A solid surface
protecting the undergrowth.
The ice crumbles on frozen puddles, spikes on branches
frozen
like fingers trying to crack the air.
Sun beaming through a line
of gleaming frost,
lost
in a crystal clear desert of ice.
Cracked and empty.

The child's conceptual connection between the frozen twigs and 'fingers trying to crack the air' was an entirely natural process. Once a sense of trust is established between teacher and child in a supportive language environment children can be encouraged to capture observations on paper along with associated thoughts, dreams, imaginings and connections, making it possible to arrive at a raw palette of words and ideas which can then be mixed, combined and developed in a variety of ways for poetic ends.

Finally, wherever possible teachers should look for opportunities to bring children into contact with published and working poets. These sessions are invaluable, not least because the children's perceptions of what a poet looks like are always proved entirely wrong. More famous (and expensive) poets are unlikely to be within the financial reach of many primary schools, but there are ways of working around such problems. For more immediate results it is worthwhile to contact writing groups (addresses will be in local libraries) or scouring local newspapers for regular contributors of poetry. Typically, these people are flattered to be recognised as authors, and quickly accept any offer of an opportunity to come into school and talk to children about their work. It is useful to ask for some copies of work in advance so that the children can familiarise themselves with it prior to the visit and think about the kinds of questions they want to generate. Any such visit should include times where the writer reads some of the work out loud (a particularly important feature of any poetry session), and hopefully there would be some opportunity for children to write themselves, under the direction of the guest. Where professional poets cannot be afforded, at the very least these kinds of arrangements bring children into contact with adults who have an active and profound relationship with poetic forms of language, offering models of communication beyond the mundane and predictable:

> Almost everybody, at some time in their lives, can produce poetry. Perhaps not very great poetry, but still, poetry they are glad to have written.
>
> (Hughes, 1967: 33).

A particularly strong resource for teachers interested in contemporary poetry would be a membership to the Poetry Book Society. This society was established by T. S. Eliot in 1953. For a one-off nominal yearly payment, members receive regular magazines and poetry publications which provide valuable starting points for older children. In addition, the Society has begun to publish optional teaching booklets (called 'Classroom Choice') to accompany some of the selections. Further resources can be obtained through the website, and these include materials (such as posters, poetry notes, teaching ideas) all specifically aimed at teachers who are keen to raise the profile of poetry in the classroom and the level of their children's analytical skills.

Practice points

- Plan regular use of a large selection of varied poetry books for choosing, reading, learning and performing.
- Mix structured poetry writing activities with opportunities for free poetry writing.
- Experiment with poetry work that combines drama, music, dance and visual artwork and always look for opportunities for children to publish or perform their work.

Glossary

Alliteration – phrases which include words that begin with the same phoneme.
Cinquain – American originated poetry form with five lines, 22 syllables in a 2, 4, 6, 8, 2 pattern.
Haiku – Japanese poetry form with three lines, and 17 syllables in a 5, 7, 5 pattern.
Inference – the knowledge of textual meanings beyond the literal or 'obvious'.

References

Department of Education and Science (DES) (1975) *A Language For Life (The Bullock Report)*. London: HMSO.
Hughes, T. (1967) *Poetry in the Making*. London: Faber and Faber.
Rosen, M. (1989) *Did I Hear You Write?* London: Andre Deutsch.
Sedgwick, F. (1997) *Read My mind: Young Children, Poetry and Learning*. London: Routledge.

Annotated Reading

Brownjohn, S. (1980) *Does it Have to Rhyme?* London: Hodder & Stoughton.
Brownjohn, S. (1982) *What Rhymes With 'Secret'?* London: Hodder & Stoughton.
Two small books packed full of interesting ideas to develop an ongoing approach to poetry writing in the primary school. Each section is richly supported by examples of children's work.
L1 *
Carter, D. (1998) *Teaching Poetry in the Primary School*. London: David Fulton.
Detailed provision of links between planning, assessing and the study of poetry and planning for the National Literacy Hour.
L2 *
Opie, I. and Opie, P. (1951) *The Oxford Dictionary of Nursery Rhymes*. Oxford: Oxford University Press.
The Opies have made an outstanding contribution to our understanding of children and childhood. If you are interested in the origins of nursery rhymes this is a fascinating book.
L2 ***

Chapter 31

Media

Children's wide exposure to media (☞) texts in everyday life means that it is important that media study forms part of their English work. Reflections on the use of newspapers is followed by examples of the use of film. Our review of research reminds you about the multimedia perspective.

The study of the media in primary schools has not had the same impact as in secondary schools. Secondary English departments have long recognised the importance of media as an aspect of English that has direct links with pupils' daily lives. For primary teachers the difficulties have included the fact that much print media requires the ability to read between the lines. However, for children at the top end of Key Stage 2 this is actually a good reason to use media sources, as it challenges children's understanding and encourages them to make inferences and deductions (➡ Chapter 5, 'Analysing texts').

The range of media, particularly since the creation of the internet, presents teachers with great opportunities and at times a bewildering array of choices. If we include advertising and other environmental print in our range of media, it is possible to see how children from two years old are aware of and can talk about media. Media has a significant influence on our lives and for this reason it is important that it forms part of the primary curriculum. One area that has been exploited well in the past is newspapers.

NEWSPAPERS IN THE CLASSROOM

The Newspapers in Education scheme was a successful strategy for involving schools and local newspapers in partnership. One of the important ideas behind the scheme was the Reading Passport. This was a little booklet of passport size that contained 20 or so activities that encouraged children to analyse newspapers. As they completed the activities an adult would sign them off; this finally lead to a 'reading certificate'. Examples of the activities include the following:

Assignment One

MAKE A CHANGE!
Find four people in the news today who have made something change.

Write their names and circle if what they did was GOOD or BAD. Are all your choices easy to make or are some difficult? Talk to your teacher about this.

Assignment Nine

CAN YOU FIND?
Something hard, something cold, something bigger than your house, something alive.
Write the names of the things that you find in each part of the cross [Carroll diagram]. Make up some more crosses of your own with different choices.

Assignment Fourteen

BARGAIN BASEMENT!
Newspapers carry lots of special offers and bargains. Find one in the newspaper you are using and describe it here.

(Van der Weijden, 1996: 4, 12, 17)

These kinds of activities help children to begin to understand some of the main structures of newspapers. Even with Key Stage 1 children, the photographs in newspapers can provide powerful opportunities for discussion and the writing of short texts such as headlines or captions.

One of the most important aspects of newspapers is that they tell stories, 'true' stories perhaps. Children's lives are full of stories and the collection of their experiences – sometimes as tape-recorded oral accounts – can provide rich material for class newspapers designed to mimic their adult counterparts. The use of tape recorders to support the interviewing of various people throughout the school community can also offer important learning opportunities in relation to speaking and listening. For example if children are involved in transcribing tapes they get first-hand knowledge of the differences between speech and writing. The widespread use of desktop publishing packages offers the chance for sophisticated presentation techniques with some schools using industry standard packages such as 'Quark Express'.

The internet presents a huge advantage for accessing examples of newspapers which can help children to familiarise themselves with the language of news stories. For example, the 'Guardian Unlimited' site (http://www.newsunlimited.co.uk/), featured pictures linked to headline stories; one of these was about the historic vote to remove the hereditary lords from British politics. Another option was to view a longer list of top stories; the following was cut from one of the stories:

Calls Grow To Extend Smaller Classes Programme

From the Press Association
Thursday October 28, 1999 07: 57 am

The Government is facing calls to extend its class-size reduction programme beyond the early years of primary education, as figures showed it is well on track to hit its General Election target.

But education minister Estelle Morris said that reducing class sizes for older primary and secondary children was not a Government target.

(Press Association, 1999)

For older children the use of presentation software (such as desktop publishing) can be made more realistic with the use of news office simulation software (☞). The essence of such software can be quite simple. 'Hotline' is a package that sends breaking news stories in real time which are printed off as they arrive. The job of the news team is to organise the front page of the newspaper. The advantage of working in real time is that this creates a feeling of urgency and realistic deadlines can be set for the work. The activity also encourages teamwork and collaboration, so a typical team might consist of: editor, one sub-editor, leader writer, picture editor and two reporters. The structure of the teams may to a large extent depend on the computer hardware that is available and the teamwork skills of the class.

FILM

Film is an extremely important form in children's lives. Children of age 3 can quickly identify their favourite videos which they want to watch again and again. This is related to their interest in stories: there are many similarities between films and story books. Another reason for using film in the classroom is that it can create a bridge to aid understanding of an original book. Many people are inspired to read books having seen the film and vice versa. For children the prior knowledge they gain by watching the film version can help them access the book more easily. One example of this is the superb BBC adaptation of C. S. Lewis's *The Lion, the Witch and the Wardrobe*. The original book is a demanding read for upper Key Stage 2 children, partly because it was written in 1950 and the use of language is both old fashioned and at a high level. When children have seen the film version and have been given the opportunity to carry out activities to extend their understanding this can improve their confidence to attempt the book.

Walt Disney films offer excellent opportunities for thinking about media in general and looking at adaptations in particular. A National Association of English Teachers (NATE) publication offers advice on using *The Little Mermaid*. *The Little Mermaid* was originally a story by Hans Christian Anderson which has been translated into many languages and has undergone many versions. Disney produced a cartoon film version and a book to accompany the film. NATE suggest the following kinds of activities:

2. Working with the original text
As a whole class, select five or six key moments in the narrative which are essential to the story. Allocate one segment to each working group, and distribute the appropriate extract from the original Hans Christian Anderson story in translation. Ask each group to discuss and prepare to report back on:

- any differences between the abridged (☞) and full versions of their story, with reasons for the changes
- their ideas and draft storyboard (☞) for a film version of their extract, which may be based on either of their two print versions, or an amalgam of both.

4. Working with another medium
(a) Screen the opening of the Disney film. This involves an entirely original narrative sequence establishing the Mer King's patriarchy, the Little Mermaid's enquiring personality and sublime voice, and introducing a new range of archetypal Disney characters – Sebastian, the Jamaican crab music master, Ariel's confidante Flounder, and her mentor Scuttle the Seagull. Ask pupils to discuss the function of this opening sequence, the poetic license it takes with the original text, and why such changes might have been considered necessary.

(Grahame, 1996: 41)

Another interesting area of analysis is the extent to which Disney films distort the cultural perspectives of the original stories. It has been alleged by some that some of Disney's work represents cultural imperialism where the dominant white American cultural norms pervade the films. Stereotypes are always something to critically examine in films: for example to what extent do you think Sebastian the crab in *The Little Mermaid* is a stereotypic character?

Although the in-depth work required for learning about media is better suited to activities outside the literacy hour you have probably realised that the NATE suggestions could be used within the literacy hour. For example, the identification of the key moments in *The Little Mermaid* could be linked with the year 5 term 2 objective. 'Fiction and Poetry: Reading Comprehension: 2 to investigate different versions of the same story in print or on film, identifying similarities and differences; recognise how stories change over time and differences of culture and place that are expressed in stories . . . ', and could be part of shared reading initially. There are other more general objectives that might be linked to film work (e.g. year 6 term 2 objective 'Fiction and Poetry: Reading comprehension: 1 to understand aspects of narrative structure' or year 4 term 1 'Fiction and Poetry: Reading comprehension: 3 to explore chronology in narrative using written *or other media texts* . . . ' [our emphasis]) but it seems unusual that the use of film is only specifically mentioned twice in the Framework for Teaching and only from year 5 onwards.

LEARNING AND MEDIA

Parker (1999) suggests that there is a positive link between moving image media and literacy development. His research featured a project that involved year 3 children adapting Roald Dahl's story *Fantastic Mr Fox* into an animated film. One aspect of the programme of study involved some children working towards a simplified version of the book for younger children, and others were getting ready to use the animation package on the computer. Parker felt that some of the children's first person writing to support the script had particularly strong visual characteristics.

1   'I saw some metal in the moonlight night.'
2   'All I can see is the 4 walls. Brown, dim and muddy like a pison.' [prison].
3   'I can see the opening to our den. Its daytime the light light is coming in.'

(Parker, 1999: 31)

In Chapter 28, 'Information and communications technology' we explored the way that new media tend to provoke extreme reactions. David Buckingham has done much work on the influence of television, and more recently has written about multimedia technologies. He suggests that society – and ironically the media – tend to take up two main positions: either that new technologies are a very good thing or that they are dangerous. He points out that neither position is satisfactory as the real picture is much more complex.

Buckingham's (1999) recent research has focused on two areas: computer games and creative use of multimedia. In contrast to public concerns he found that games playing was very much a social activity. Although games were played alone they were also played collaboratively. The games also provided a topic for much discussion that included swapping games, sharing cheats and hints, and discussion about the wider world of games playing such as TV programmes about the subject, games shops, games arcades and magazines. Buckingham also added a cautionary note that a great deal of the discussion was influenced by consumerism. This perhaps adds further justification for helping children to become critical consumers of media messages so they are not unfairly influenced by advertising messages.

In another piece of research Buckingham tried to find out 'to what extent, and how, were children using computers for digital animation, design work, sound or video editing, or for what is sometimes called "multi-media authoring"?' Some of this survey's results mirrored the previous piece of research, for example, overall he found that 'boys were generally more interested and involved' in the area than girls. He also found that although many of the children claimed to be involved in multimedia authoring it was rarely a creative process. For example, although some of the children thought that they had made animations, they confused their own input with examples that were already available on the computer. The lack of creativity was caused by parents' lack of skill and therefore ability to help their children, the children's view that computers were mainly to be used for 'messing about' when they were bored, and the lack of meaningful audiences for their work. This kind of work at home is an area that teachers can actively build on.

Practice points

- The media is a powerful influence on all out lives and for that reason needs to be understood and analysed.
- Film and moving images should be regularly explored.
- The creation of media texts in the classroom should be balanced with the analysis of media texts.

Glossary

Abridged – shortened version of a text.
Media – different ways of communicating information and ideas to large numbers of people.
Simulation software – computer packages designed to simulate real life situations
Storyboard – a film planning device. A linear series of rectangular boxes which include a picture and captions and/or short notes. Can be used for planning other narrative texts.

References

Buckingham, D. (1999) 'Superhighway or road to Nowhere? Children's Relationships with Digital Technology'. *English in Education*, 33(1): 3–12.
Grahame, J. (1996) *The English Curriculum: Media 1: Years 7–9* (updated edition). London: English and Media Centre.
Parker, D. (1999) 'You've Read the Book, Now Make the Film: Moving Image Media, Print Literacy and Narrative'. *English in Education*, 33(1): 24–35.
Press Association. News Unlimited. London: *Guardian* newspaper. [online – cited 28-10-99]. Available from:
    http://www.newsunlimited.co.uk/0,2221,,00.html
Van der Weijden, G. (1996) *Newspapers in Education: Reading Passport.* Huntingdon: Creative Media Concepts.

Annotated bibliography

British Video Association (1999) *Reel Lives.* (Place of publication not given) British Video Association.
    A free resource that has a video of film clips from children's classics and photo-copiable worksheets to accompany it.
    L1 *
Grahame, J. (1996) *The English Curriculum: Media 1: Years 7–9* (updated edition). London: English and Media Centre.
    Although this is aimed at secondary English departments it contains all the principles that should underpin good media education. The important focus on things like bias is supported by many practical suggestions.
    L2 *

Mayall, B. (1994) *Children's Childhoods Observed and Experienced*. London: Falmer Press.
David Buckingham is one of the contributors to this book. In his chapter he uses the killing of Jamie Bulger to reflect on the influence of television on children.
L2 ***

Appendix
The links with Circular 4/98
Annex C

Throughout the book

11a and 12d – professional/technical terms: throughout supported by glossaries;

2a – word/sentence/text levels: different emphases in different chapters;

5a – explicit and systematic teaching of reading, writing, and speaking and listening: issue throughout

5c – enthusiasm for reading: various chapters

7c – inspection/research evidence: throughout

11b – relationship between spoken and written English: various chapters

11c – explicit reference to subject knowledge: throughout

Part One—Introduction to language, literacy and english

The history of English, langauge and literacy	7c – inspection/research evidence; 2b – relationship between word/sentence/text levels
Theories of learning	5v – direct instruction

Part Two—Reading

The development of reading	1 – Essential stages of development; 1e – adult intervention and independence; 2c – emphases of word/sentence/text level; 5b – word level up and text level down
Texts for children	5eiv – critical and imaginative responses to texts; 12b – textual knowledge
Analysing Texts	3di,ii,iii – meaning of whole texts; 4 – range, structures and features of texts; 12b textual knowledge; 12c – analyse texts critically
Listening to children read	3aiii – hearing, discussing, retelling, inventing stories; 5eii – discussing key features of texts; 5eiii, iv, v – guided and focused reading; 6bi – reading strategies
Phonics	3bi,ii,iii,iv – phonemes and graphemes; 5di to iv – essential core of phonic knowledge; 12b – lexical knowledge

Routines for reading	5ei – shared reading
Reading for information	5evii – locate information
Reading recovery	5vi – Multi-sensory approaches; 5J – learning difficulties
Assessing reading	3ci,ii – graphic, syntactic and contextual cues; 6ai,ii – pupils errors and reading strategies; 7a – formative, summative, diagnostic assessment; 7bi to iii – standards of attainment

Part Three—Writing

The development of writing	1 – Essential stages of development; 1e – adult intervention and independence; 3av – the conventions of writing
Composition	1c – awareness of audience; 5fi – teach compositional skills
Genre and the process of writing	5fi – the writing process; 6v to vii – pupils errors written structure
Spelling	1d – non-conventional and conventional writing; 3aiv – relationship between spoken and written language; 3bv,vi – patterns of spelling; 5fiv – teach spelling; 6bi – pupil errors generalising spelling patterns; 12b – lexical knowledge
Handwriting	5fv – teach handwriting
Punctuation	3ciii – syntactic boundaries including punctuation; 5fiii – teach punctuation; 6aiii – pupil errors and punctuation; 6biii – pupil errors puncuation and meaning; 12b – grammatical knowledge
Grammar	1a – implicit to explicit knowledge; 3civ – meanings of phrases and clauses; 3ei to v – structure of language; 5fii – teach grammar systematically; 6aiv – pupil errors verb tenses; 12b – grammatical knowledge
Assessing writing	7a – formative, summative, diagnostic assessment; 7bi to iii – standards of attainment

Part Four—Speaking and listening

The development of talk	1 – essential stages of development; 1e – adult intervention and independence; 3aii – sounds, structures and patterns
Accent, dialect and standard english	1b – Informal and formal language; 12a – nature and role of standard English;
Planning for talk	5g – teaching speaking and listening through planned activities
Play and language	3ai – spoken language in a variety of contexts
Drama	5g – teaching speaking and listening through planned activities
Assessing Talk	7a – formative, summative, diagnostic assessment; 7bi to iii – standards of attainment

Part Five—General issues

Planning

Home/school links

Information and   5eviii – using ICT to develop reading; 5fi – use of
communications technology   word processors; 11d – awareness of strengths
                                        and limitations of ICT

Supporting black and   5l – provision for pupils not yet fluent in English
multilingual children

Poetry   5vii – sound patterns, rhymes and poems;
                                        5h – develop language through imagery and
                                        figurative language

The media   12b and c – analysing texts

Index